ESSAYS ON
THE FICTION OF A. S. BYATT

ESSAYS ON
THE FICTION OF A. S. BYATT
Imagining the Real

Edited by

Alexa Alfer and Michael J. Noble

Contributions to the Study of World Literature, Number 110

Greenwood Press
Westport, Connecticut • London

Library of Congress Cataloging-in-Publication Data

Essays on the fiction of A. S. Byatt: imagining the real / edited by Alexa Alfer and
Michael J. Noble.
     p. cm. — (Contributions to the study of world literature, ISSN 0738–9345 ; no. 110)
    Includes bibliographical references and index.
    ISBN 0–313–31518–3 (alk. paper)
    1. Byatt, A. S. (Antonia Susan), 1936– —Criticism and interpretation. I. Alfer, Alexa,
    1968– II. Noble, Michael J., 1968– III. Series.
    PR6052.Y2 Z64   2001
    823.'914—dc21   2001023321

British Library Cataloguing in Publication Data is available.

Library of Congress Catalog Card Number: 2001023321

ISBN: 0–313–31518–3
ISSN: 0738–9345

First published in 2001

Greenwood Press, 88 Post Road West, Westport, CT 06881
An imprint of Greenwood Publishing Group, Inc.
www.greenwood.com

Printed in the United States of America

COPYRIGHT ACKNOWLEDGMENTS

From Sigmund Freud, *New Introductory Lectures on Psychoanalysis*, *The Standard Edition of the Complete Psychological Works of Sigmund Freud*, trans. and ed. James Strachey (The Hogarth Press and The Institute of Psycho-Analysis, 1953-74). Translation copyright © 1965, 1964 by James Strachey. Sigmund Freud © Copyrights. Reprinted by kind permission of The Random House Group Ltd., and W.W. Norton, Inc.

From *The Letters of Arthur Henry Hallam*, ed. Jack Kolb (Ohio State UP, 1981). Reprinted by kind permission of Jack Kolb.

From C. G. Jung, *Alchemical Studies*, trans. R. F. C. Hull (1967; Routledge and Kegan Paul, 1983). Reprinted by kind permission of Routledge.

From Doris Lessing, *The Golden Notebook* (Michael Joseph, 1963). Copyright © 1962 by Doris Lessing. US Copyright © renewed 1990 by Doris Lessing. Reprinted by kind permission of Simon & Schuster, and Jonathan Clowes Ltd., London, on behalf of Doris Lessing.

From Maurice Mætterlinck, *The Life of the Ant*, trans. Bernard Miall (Allen & Unwin, 1958). Reprinted by kind permission of HarperCollins Publishers Ltd.

From V. S. Naipaul, *The Enigma of Arrival* (Penguin, 1987). Copyright © 1987 by V. S. Naipaul. Reprinted with the permission of Gillon Aitken Associates.

From Wallace Stevens, "Notes Toward A Supreme Fiction," *Collected Poems* (Faber, 1984). Reprinted by kind permission of Faber & Faber, and Random House Inc. on behalf of The Estate of Wallace Stevens.

From Boyd Tonkin, "Antonia S. Byatt in Interview with Boyd Tonkin," *Anglistik* 10.2 (1999). Reprinted by kind permission of Boyd Tonkin, A. S. Byatt, and Rüdiger Ahrens on behalf on *Anglistik*.

From Nicolas Tredell, *Conversations with Critics* (Carcanet, 1994). Reprinted by kind permission of Carcanet Press Ltd.

From Eleanor Wachtel, *Writers and Company* (Knopf, 1993). Copyright © 1993. Reprinted by permission of Alfred A. Knopf Canada, a division of Random House of Canada Limited.

The editors and publishers would also like to thank Walter De Gruyter & Co. for permission to include material from Sally Shuttleworth, "Natural History: The Retro-Victorian Novel," *The Third Culture: Literature and Science*, ed. Elinor S. Shaffer (Walter De Gruyter, 1998), which forms part of Sally Shuttleworth's contribution to this book.

We further acknowledge kind permission to reprint the following two contributions to this book:

Jean-Louis Chevalier, "Conclusion in *Possession*," *Fin de Romans: Aspects de la conclusion dans la littérature anglaise* (Presses Universitaires de Caen, 1993). Reprinted by kind permission of Lucien Le Bouille on behalf of Presses Universitaires de Caen.

Jackie Buxton, "'What's love got to do with it?': Postmodernism and *Possession*," *English Studies in Canada* 22 (1996). Reprinted by kind permission of *English Studies in Canada*.

Grateful acknowledgment also to Michael D. Crane, co-author (with Alexa Alfer) of the comprehensive *A. S. Byatt: An Annotated Bibliography* (http://www.asbyatt.com), for making this material available for our select bibliography. (Copyright © 1999 by Alexa Alfer and Michael D. Crane.)

For
Ruth Becker
and
Evan Victoria Noble

Contents

Acknowledgments

We would like to thank the following friends and colleagues for their ideas, encouragement, and help in realizing this project: Rosemarie and Dieter Alfer, Hazel Bell, Darrell Bourque, Tiffany Bunker Noble, Michael Danner, Nattie Golubov, Claudia Harris, Elizabeth Maslen, Gill Marsden, and Gráinne Walshe. We are particularly grateful to Michael D. Crane for his collaboration on matters bibliographical.

Special thanks are due to all our contributors for their patience, goodwill, and much mutual inspiration—it has been a joy working with all of them. Finally, we are deeply indebted to A. S. Byatt for her enthusiasm, generosity, and unfailing support.

Alexa Alfer and Michael J. Noble

Abbreviations

Works by A. S. Byatt, cited parenthetically throughout this book, are abbreviated as follows:

AI   *Angels and Insects* (London: Chatto & Windus, 1992).

BG   *The Biographer's Tale* (London: Chatto & Windus, 2000).

BT   *Babel Tower* (London: Chatto & Windus, 1996).

DNE *The Djinn in the Nightingale's Eye: Five Fairy Stories* (London: Chatto & Windus, 1994).

E   *Elementals: Stories of Fire and Ice* (London: Chatto & Windus, 1998).

G   *The Game* (London: Chatto & Windus, 1967).

IC   with Ignês Sodré. *Imagining Characters: Six Conversations About Women Writers*, ed. Rebecca Swift (London: Chatto & Windus, 1995).

MS   *The Matisse Stories* (London: Chatto & Windus, 1993).

PM   *Passions of the Mind: Selected Writings* (London: Chatto & Windus, 1991).

POa *Possession: A Romance* (London: Chatto & Windus, 1990).

POb *Possession: A Romance* (New York: Random House, 1990).

S   *Sugar and Other Stories* (London: Chatto & Windus, 1987).

SS   *The Shadow of the Sun* (London: Vintage, 1991). Rpt. of *Shadow of a Sun* (London: Chatto & Windus, 1964).

ST   *Still Life* (London: Chatto & Windus, 1985).

VG   *The Virgin in the Garden* (London: Chatto & Windus, 1978).

ESSAYS ON
THE FICTION OF A. S. BYATT

Alexa Alfer and Michael J. Noble

Introduction

"It occurred to me that it was a delicious, delicate tact, being, so to speak, the third in line, organising my own attention to the attention of a man intent on discovering the whole truth about yet a third man" (*BG* 24). Thus reflects the protagonist of A. S. Byatt's latest novel, *The Biographer's Tale* (2000). Phineas Nanson, disenchanted postmodernist critic and failed postgraduate student, has just embarked on a biographical study of a 1950s scholar who is, in turn, the biographer of an eminent Victorian polymath. "I need a life full of *things*," Phineas declares, "full of facts" (4), and the "almost impossible achievement of contact with the concrete world" (18) that Scholes Destry-Scholes's biography of Elmer Bole seems to afford holds out the promise of intellectual refuge in "the shining *solidity* of a world of facts" (4). Soon enough, however, Phineas realises that he is "acquiring only second- and third-hand facts," that he "was not discovering Destry-Scholes, beyond his own discoveries" (30). Such, it would seem, is the inevitable fate of the biographer's biographer, the critic's critic. But if the fictional biographer's biography seems doomed to remain unwritten, his *tale*, and that of his would-be biographer, is not. A. S. Byatt has written it.

Readers of Byatt's earlier fiction are already well accustomed to the "delicious, delicate tact" required of those who, as readers, must always stand "third in line." It is a predicament they share with many of Byatt's characters who, as readers, writers, and critics, ponder the fictional world with an intellectual intensity and critical astuteness that not only has the "shining solidity of the world of facts" perched at a precarious angle, but also inevitably complicates the business of recovering a critical vantage point beyond the text's own acute awareness of its fragility as fiction.

The Biographer's Tale, published just when our work on this collection was nearing completion, seems a poignant reminder of both the difficulties that we encountered as editors and the endlessly new and fascinating vistas that opened themselves up to us during the long process of realising this project. How, we had to ask ourselves, does one critique fictions that are always already critiquing themselves? How to "discover" beyond the texts' own rich discoveries? The present volume is in large part the result of our own as well as the various contributors' retracing and probing of this familiar dilemma. Above all, however, it is the record of a three-way conversation that takes its cue from our encounter with Byatt's fiction itself. "The novel is an agnostic form—it explores and describes," she writes, and "the novelist and the reader learn more about the world along the length of the book."[1]

A. S. Byatt's books project worlds that are both richly sensual and intensely intellectual, and her writings habitually emphasise the creative potential of an intersection—rather than mutual effacement—of storytelling and critical thought. Her "thinking" characters are a case in point, as are her recurrent forays into the realm of science and other academic discourses that enrich rather than stifle the creative potential unleashed by her fictions. And yet, when Phineas in *The Biographer's Tale* returns again and again to the intellectual and ontological dilemma of finding himself only "third in line," he is in good company. By placing characters and readers alike in the midst of such quandaries, Byatt exploits the make-believe of fiction with the express intention of aesthetic learning. It is in a similar spirit of learning that this collection sets its respective essays within a larger context, that of a mutually informative interchange between the scholarly and the imaginative. By seeking to explore, inhabit, and expand the fictive (and fictitiously critical) space that Byatt's work affords, this volume aspires to bring the reader, together with the multiple authors of this work, to a more comprehensive understanding of what is perhaps the most recurrent and idiomatic of Byatt's intellectual and aesthetic concerns: the nature of fiction as the proxy of thought and as an object of knowledge in its own right.

A writer with a long and varied career, A. S. Byatt is undoubtedly best known, at least internationally, for her re-imaginings of the Victorian past, prefigured in short stories like "Precipice-Encurled" from the 1987 collection *Sugar and Other Stories*, culminating in the virtuoso poetic ventriloquism of her award-winning novel *Possession: A Romance* (1990), and continued and refined even further in the two novellas that comprise *Angels and Insects* (1992). In a recent review for the German weekly *Die Zeit*, Dieter E. Zimmer writes:

One would have to go a long way before finding a contemporary writer to whom the literary classics of the past are so little "classic," so much alive and near and immediately relevant as they are to A. S. Byatt. One would have to go an even longer way before finding a writer who insists on making the relation of our own present to those literary classics one of the central and recurring themes not of her essays, but of her fictions.[2]

In the context of Byatt's work, such comments are more literal than figurative. The relation of our own present to the past (and its textual traces) is indeed not a mere subtext but the subject proper of many of her works, and reviewers and critical commentators alike repeatedly emphasise Byatt's joyful yet erudite fictional analyses and negotiations of history, and of literary history in particular.[3] In recent years, scholarly attention has increasingly focused on *Possession* in this context, and critics are drawn as much by this novel's exuberant excess of plot as by the critical astuteness that runs as a powerful undercurrent to its author's storytelling imagination. Indeed, as Byatt herself notes in her contribution to this volume, the difficult, often uneasy, yet potentially infinitely productive "relations of precise scholarship and fiction" are as integral to her work as they are to the critical debates that her fictions engender and in which they participate.

Amidst the intense theorising A. S. Byatt's fiction has inspired, one interpretative paradigm in particular—namely, that of "postmodernism"—enjoys unrivalled currency in discussions of her work. When Frederick Holmes compares *Possession* with John Fowles's *The French Lieutenant's Woman*[4] and places both novels within a "sub-species of postmodernism,"[5] specifically that class of text Linda Hutcheon terms "historiographic metafiction" or "novels which are both intensely self-reflexive and yet paradoxically also lay claim to historical events and personages,"[6] he offers a characterisation that has met with an almost uncanny consensus amongst critics of Byatt's historical fiction.[7] We shall return to the question of paradox further on and, indeed, throughout the course of this collection. Interesting at this point are the conclusions postmodern literary theory offers to draw from the conjunction of critical astuteness and the "primitive sensuous"[8] delight in storytelling that characterises A. S. Byatt's work. Within the theoretical framework envisaged by Hutcheon, the literary return to/of the past is essentially parodic in character; it subverts, her argument runs, poetic as well as historical conventions by working within them so that fiction assumes a critical function.[9] It is the postmodern awareness of this critical function on the part of the writer as well as the reader that accounts for the blurring of boundaries between literary and critical genres in the postmodern text.[10]

A. S. Byatt's ironic mimicry of contemporary criticism, her precise and gleefully assertive reinventions of Victorian poetry, the unashamedly constructed parallels between Victorian and contemporary story-lines—in short, the deft yet eclectic mix of genres, forms, and styles that make up the multilayered narrative of *Possession* certainly suggest strong—and almost suspiciously blatant—allegiances to what we have become accustomed to categorise as distinctly postmodern. Byatt's narratives even participate in this theory game, taking it one step further and confounding notions of the "well-made" postmodern text by boldly assuming narrative voices that seem to have travelled—unfiltered—straight out of the nineteenth-century novel: a happily omniscient narrator intrudes midway through the meticulously contrapuntal texts of *Possession* to confuse the parody with its original, while the two novellas comprising *Angels and Insects* dispense altogether with any narrative framework of overt self-reflexivity.

And yet, at a deeper level, A. S. Byatt's novels seem to defy, even defeat critical labelling. Jackie Buxton, in her contribution to this book, retraces and problematises the debate over Byatt's postmodernism and uncovers a critical tendency to "possess" or to name Byatt's historical fictions as "postmodern" that ignores an inscribed resistance to any easy appropriations of either the historical past or literary fiction. Most importantly, Buxton reminds us that the theory game in *Possession* ought not be taken at face value. When Roland, one of the novel's twentieth-century academic characters, asks himself whether there might not "be an element of superstitious dread in any self-reflexive, inturned postmodernist mirror-game or plot-coil that recognises that it has got out of hand," Buxton takes *him* at his word and reads his "precise postmodernist pleasure" and his frightening desire for closure as more than just another twist in the coil (*POb* 456). On the subject of Byatt's postmodernism, Buxton is thus able to conclude: "If *Possession* is a postmodern text then it is one that is deeply suspicious of *postmodernism*, whether it is construed as an aesthetic practice or as a historical condition. *Possession* may not celebrate the postmodern, but what it does do as a literary text is to seduce the reader into the consumption of Victorian poetry (or its simulacrum!)."

What postmodernism theorises as a paradox with considerable and almost automatic subversive potential can thus also be seen in a somewhat different and perhaps less blinding light. An alternative conceptualisation of the interlinking narrative claims to "intense self-reflexivity" and "historical events and personages" is suggested by A. S. Byatt's own essay for this book. In "True Stories and the Facts of Fiction," Byatt ponders the ambitious attempt to truly embody an earlier narrative mode or historic event—to analyse not so much through subversion of convention but through faithful, scrupulous adherence to it. Taking her cue from Robert Browning, she writes:

It is always said of Browning's various resurrected pasts in his dramatic monologues that they are about Browning and the nineteenth century, and of course this is true— but it is not always added that they are also truly about the time when the New Testament was written, or Renaissance Christianity and Art, though they are, and are illuminating about those matters. It is not either–or. At its best it is both–and. I do believe that if I read *enough*, and carefully enough, I shall have some sense of what words meant in the past, and how they related to other words in the past, and be able to use them in a modern text so that they do not lose their relations to other words of their own vocabulary. . . . Serious historical fiction today seems to me to have something in common with the difficult modern enterprise of Borges's *Pierre Menard*, rewriting the Quixote, in the "same" words, *now*.

In her own fiction, Byatt boldly dares to venture that despite the necessary and irreducible difference between the "then" and the "now," it is possible to recuperate the past and to give it a voice. Rather than celebrating postmodern parody and pastiche, Byatt joins in the serious and "difficult modern enterprise" of writing and rewriting "in the 'same' words, *now.*" As Sally Shuttleworth shows in her contribution to our collection, Byatt's historical fictions are indeed "both–and" rather than simply "either–or." Shuttleworth's specific focus is on Byatt's engagement with Darwinism and natural history in her novella "Morpho Eugenia" from *Angels and Insects*. There, "we are given not only the details of a Victorian natural history text" in Matty Crompton and William Adamson's study of the ants, "but a natural history of the lives and beliefs of the protagonists who are alike subjected to the scrutiny of the magnifying lens." Most importantly, however, the novella itself, moving "increasingly inward with a dizzying sense of detail," takes the textual form of a Victorian natural history. Natural history thus becomes both trope and narrative model in "Morpho Eugenia," and, according to Shuttleworth, this is a feature the novella shares with a number of its contemporaries. Refuting Fredric Jameson's hypothesis of the "historical deafness" of the postmodern age, she shows how *Angels and Insects* can be read as *both* "a symptom," as Jameson would claim, "of the poverty of our own culture" *and* "an antidote to that poverty." It thus seems permissible, appropriate even, to apply what Byatt says about Browning to Byatt's own "various resurrected pasts"— they are about Byatt and the twentieth century, but they are also truly about the Victorian age, Browning and Tennyson, Darwin and Swedenborg.

Like Browning, A. S. Byatt is a "witness of difference," and her re-imaginings of the past are fictional "resurrections" not only of past men and women, but also of texts, "all separately incarnate, all separately aware in their necessarily and splendidly limited ways, of infinite passion and the pain of finite hearts that yearn" (*PM* 71). Such a strong impulse to separate is also a desire to give definition, to give form, to make distinctions. If the resurrected past is *both* living *and* dead, this condition is not achieved by blurring the boundaries but by plotting them out in detail. Michael Levenson's contribution to this volume, which complements and connects with the pieces by Byatt and Shuttleworth, explores Byatt's commitment to this fundamental concept of difference—the indwelling difference between past and present, theory and fiction, text and intertext that alone can make full sense of their relation to each other. "In a more than clever analogy," Levenson has written elsewhere on *Angels and Insects*, "Byatt has drawn a connection between the 'afterlife' of the Bible and the 'afterlife' of the nineteenth-century novel. We live in the shadow of both. But the task, as Byatt sees it, is not to get out from under the shadow into the white modern light. It is to respect and to love our old shadowy needs, to keep faith with faith, and with realist fiction."[11] The difficulty, as Levenson muses in the pages of the present collection, lies, however, "in finding figures for this continuity," figures of thought and language that reach beyond mere nostalgia and easy analogy. Matty Crompton's "realist fable" of insect life in "Morpho Eugenia" is one such figure. In Matty's tale of "incarnation and metamorphoses," the rupture of the cocoon and the emergence of the newly born moth becomes a metaphor for Byatt's own particular vein of historical fiction. Ultimately, however, it is within language itself that Levenson recovers "the resources that bind us to the unsurpassable struggles of the nineteenth century." In *Angels and Insects*, metaphor, quite literally, becomes metamorphosis, language incarnation, so that the reading and writing of fiction, then as now, "might not only be *about* the act of faith in an age of doubt; it can itself *be* the act."

The amount of critical attention paid to A. S. Byatt's overtly historical fictions in the wake of *Possession*'s overwhelming public success has tended to obscure somewhat the view onto a larger project of novelistic reclamation that is, in our opinion, nevertheless ubiquitous to Byatt's work as a writer. The fictional resurrection of the Victorian past represents but one facet of the cultural and literary inheritance Byatt accepts and elaborates. Part of this inheritance is the novel form itself, and it is indeed possible to read Byatt's œuvre as an ongoing series of re-imaginings of the novel and its various (dis)contents. Here, Byatt may herself be said to stand "third" (or fourth, fifth, etc.) in a line of literary predecessors—yet here, too, she is above all a "witness of difference."

Characteristically, then, it is not the novelist but, rather, her characters who are troubled by what Harold Bloom has theorised as the "anxiety of influence." In the Prologue to *The Virgin in the Garden*, the poet and playwright Alexander Wedderburn is prompted to ponder "the nature of modern parody" by the crowd of eclectically attired hippies—"variously uniformed, uniformly various"—populating the steps leading up to the National Gallery: "Alexander himself had considerable knowledge about the history of clothing, could place a shift of seam or change of cut in relation to *tradition and the individual talent* almost as well as he could a verse-form or a vocabulary. He watched his own clothes and his own poetry in the light of these delicate shifts of subdued innovation. But he was apprehensive that at this time there was no real life in either" (11; emphasis added). The reference to T. S. Eliot is carefully placed early on in the novel and sets the tone for what lies ahead. What Eliot wrote in 1919 not only provides a fitting metaphor for A. S. Byatt's ongoing meditation on and reinventions of the novel form, which cut across her entire body of work, notably her projected tetralogy, which so far comprises *The Virgin in the Garden* (1978), *Still Life* (1985), and *Babel Tower* (1996).[12] Eliot's "Tradition and the Individual Talent" is also one of the principal texts Byatt writes back to in *The Virgin in the Garden*—sceptically, yet with nostalgia, "in the 'same' words, *now*." In Eliot, we read:

No poet, no artist of any art, has his complete meaning alone. His significance, his appreciation is the appreciation of his relation to the dead poets and artists. You cannot value him alone; you must set him, for contrast and comparison, among the dead. I mean this as a principle of aesthetic, not merely historical criticism. The necessity that he shall conform, that he shall cohere, is not onesided; what happens when a new work of art is created is something that happens simultaneously to all the works of art which preceded it. . . . The existing order is complete before the new work arrives; for order to persist after the supervention of novelty, the whole existing order must be, if ever so slightly, altered; and so the relations, proportions, values of each work of art toward the whole are readjusted; and this is conformity between the old and the new.[13]

Here, we have an almost uncannily accurate image also of the *internal* structure of *The Virgin in the Garden*. In this novel of stunning verbal and intellectual complexity, whose plot evolves, tellingly, around the production of a modern verse-drama on Elizabeth I, literary allusions and quotations abound to form an elaborate fictional commentary on the history of modernity. Indeed, as Byatt writes in her essay "Still Life / Nature morte," *The Virgin in the Garden* was intended in part as a fictional "response to T. S. Eliot's ideas of the history of poetic language and the nature of the poetic image," as well as to his almost mythical dictum of modernity's "dissociation of sensibility" (*PM* 9). *The Virgin in the Garden* is essentially written *into* an intricate and already existing web of literary predecessors which it simultaneously reimagines as the narrative unfolds, and here, too, "the relations, proportions, values of each work of art toward the whole are readjusted" with every new/old line of poetry, every figure of thought that (re)enters the richly textured fabric of this novel. Such is "the conformity between the old and the new" that *The Virgin in the Garden* celebrates at the same time as it deeply distrusts its seeming promises of a perpetual golden age of literature.

In this volume, Judith Plotz counts the casualties of such "conformity" in her essay on one of this novel's most puzzling characters, Marcus Potter. A troubled teenager prone to overwhelming moments of geometric apprehension and "floods of light," Marcus is gifted or cursed with a perceptual capacity for "spreading himself" to the extent that "sometimes, for immeasurable instants he lost any sense of where he really was, of where the spread mind had its origin" (27). Marcus has attracted curiously little attention in criticism of Byatt's tetralogy. Perhaps, as Plotz muses, this silent, "resolutely incommunicative" and so exclusively mathematically minded character is not only a stranger in the fiercely literary and "densely verbal universe the novel projects; perhaps he must also seem alien and inaccessible to the literary critic." Yet, as Plotz demonstrates, "in his isolation, his seeming self-sufficiency, his private interior world, his visions of pure form, and his apprehensions of a world charged with life, Marcus resembles a Romantic wise child" with distinct Wordsworthian overtones. In the course of the novel, however, Marcus emerges not as a modern "seer blest," but bruised and abused not only by his increasingly insane friend and mentor Lucas Simmonds, but also by a family environment that is much better at literature than at life and repeatedly, perhaps ironically, fails to provide a meaningful context for Marcus's experience. Unlike Byatt's other grand visionary, the novelist Henry Severell in *The Shadow of the Sun* (1964)—and not so very unlike the character of Cassandra Corbett in *The Game* (1967)—Marcus's visions fail to resonate with meaning. A clinical synaesthetic, yet his remains a profoundly "dissociated sensibility" at sea in a fictional world that has so much invested in Eliot's myth of modernity's fall from "undissociatedness."

It is precisely the visionary figures in Byatt's earlier fiction to which Kuno Schuhmann turns his attention in his contribution to this book. If Marcus's post-Romantic gifts of perception in *The Virgin in the Garden* only highlighted the "terrors and loneliness of childhood" brought on by a painful lack of self-knowledge, such lack of self-knowledge provides intense creative impetus for Byatt's first and far more classically Romantic artist-character. In *The Shadow of the Sun*, Henry Severell is a novelist of genius, famous and—crucially—only too aware of the traditions and layers of intertexts that legitimise his own visionary spells as "a direct source of power" (*SS* 59). Schuhmann aptly describes the loss of identity underlying Severell's visions as seminal to his creativity: following Henry on one of his highly imaged solitary walks, he retraces "a gradual progress via several stages to a loss of personal identity, a merging with nature in which natural objects keep their characteristics while the observing wanderer becomes 'unrecognizable' and is transformed into a 'grotesque figure,' . . . blurring the boundaries between man and animal existence." Here is transfiguration of another kind—not from an abstraction to an incarnate representation in art, but from visionary to vision, from artist or author to that which is represented. Schuhmann's dissection of "self-actualisation," in which the self is made real or made *actual*, goes beyond the psychobabble so often connoted by "self-fulfilment" to show how Severell's art functions as a medium to capture or arrest the self in a silent moment of pure language. The transfiguration is not necessarily or innately ennobling, however. Extending his discussion to an analysis of scholarly Cassandra in *The Game*, Schuhmann contrasts this long-suffering character's extreme and ultimately suicidal selflessness with the essential self-assertion of her novelist sister Julia and arrives at a reading of *The Game* as a late-twentieth-century commentary on Keats's concept of *negative capability*. When, as in Cassandra's case, there is complete extraction or effacement of self, there is also no meaning. At the same time, Julia's literary endeavours demonstrate that if the self prevails, there is no art.

Again, the central question is one of representation, its reality and truthfulness, manifest through the *visionary* but also through the *visual*. In a fascinating passage from *Still Life*, Alexander Wedderburn and/or the narrator, in one of the novel's recurring instances of fused narrative consciousness, ponder that "Language might relate the plum to the night sky, or to certain ways of seeing a burning coal, or to a soft case enwrapping a hard nugget of treasure. Or it might introduce an abstraction, a reflection, of mind, not of mirror." Paint, on the other hand, "declares itself as a force of analogy and connection, a kind of metaphor-making between the flat surface of purple pigment and yellow pigment and the statement 'This is a plum'." And yet, the narrative goes on to reflect, "it is impossible *not* to think about the distance between paint and things, between paint and life, between paint and the 'real world' (which includes other paintings). It is not at all impossible, it is even common, not to think about the distance between words and things, between words and life, between words and reality" (*ST* 165).

In *Still Life*, the intellectual focus is on Van Gogh's paintings, and throughout the book, as again in *The Matisse Stories* (1993) and *Elementals* (1998), "there runs a concern for the relation between visual perception, predominantly the perception of colour, and its representation in language."[14] Michael Worton conceptualises Byatt's approximations of this relationship in his contribution to this volume. Through a reading of the "necessarily absent" paintings that abound in Byatt's "inter-generic fictions," Worton uncovers a much neglected and perhaps unexpected facet of intertextual practice in her work. In *Babel Tower*, a novel not explicitly discussed by Worton, it is again one of the characters who grapples with the tension between textual absence and intertextual co-creation. Teaching a class on *Women in Love* to a group of young artists, Frederica Potter elaborates on how "This novel is made of visual images—the lanterns, the moon, the white flowers—which you might think were like painted images, but they are not for they have to be *unseen visible images* to be powerful. They are made out of language but that is not all they are" (213). Where Frederica (and, one might add, D. H. Lawrence) tries—and, for the time being, fails—"to make the painters and sculptors see how a novel is a work of art and is not a painting," A. S. Byatt succeeds. As Worton demonstrates, her writings "reveal themselves as performative responses to paintings," so that "the (creative) tension between art and literature is much more than a struggle for interpretative priority, and the . . . debates around *ut pictura poesis* lead us beyond evaluations of the relative merits of illustration, commentary, or ekphrasis into considerations of the cognitive status of both reading and viewing." To say that writing is like painting, in this sense, is to undo the analogy, to deconstruct both the opposition between, and the creative conflation of, the visual and the verbal. The key, it seems, is a writerly practice that retains at the same time as it supersedes the "distance between paint and things," between paint and words, and between "words and reality."

Seemingly at odds with Byatt's long-standing fascination with "the problems of the 'real' in fiction, and the adequacy of words to describe it" (*PM* 3–4) is her simultaneous engagement with the impossible and fantastic realms of the fairy tale.[15] Recent collections of short stories, namely *The Djinn in the Nightingale's Eye* (1994) and *Elementals*, contain several traditional fairy stories—*traditional* in the sense that they take up and expand upon the conventions of the genre. Such tales have been a continually present subtext also to Byatt's historical fiction. Embedded within *Possession*, for example, is the story of "The Glass Coffin," part of the fictitious *Tales for Innocents*. Likewise in "Morpho Eugenia," Matty Crompton pens her "Things Are Not What They Seem," which she intentionally writes as "a fabulous Tale, not an allegory" (161).

Richard Todd, in his 1996 monograph on A. S. Byatt, suggests that rather than "fairy stories," these forays into fantasy are more appropriately placed within the German tradition of the "wonder-tale," a term altogether more conducive "to the feel of the marvellous."[16] Indeed, Byatt herself writes about the "wonder-tale" in one of her essays on Browning, arguing that the (Christian) concept of Incarnation is "inextricably connected, consciously and unconsciously" to this tradition

(*PM* 83). It is not surprising then that Byatt's own *märchen* habitually reveal themselves as magical transformations, marvellous "reincarnations" of their own narrative format.

In the current volume, both Jane Campbell and Annegret Maack turn their attention to Byatt's *The Djinn in the Nightingale's Eye: Five Fairy Stories* (1994). Jane Campbell examines the collection as a whole and proposes a feminist reading of its tales as re-visions of the traditional female plot. In "Wonder-Tales Hiding a Truth," Annegret Maack explores the volume's title story as a tale of human freedom and fate, in which texts and intertexts oscillate between narrative experiences of entrapment and empowerment. Both critics, however, view the transformation of the narrative form as a significant counterpoint to the transformation of character.

For Campbell, the transformational force of *The Djinn in the Nightingale's Eye* manifests itself as a strategic plotting of gender and identity that reveals the patriarchal ideology inherent in the genre. By breaking some of the key conventions of the fairy-tale form, Byatt upsets the formulaic plot, and the tension between form and formula does not go unnoticed by the protagonist of the collection's title story. Gillian Perholt, a professional narratologist, reflects on the predicament of fairy-tale characters whose wishes are granted: "We feel the possible leap of freedom . . . and the perverse certainty that this will change nothing; that Fate is fixed" (259). It takes Gillian's physical journey to the East and her magic encounter with the djinn—the embodiment of the stories she studies—to reveal the full power of the storytelling imagination and its capacity to take narrator, narratologist, and reader alike beyond such paralysing paradox. As Maack suggests, stories, and fairy stories in particular, articulate this paradox, and "The Djinn in the Nightingale's Eye" is a tale that not only speaks of wish-fulfilment and its limitations, narrative desire and containment, but also about itself as a story told and retold. Noting a gradual thinning of the boundary between the (re-)telling and the tale, Campbell goes on to show how Gillian herself becomes, quite literally, a magical figure in a tale. By reinventing the form of the frame story with which Gillian herself has some expertise, both teller and tale spin and are spun in concentric circles, intersecting with Chaucer, Perrault, Scheherazade, and the "Ancient Mariner," one within another, and/or one on top of the other. And like the glass paperweight Gillian ponders at the end of "The Djinn in the Nightingale's Eye," this wonder-tale is somehow, marvellously, "not possible, it is only a solid metaphor, it is a medium for seeing and a thing seen at once" (274–75).

"What do words mean? What do they wish to mean? What do they mean without wishing? And how to read them?" Jean-Louis Chevalier is prompted to ask in this volume. He refers specifically to Byatt's *Possession*. This novel is, as Chevalier writes, above all else "a story of words: a famous poem of stealth by a famous poet, and unknown manuscripts stolen by an unknown scholar, all amount to words of the self-same poet, words public and words private, words poetic and domestic, or not quite domestic, not homely, but comely, attentive, assiduous, and seductive."

In *Possession*, the famously fictitious Randolph Henry Ash tells the adventure of Herakles in his poem "The Garden of Proserpina," but Byatt (via Ash) casts this adventure against a very word-heavy legacy of mixed metaphors and mythologies. Proserpina's garden is every garden—it is the forest of Arcady, it is the garden of the Norse goddess Freya, it is the Garden of Eden, and it is the Hesperidean grove:

> These things are there. The garden and the tree
> The serpent at its root, the fruit of gold
> The woman in the shadow of the boughs
> The running water and the grassy space.
> They are and were there. . . .
>
> (*POb* 503)

The tree may be the tree of the knowledge of good and evil, or it may be the tree growing the golden apples. The serpent at the tree's root may be the guardian Ladon or the spirit of Lucifer, and the woman may be Eve or one of the many Hesperidean nymphs. All of them "are and were there." Or are they?

> And are these places shadows of one Place?
> Those trees of one Tree? And the mythic beast
> A creature from the caverns of men's minds . . . ?
>
> (504)

Chevalier finds in Ash's garden the beginning of a quest, not only for the possession of knowledge but for the conclusion that will engender meaning. In what Chevalier identifies as a *trying for* and a *trial of* conclusions, the multiplicity of the narrative veils meaning as it seeks to reveal it, so that conclusion retreats infinitely, as mirror images of a mirror image. For Chevalier, *Possession* is thus also a story of words missing or gone missing, like the golden apples. Above all, however, it is a story of conclusion held out, withheld, and reached only "outside the narrative, yet at the very heart of the story."

Perhaps a similar quest for conclusion underlies the enterprise of this collective endeavour. Feminist polemic and/or post-postmodern critique, literary metacriticism and/or artistic–scientific postulation, Byatt's fiction is, and inspires, not "either–or" but emphatically "both–and." Taken together, the various essays in this volume cannot be subsumed into a larger conclusion or key to interpreting Byatt's work. They can, however, offer a cumulative context for additional critical inquiry and a sounding board for individual readers. Where there are differences—and there are significant differences—they reflect the spirit of inquiry that lies not only at the "heart of the story" but also at the heart of *story* itself, narrative and metanarrative exquisitely conjoined. Byatt's own contribution underscores this spirit of inquiry, suggesting as it does that interpretation need not be "imposed," that it might also be "found" through careful scrutiny *and* the work of the creative imagination. Our joint critical aspiration is thus as ambitious as the steep narrative terrain of Byatt's fiction: to explore and map out "the hard idea of truth," to discover form through the power of thought and of imagination, to realise the imagined and to imagine the real.

NOTES

1. A. S. Byatt in Christopher Hope (ed.), *A. S. Byatt* [pamphlet], Contemporary Writers Series (London: Book Trust in conjunction with the British Council, 1990) 1.

2. Dieter E. Zimmer, "Intelligente Landschaften," rev. of *Die Jungfrau im Garten* [*The Virgin in the Garden*], *Die Zeit* (10 Dec. 1998): 60 [translated for this edition].

3. See, for instance, Ivana Djordjevic, "In the Footsteps of Giambattista Vico: Patterns of Signification in A. S. Byatt's *Possession*," *Anglia* 115 (1997): 44–83; Sabine Hotho-Jackson, "Literary History in Literature: An Aspect of the Contemporary Novel," *Moderna Språk* 86.2 (1992): 113–19; Del Ivan Janik, "No End of History: Evidence from the Contemporary English Novel," *Twentieth Century Literature* 41.2 (1995): 160–90; Dana Shiller, "The Redemptive Past in the Neo-Victorian Novel," *Studies in the Novel* 29.4 (Winter 1997): 538–60.

4. Cf. A. S. Byatt, "The Reader as Writer, the Writer as Reader," The Beall-Russell Lectures in the Humanities, Baylor University (1 Nov. 1993), published as an untitled pamphlet by Baylor University (1993), 18 pp, in which Byatt comments at length on literary models and predecessors to *Possession* and discusses *The French Lieutenant's Woman* in a not entirely favourable light.

5. Frederick M. Holmes, "The Historical Imagination and the Victorian Past: A. S. Byatt's *Possession*," *English Studies in Canada* 20.3 (1994): 320.

6. Linda Hutcheon, *A Poetics of Postmodernism: History, Theory, Fiction* (London: Routledge, 1988) 5.

7. See, for instance, Elizabeth Bronfen, "Romancing Difference, Courting Coherence: A. S. Byatt's *Possession* as postmodern moral Fiction," *Why Literature Matters: Theories and Functions of Literature*, ed. Rüdiger Ahrens and Laurenz Volkmann (Heidelberg: C. Winter, 1996), 117–34; Kate Flint, "Plotting the Victorians: Narrative, Post-modernism, and Contemporary Fiction," *Writing and Victorianism*, ed. J. B. Bullen (Harlow: Longman, 1997), 286–305; Giuliana Giobbi, "'Know the Past, Know Thyself': Literary Pursuits and the Quest for Identity in A. S. Byatt's *Possession* and F. Duranti's *Effeti Personali*," *Journal of European Studies* 24.1 (March 1994): 41–55; Kelly A. Marsh, "The Neo-Sensation Novel: A Contemporary Genre in the Victorian Tradition," *Philological Quarterly* 74.1 (Winter 1995): 99–123; Shiller 1997; Richard Todd, "The Retrieval of Unheard Voices in British Postmodernist Fiction: A. S. Byatt and Marina Warner," *Liminal Postmodernism: The Postmodern, the (Post-) Colonial, and the (Post-) Feminist*, ed. Theo D'haen and Hans Bertens (Amsterdam: Rodopi, 1994) 99–114.

8. Kuno Schuhmann, introductory talk, British Council New Writing Festival, Literaturhaus Fasanenstraße, Berlin, 26 Nov. 1998.

9. Linda Hutcheon, "Beginning to Theorize Postmodernism," *A Postmodern Reader*, ed. Linda Hucheon and Joseph Natoli (New York: State U of New York P, 1993) 246.

10. Hutcheon, "Beginning to Theorize" 250.

11. Michael Levenson, "The Religion of Fiction," rev. of *Angels and Insects*, *New Republic* 209 (2 Aug. 1993): 41–44; rpt. as "Angels and Insects: Two Novellas by A. S. Byatt," in

A. S. Byatt, *Degrees of Freedom: The Early Novels of Iris Murdoch* (London: Vintage, 1994) 337–44; here 343.

12. The fourth and final volume in the series, *A Whistling Woman*, was nearing completion at the time the present collection of essays went to press.

13. T. S. Eliot, "Tradition and the Individual Talent," *Selected Essays*, 3rd ed. (London: Faber & Faber, 1963) 15.

14. Michael Westlake, "The Hard Idea of Truth," *PN Review* 15.4 (1989): 33.

15. See Ann Ashworth, "Fairy Tales in A. S. Byatt's *Possession*," *Journal of Evolutionary Psychology* 15.1–2 (March 1994): 93–94; and Victoria Sanchez, "A. S. Byatt's *Possession*: A Fairytale Romance," *Southern Folklore* 52.1 (Spring 1995): 33–52.

16. Richard Todd, *A. S. Byatt* (Plymouth: Northcote House in association with the British Council, 1997) 39.

Michael Worton

Of Prisms and Prose: Reading Paintings in A. S. Byatt's Work

A. S. Byatt's work is amongst the most intricately texted and richly intertextual of contemporary writing. Her novels and stories persuade, seduce, amuse, educate, and occasionally confound readers. It can, however, easily be forgotten that at the heart of her enterprise is a desire to tell stories and to tell stories that not only impart knowledge and ideas but also generate thinking and inspire speculative curiosity. Byatt does *know* a lot, but comparisons of her work with, say, that of Umberto Eco, which dwell on "the extent and ostentatiousness of [her] learning"[1] can be misleading. Byatt does not so much wear her learning showily as communicate in all of her writings the intense excitement that she herself finds in learning. In other words, she is concerned more with the process of acquiring knowledge than with the state of having gained it, since for her to know is always to recognise that more is to be learned. If Byatt's joy in knowledge is coupled with an anxious regret about the loss of the *presence* of the cultural, and especially the literary past,[2] it is also informed by a passionate commitment to the reader—who is always a co-creator rather than a passive receiver of her texts.

In the introduction to *Passions of the Mind*, Byatt tells us that from her early childhood, reading and writing were not distinct activities but rather "points on a circle," stating that: "Greedy reading made me want to write, as if this was the only adequate response to the pleasure and power of books." Such an attitude is not uncommon in writers, but Byatt goes on to make a striking, more original point: "Writing made me want to read" (*PM* 1). In other words, for Byatt the writing process is a centrifugal rather than a centripetal process, one that constantly takes her beyond the orbit determined by her own writing needs and into realms of otherness. Her literary enterprise is marked by an abiding curiosity,

both epistemological and simply, joyfully natural. As a practice, it is characterised also by generosity, since, although her fictional texts are carefully crafted,
they do not confront their readers with closure; rather, they offer narratives that
are *seamed through* with openings onto other worlds existing outside that of the
tale.

In this "exorbitant" universe, intertextual reference is paradoxically anchor
and sail, simultaneously providing the fixity and certainty of context for the tale's
wanderings and enabling it to fly off in different directions, carried off by the
winds of chance cultural—and other—encounters. Now, it is in the nature of
every literary text to generate uncertainty, for every text is built on references to
texts and events outside itself, references that no individual reader can ever
completely understand or follow up. In Byatt's case, the extra-textual references
are many and complex, and these references are not purely textual. Indeed, one of
the shortcomings of much Byatt criticism is the concentration on the textual and
intertextual at the expense of the more broadly cultural and intergeneric.

Byatt has often spoken passionately about both the worth of art and the role of
the artist. For her, the issue of *how* and *why* artists create is "a serious and terrible
problem" (*MS* 52), one that is perhaps best articulated in "Art Work" in *The
Matisse Stories* in the searing question: "why bother, why make representations
of anything at all?" (52). She is haunted by "the impossibility of pure representation" (*PM* 6) yet also clings to the belief that "accuracy of description is possible
and valuable. That words denote things" (*PM* 11).

Her fictional universe is complex and full of people and events, many of which
are drawn in minute detail. However, critics are perhaps over-ready to privilege
the verbal and linguistic when considering her work, even when studying her
engagement with painting and painters. For instance, in speaking of *The Matisse
Stories*, Silvia Bigliazzi argues that Byatt seems to "endow Matisse's painting
with specifically linguistic functions."[3] This seems to me seriously to misread
how the paintings function semantically in Byatt's work: Bigliazzi pre-emptively
accords primacy to the verbal in her analyses and consequently fails to allow that
there can be any significant semantic functioning that goes beyond the hallowed
linguistic.

Byatt's universe is a highly referential one in which language not only is used
with pleasure as a means of giving presence to stories, ideas, and cultural
concepts, but also refers the reader outwards *from* the text to a world that is
decidedly non-verbal. One particularly significant part of this non-verbal extra-
text or paratext is painting. The references throughout Byatt's writings to works
of art and especially to paintings are crucial both to the narrative drive of her
fictions and to the central image-clusters of the individual texts. However, the
paintings themselves are necessarily *absent* from the texts (although some of
them figure on the covers of her books, e.g., *The Matisse Stories*). This textual
absence both fractures and creatively complicates the text, since, in order fully to
understand the narrative, the reader has to visualise the painting—and this often
means leaving the reading of the text to seek it or its reproduction out.

Having seen the painting, the reader then returns to the text with an altered perspective. Byatt's textual inscription of paintings takes a variety of forms, ranging from description and interpretation through evocation and allusion to creation and invention. Perhaps unsurprisingly, critics strive to make narrative sense of the paintings, inscribing them into the meaning of the text. However, I would argue that it is not so much a question of textual meaning as one of textual *meaningfulness*. Byatt's inter-generic fictions reveal themselves as performative responses to paintings, which challenge the reader both to *read* for him/herself and to recognise that all reading, be it of a painting or a text, is the trace of an encounter, and will, indeed must, lead to a writing of and for the self.

UT PICTURA POESIS?

The debates about the validity of the Classical maxim *ut pictura poesis* have raged for centuries, with Lessing, for example, asserting in his *Laocoön* that literature and painting are based on wholly irreconcilable principles, or Valéry arguing repeatedly that paintings necessarily call up verbal responses,[4] or Lyotard opening his *Discours/Figure* with the trenchant statement that "One does not read, one does not hear a painting."[5] However important these debates are, they often tend towards the universalising, and the very vastness of their scope and targets can lead to a suspect process of essentialising. Nonetheless, we need to speak of art, even if, as Louis Marin reminds us, "Discourse about painting is always academic, which essentially means that it is metadiscursive."[6] For Marin, any discussion of painting is necessarily based on one or more system(s) of norms and principles of aesthetic judgement—and also, one might add, on socio-historically constructed taxonomies and codes of thinking and saying. And if painting both has and is its own rhetoric(s), it too inescapably functions—in relation to the spectator—through the mediation of the structures of and in language.

In the modern world, we tend increasingly to narrativise, despite the fact that the image is ever more dominant and *immediately* important. Or perhaps precisely because of this fact—because the images that saturate today's mediatised society *supplant* verbal narratives while purporting to supplement them, thus leaving us momentarily bereft of the means of making sense of the world. The compulsion to narrativise is a particularly modern phenomenon, but Byatt is acutely aware of the need for other, non-linear and non-linguistic modes of both representing and being in the world. She sees painters and novelists as interpreters, affirming that they are "secondary beings, not primary beings. They are recorders. They work, and work is understanding, work is representing, work is making an object which allows you to consider, rather like a microscope, the world from a different angle."[7]

It is undeniable that Byatt *reads* paintings. She also regards them as radically different from fiction: "painting, unlike writing, is a science as well as an art— that is one of the reasons I so love painting; the precision of it, the analytic quality of it."[8] However, she does not only read them: she experiences them "sensation-ally," allowing colour, shape, and line to move her emotionally. Furthermore, she knows that painting is ultimately not translatable into words: "I have come to see painting as, in a sense, the opposite of literature. I think almost all writers who write about painting write about it as though it was narrative or at least poetry, yet what I like about it is that element in the visual which completely defeats language."[9]

In this, she is expressing a view shared by critics, theorists, and artists alike. For instance, John Gage writes of two artists for whom Byatt has a particular affinity: "One cannot but be struck . . . by the poverty of idea and expression in, say, Mondrian's writings between 1917 and 1944, or Matisse's between 1908 and 1947, compared to the richness and variety of the works to which these writings ostensibly relate. In the case of Matisse we are dealing with a far more sophisticated thinker than Mondrian, but the simplifications that arise from an essentially propagandist intent are no less evident."[10] Matisse himself recognised the problem, stating in his influential "Notes of a Painter" of 1908:

A painter who addresses the public not just in order to present his works, but to reveal some of his ideas on the art of painting, exposes himself to several dangers.

In the first place, knowing that many people like to think of painting as an appendage of literature and therefore want it to express not general ideas suited to pictorial means, but specifically literary ideas, I fear that one will look with astonish-ment upon the painter who ventures to invade the domain of the literary man. As a matter of fact, I am fully aware that a painter's best spokesman is his work.[11]

Jacques Derrida takes a similarly caustic view: "As for painting, any discourse on it, beside it or above, always strikes me as silly, both didactic and incantatory, programmed, worked by the compulsion of mastery, be it poetical or philosophi-cal, always, and the more so when it is pertinent, in the position of chit-chat, unequal and unproductive in the sight of what, at a stroke [*d'un trait*], does without or goes beyond this language, remaining heterogeneous to it or denying it any overview."[12] However, there is always also the desire to talk of a painting, to put it into words, and Derrida himself elsewhere adopts a Valéryan position when speaking of "silent works" of art that are "talkative, full of virtual dis-courses."[13]

The (creative) tension between art and literature is much more than a struggle for interpretative priority, and the contemporary debates around *ut pictura poesis* lead us beyond evaluations of the relative merits of illustration, commentary, or ekphrasis into considerations of the cognitive status of both reading and viewing.

Matisse offers a clear statement of the importance he accords to composition:

Composition is the art of arranging in a decorative manner the diverse elements at the painter's command to express his feelings. In a picture every part will be visible and will play its appointed role, whether it be principal or secondary. Everything that is not useful in the picture is, it follows, harmful. A work of art must be harmonious in its entirety: any superfluous detail would replace some other essential detail in the mind of the spectator.[14]

What is striking about this notion of compositional harmony as vital for the viewer as well as for the artist and the work is how similar it is to the great heuristic tradition descending from St. Augustine's *De Doctrina Christiana,* which holds that any interpretation of a certain portion of text can be accepted if it is confirmed by, and must be rejected if it is challenged by, another portion of the same text. However, all texts (and, indeed, paintings, albeit to a lesser extent) are full of what Michael Riffaterre calls "ungrammaticalities"[15]—moments when their discourse is interrupted by another discourse, when they refer outside themselves, when they contradict themselves. These ungrammaticalities send us off outside the text, back into the phenomenal world; they also alert us to the literariness, the complex textuality of the texts that we are reading and so maintain us in a speculative oscillation between a world of referring and a world referred to.

Byatt is a very "wordy" writer. She loves language and revels in the extensive lexical possibilities of English, as is witnessed by her predilection for cumulations of nouns or adjectives, her etymological plays, and her borrowings from other languages. She also savours the aurality and the implicit orality of the written word. Indeed, rhythm is crucial for her, and she regrets passionately the loss of a shared oral and written rhythmic past: "I feel lonely sometimes when I offer a little bit of biblical rhythm to my children's generation and not one of them recognises it."[16] One senses in reading her work that the process of writing her fictions is one in which sense is always interacting with sensibility and sensation. And, crucially, one realises that, as Mikel Dufrenne puts it, "The act of reading is not precisely one of seeing or of hearing."[17] Reading is a *performative* act in which one discovers the world through the prism of someone else's vision and also discovers it for oneself—by testing hypotheses and by checking extratextual references. The range of Byatt's references is vast: one cannot simply accept what she writes, one is driven by the text itself to go and encounter the world anew.

In an attack on overinterpretation, Eco warns against what he calls "an excess of wonder,"[18] which, in his view, leads to overestimating the importance of details and coincidences in a text. Eco is determined to respect the distinction between what he calls "internal textual coherence" and "the otherwise uncontrollable drives of the reader."[19] According to him, the former must control the latter, and the only way to check an interpretative conjecture against the *intentio operis* or intention of the text[20] "is to check it upon the text as a coherent whole."[21] This moderate, Augustinian position strikes me as suspect in general terms, and in thinking on how reading can best function, I have argued elsewhere for speculative risk-taking as the essential mode of reading.[22]

In its celebration of knowledge and culture, Byatt's fiction is a testament to what some might call "an excess of wonder," and it wondrously generates speculative responses in its readers, making them want to know and go and *see*. Occasionally, Byatt invents a painting, as is the case in "'Crocodile Tears,'" where she describes a seaside scene that is entitled *The Windbreak*. Patricia and Tony have violently differing responses to this work, Patricia considering it to be banal and clichéd, whereas, for Tony, "It's a perfectly good complete image of something important" (*E* 6). Both advance good reasons for their positions, but what is significant is that the reader can *see* it: Byatt gives a minute description, which is rich not only in colour adjectives but also in evocations of texture (5–6). It has such a sense of reality that one is certain that one has seen it—and indeed one has, in slightly different versions, at the Royal Academy Summer Show and art exhibitions across the country, for what is being described here is a *type* of work, a generic collage seascape of the 1960s and 1970s, complete with tiny seashells and bits of plastic bucket. Yet it is also absolutely absent and resistant to any attempt to check the accuracy or completeness of Byatt's description against a real work in canvas, oils, and plastic. Like Byatt, one sees the painting in one's mind's eye; then, on realising that it is a mere figment of an author's imagination, one scrutinises with suspicion all later references to artworks, such as those of the very real Sigmar Polke, which are equally well—and verifiably—described (*E* 50–52).

In the majority of cases, though, Byatt is not playing with her reader in this way, and her references are to real artists and works. While she refers to a host of artists from the classical to the contemporary, the work of three artists seems to me to be particularly important for an understanding of how references to painting function in her work: Van Gogh, Matisse, and Velázquez.

VAN GOGH

One of Byatt's abiding concerns is with balance—psychic, artistic, formal, metaphysical, ontological balance. She sees in Van Gogh's best work an ability to hold things together in "a kind of creative or poetic balance," going so far as to define this as "human sanity, which is always threatened by forces from inside and outside itself" (*PM* 330). Fascinated almost as much by his "great, wise, intelligent letters" as by his paintings (*PM* 292), Byatt cites these in *Still Life* even more often than she gives descriptions of his paintings. Through these citations and allusions, Byatt reveals to the reader a Van Gogh who is much more than the painter whose luminous works are familiar from art galleries, hospital wards, greetings cards, chocolate boxes. To see or read about his paintings is inevitably to have an experience of *déjà vu*. Yet Van Gogh is a much more complex—and more anxiously powerful—artist and thinker than is often realised by those admiring his straw-yellow sunflowers, bright irises, or rippling cornfields. In *Still Life*, Byatt reveals how important to the painting Van Gogh is the writing and thinking Van Gogh. While she refers in the novel to many painters, ranging from

El Greco and Vermeer to Mondrian and Jackson Pollock, Van Gogh dominates the novel: his painting *Still Life with Books* is reproduced on the cover (and described on page 69); Alexander's 1957 verse play, *The Yellow Chair*, which dramatised the last years of Van Gogh's life and especially the dispute between Gauguin and Van Gogh, is the focus for many debates about the adequacy of language to describe—to *say*—the visual; Alexander himself is "obsessed by the yellow chair," by its meaning and how to render it (*ST* 69); Van Gogh's use not only of colour but also of colour adjectives influences both Alexander and the way that *Still Life* itself is written. Alexander's aesthetic concerns are those that deeply concern the novelist herself. The novel is self-reflexive, albeit subtly and complexly so, as the fiction tells its tales while also interrogating both the world and its own possibilities for rendering that world. Alexander's (and Byatt's) anxiety about how to write about Van Gogh's work is clearly articulated at the start of the novel:

He had had trouble finding an appropriate language for the painter's obsession with the illuminated material world. . . . At first he had thought that he could write a plain, exact verse with no figurative language, in which a yellow chair was the thing itself, a yellow chair, as a round gold apple was an apple or a sunflower a sunflower. . . . But it couldn't be done. Language was against him, for a start. Metaphor lay coiled in the name sunflower. (*ST* 2)

Speaking of Van Gogh's sunflowers in her essay "Still Life / Nature Morte" and pointing out that they are both symbols and concrete things, Byatt states that "to write language about their thinginess can be to comment on the doubleness of a metaphor that is both mimetic, and an exploration of the relation between identity and difference" (*PM* 16). For her, Van Gogh incarnates the duality of the artistic endeavour, which is always caught in a tense oscillation between the search for identity and difference—and on all levels.

For this novelist, whose thinking is haunted by her anxiety about "the impossibility of pure representation" in language, Van Gogh's work has almost totemic status. She explains in her essay "Sugar / Le Sucre":

A leitmotif in that novel [*Still Life*] was Vincent Van Gogh's painting of the yellow chair, which I took at first as a work of art which was made for the pure pleasure of exact mimetic knowledge—the chairness of the chair, the colour, the form. Later, of course, one discovered cultural and personal connotations. Van Gogh's chair was yellow and blue (colours of day) in contradistinction to Gauguin's, which was red and green (the "terrible human passions" of the night). He had bought twelve, for the disciples of the new religion of secular art. And so on. But nevertheless it shone in its exact simplicity of representation. (*PM* 25)

Van Gogh's yellow chair is complex, the site of multiple interpretation and semantic undecidability; it is also an icon of the achievability of representation. It is—simply—"yellow and wholesome" (*PM* 299). This one can know, but how can one say it—at least in a way that others will understand?

The painter himself strove to show and express humanity and its predicament. At the heart of this enterprise lies his abiding, impassioned study of colour. For him, painters can speak a symbolic language through their use of colour, while also making present and real the world through the intense rightness of the chosen colours. The belief in "a universal language of colour, a primary language, a divine alphabet of colours and forms" (*ST* 79) was, of course, shared by all the symbolists of Van Gogh's time, but what is distinctive about him is his insistence on maintaining identity and difference as both dialectic and harmony through the use of colour: "I am always in hope of making a discovery there [in the study of colour], to express the love of two lovers by a wedding of two complementary colours, their mingling and their opposition, the mysterious vibrations of kindred tones."[23]

The "universal language of colour" is, we now know, a mere fantasy. Individuals have different biological—and gender-determined—capacities to see colour (colour-defective vision is nearly a hundred times more common among white males than among white females).[24] Furthermore, as Byatt puts it: "Our perception of colour, like our language, like our power to make representations, is something that is purely human. We know now that other creatures see different wave-lengths" (*PM* 329). Furthermore, colours are culture-specific (compare, for example, the number of words for white in any European language and in Eskimo). They are even individual-specific, with colours and shades having particular personal associations. Speaking about the cyclamen in *Still Life*, Byatt writes: "The mental colours shifted very beautifully from various rosy cyclamens to a distressing purple I associate with death and depression" (*PM* 13). And Frederica states: "Pigment is pigment and light is light in any culture. But words, acquired slowly over a lifetime, are part of a different set of perceptions of the world, they have grown with us, they restrict what we see and how we see it" (*ST* 59).

Given the range of colours and hues that exists, it is astonishing that, as philologists have realised for centuries, we have an extraordinarily impoverished vocabulary to speak of them. As Alexander muses one morning at breakfast: "How would one find the exact word for the colour of the plum-skins? . . . Do we have enough words, synonyms, near synonyms for purple?" (*ST* 164). Pondering once more the difference between painting and language, the narrating voice responds to this question: "We know paint is not plum-flesh. We do not know with the same certainty that our language does not simply, mimetically coincide with our world" (*ST* 166).

There is no single way of seeing or saying colour: "We are not in possession of an objective colour key. Colour is studied in relation to its chromatic environment."[25] The cognitive status of colour has been the subject of debates for centuries, with thinkers such as Bishop Berkeley and Goethe arguing that our understanding of the world is conditioned by our understanding of its coloured surfaces, and others such as the Classical sceptics and Locke regarding colour as merely an accidental attribute of the phenomenal world, and visual phenomena as cognitively unreliable. Ernst Gombrich tells us that the interpretation of form and colour is closely associated with our elementary biological life.[26] However, we know also, as does Byatt (see *ST* 108), that children learn to name colours much later than things and that they learn the words for colours, shades, and hues gradually and sequentially—and never completely. This is the drama of writing about painting: the words simply are not there, even when the eye is. Yet there is a compulsive need to *say*, and words must be found. In Byatt's case, the verbal palette is a genuine artist's one. There is a precision in her usage—and a marvellous metaphoricity, since terms such as "cobalt blue" evoke minerals and mines as much as a deep bright blue (*MS* 35, 63, 67; *E* 6, 86, 159).

Byatt is ardently concerned with how to communicate colour and shape through language; she is also aware that the tensions caused by language's (in)adequacy can lead to a dynamic balance. She does not seek any resolution that would allow triumph of either side; rather, she is constantly seeking an equivalent in language of the "creative or poetic balance" that she finds in Van Gogh's work. Two paintings repeatedly draw her back: "The pictures to which I always return again and again when thinking about this balance, of human and inhuman, vision and artifice, are the purple and yellow sower, painted in June 1888, and the reaper of St-Rémy" (*PM* 330). Just as *Still Life* opens with a Van Gogh painting, a *Poets' Garden*, so it closes with two more: "On his walls Alexander had large images of the Sower and the Reaper, . . . swarming with yellow and violet light. He knew very well that a casual visitor, most visitors, might see in them the usual bourgeois brightening-up. He knew also that the painter had wished to make images that anyone, that everyone, could hang in their room to cheer themselves up" (357–58). For Van Gogh, the two figures of the sower and the reaper are opposites, but also complementary, as the novel acknowledges explicitly in citing from Van Gogh's letter on them (310–11). Van Gogh's view has been prefigured earlier in the novel, where the narrating voice speculates on how the eye is never innocent but "acts and orders" the light it receives. The narrator then proceeds to consider the painter's ordering of "his world of raw and sophisticated vision," culminating in a comparison of the two paintings, which leads both narrator and reader–spectator to a recognition that the painted world of *The Reaper* is "new and the opposite of innocent: it is seen, and thought, and made" (108–9). Byatt is here both commenting on and appropriating Van Gogh's vision; she is also, crucially, making this vision textual, as the commas in the final clause foreground textuality, separating the three past particles and thus reminding the reader that to see, to think, and to make are radically different, if potentially linked, activities.

MATISSE

If Van Gogh's anxieties about colour and representation darkly illuminate *Still Life* and Byatt's essays of the late 1980s, his paintings and their verbal evocations show that resolution and representation are ultimately possible. A very different painter, Matisse, casts a bright shadow over much of Byatt's more recent work. As I have argued above, it is misguided to over-privilege the verbal when reading Byatt's art-referential fictions, since Byatt herself is acutely aware that the verbal and the pictural exist in a dialectical relationship, wherein the central issue is not one of hierarchical supremacy, but the fundamental question of the nature and adequacy of representation.

The fact that she entitles a trilogy of stories *The Matisse Stories* has led critics to explore the programmatic function of the paintings for the reader.[27] However, Matisse and his works are more than triggers for a particular reading of the stories. The paintings evoked, which figure on the front and back covers of the book, do not so much tell us *what* to read in the stories as *how* to read them. For instance, a description of the painting *Le silence habité des maisons* opens "Art Work":

Two people sit at the corner of a table. . . . The child, it may be, turns the page of a huge white book . . . with his/her lower arm. . . . It is a pity there are no colours but it is possible, tempting, to imagine them, sumptuous as they were. . . . It is a dark little image on the page. . . . We may imagine it flaming, in carmine or vermilion, or swaying in indigo darkness, or perhaps—outdoors—gold and green. We may imagine it. The darkness of the child may be black on black or black on blue or blue on some sort of red. The book is white. Who is the watching totem under the ceiling? (*MS* 31–32)

This is not pure description; rather, it is interpretative speculation beyond the image and projection both into the inspiration that created it and also, more importantly, into the inspiration of the spectator who will colour it in. The description is studded with questions and hypothetical musings on what the painting might show and mean. Indeed, even the simplest, most concrete, and seemingly empirically verifiable statements are rendered suspect by the text: the book may well be white, but what is white if black is not certainly black?[28] After the first two pages, the painting is forgotten as other artists and artworks, real and imagined, are introduced. It is, however, more than a prelude: it alerts the reader to the need to interrogate whatever is seen and read, and to focus on visual and verbal details whose ungrammaticality is the stimulus for the reader to engage in co-creating the text.

The line-drawings that precede each story are more conventionally illustrations than the paintings, since each of them can be read—retrospectively—as offering visually a thematic counterpart to the content of the stories. However, they have a more than merely illustrative function. In their position *within* the book, whose Matisse-blue cover bears images of the paintings, they engender a speculation on the relationship between painting and drawing and between the pictural and the textual. In the nineteenth century, the theorist Charles Blanc declared that "drawing is the masculine sex of art and colour is the feminine sex" (and thus only of secondary importance).[29] This hierarchical gendering of the drawing/colour relationship has underpinned thinking about colour for centuries, bolstered not only by cultural evidence but also by the biological fact of greater male susceptibility to colour-blindness. Matisse, however, saw things very differently, arguing that drawing—which he considered to be the more difficult task—was female.[30] Each of the explicitly named "Matisse stories," like another Matisse-rich tale, "A Lamia in the Cévennes" in *Elementals*, deals with gender relations. These stories all enact male/female tensions, with the "Matisse stories" having a strongly feminist drive, whereas the narrative motor in "A Lamia" is the compulsion of a male artist to solve the problem of how to (re)create colour. Byatt does play with gender stereotypes, yet these are always also mapped onto a series of other tensions and dialectics, such as those of image and identity, showing and telling, seeing and understanding, living and dying. In the encounter with these texts, their visual commentaries and semantic alternatives, the reader is engaging, albeit perhaps unwittingly, in an intergeneric debate that uses gender as one of the defining poles of artistic thought.

Van Gogh strove for a creative balance that would represent human sanity. Matisse too strove for balance, although of a very different order: "What I dream of is an art of balance, of purity and serenity, devoid of troubling or depressing subject matter, an art which could be for every mental worker, for the businessman as well as the man of letters, for example, a soothing, calming influence on the mind, something like a good armchair which provides relaxation from physical fatigue."[31] This statement has been much quoted—and much misunderstood. A typical response is that of Alison Hilton: "A painting should contain nothing exciting or excessive, and, above all, no message."[32] This is by no means what Matisse meant: he sought to express and celebrate life and beauty, but he wanted to go beyond representation. When painting a woman's body, for instance, "first of all I imbue it with grace and charm, but I know that I must give something more. I will condense the meaning of this body by seeking its essential lines."[33] For him, the imitation of nature was less important than the transfiguration of his perceptions into an image that would have enduring meaningfulness. Matisse's paintings are far from being devoid of message: they offer a distilled, often monumental view of the world rather than a detailed and anecdotal one. For him, "all is in the conception,"[34] and he reworked a painting many times before it was finished.

A striking example of this is the celebrated *Pink Nude* in "Medusa's Ankles," which draws Susannah into Lucian's hairdressing salon. This "lavish and complex creature" (*MS* 3) has a monumental quality despite its modesty of scale. The model's limbs are emphatically exaggerated, her breasts are suggested hummocks, her head is turned and held to face the painter and the spectator: all is simplified to give maximum impact. The background is no more than a pattern and the nude an outline of the human body. Matisse has achieved an extraordinary balance between organic and geometric form, curved lines and straight, warm and cold colours; through this balance, *Pink Nude* draws and holds the eye, making the spectator speculate on what lies outside the frame that cannot quite contain the woman.

Significantly, this painting went through eighteen stages over several months in 1935, as Matisse moved gradually from a realist portrayal of Lydia Delektorskaya to the final, elemental image that is *Pink Nude*. This woman is astonishing in her self-contained but generous autonomy and self-confidence; she is also one of Matisse's best-known images. In "The Chinese Lobster," the painting is cited as one of the many works that Peggi Nollett has pinned to her wall—and it is cited correctly as *Le Nu rose* (*MS* 111). However, in "Medusa's Ankles," the work is consistently called the *Rosy Nude*, whereas the conventional name in English is *Pink Nude*. Byatt's choice of colour adjective is not, of course, innocent: by substituting "rosy" for the neutral colour term "pink," she appropriates the painting and inscribes it into the textual vision of an over-prettily rosy-ruched hairdresser's salon. It thus functions as an icon, but as an icon that is always-already misread (by Lucian and his clientele). And when the *Rosy Nude* is removed and replaced by chic grey young faces, Susannah's hopes of achieving her own lavish and complex independence vanish too. The painting thus—implicitly—functions in the story like a fetish, protecting but also generating speculation, like the empty black totem in "Art Work."

Matisse is a master of colour, which he used to express emotion rather than to transcribe nature.[35] In *The Matisse Stories*, colour has an analogous function, to the extent that it has been argued that the colours serve as a kind of emotional grammar, as "the objective correlatives to both theme and character."[36] The relational aspect of Matisse's colours, like that of Van Gogh's, is clearly important to Byatt, but she is also acutely aware of the need to understand and create individual colours. This artistic quest underpins "A Lamia in the Cévennes," where Bernard wants to paint a particular, a "recalcitrant" blue that "he needed to know and fight" (*E* 83). There are more than forty occurrences of "blue" in this story, plus a host of technical artists' terms and near-synonyms for blue: Byatt's description of the sky is a particularly stunning example of how language can enact, through its repetitions and juxtapositions of colour terms, the artist's anguished quest to find the particular blue that he wants (86). Here again, Matisse is present as a cultural signifier: "he tried Matisse-like patches of blue and petunia" (87). Elsewhere, though, Byatt complicates Matisse's referential function: "Swimming was *volupté*—he used the French word, because of Matisse. *Luxe, calme et volupté*" (85). Matisse is invoked as the creator of a painting called *Luxe, calme et volupté*, yet for anyone with any French culture there lies behind and before the painting the poem by Baudelaire that inspired it: "Invitation au voyage," which contains a litany of those very words. Thus the reader, asked to visualise from language, finds another text that itself invites him/her to imagine and visualise—differently. And so it goes on. Bernard's quest for his key colour is as anxious as that of Van Gogh: "Why bother. Why does this *matter* so much. *What difference does it make to anything if I solve this blue. . . . Why bother to render the transparency in solid paint or air on a bit of board?* I could *just stop*. He could not" (87). Bernard simply cannot stop, just as Van Gogh and Matisse could not stop—because representation must be attempted and can ultimately be achieved.

VELÁZQUEZ

Influenced by Henri Bergson's theories of time and intuition, Matisse sought to evolve forms that would express the essential character of things. His work is a constant striving to transcend the "succession of moments which constitutes the superficial existence of beings and things" in order to "search for a truer, more essential character, which the artist will seize so that he may give to reality a more lasting interpretation."[37] The work of Velázquez, more than two centuries before, has the same goal. Furthermore, like Van Gogh and Matisse, Velázquez strove for balance in his paintings. His *Christ in the House of Martha and Mary* is an enigmatic painting, which juxtaposes a realistic contemporary kitchen scene with a religious scene inspired by Luke 10.40. Each of the scenes occupies its own area of space, creating a hiatus and lack of cohesion that has led critics over the centuries to speculate on whether the image of Christ and the sisters is a picture or a scene seen through a window or aperture in the wall. Byatt knows this: on seeing the painter's finished work in her story, Concepción wonders: "was it through a window, or over a sill, or was it an image of an image on a wall? it was not clear" (*E* 229).

The undecidability of the Velázquez painting is willed. It calls up speculation on the part of the spectator and leads Byatt to invent the story of its creation. Her personal involvement with the work is clear: "the expression on the face of that very angry servant girl in *Christ in the House of Martha and Mary* haunts me, and she haunts me partly because she is in the same picture as this perfectly painted egg—they balance each other. This is where the really difficult, complicated, beautiful things are, in this contact between oneself and the world."[38] Byatt's tale is about the nature of artistry, identity, and the need to accept oneself in order to produce truly beautiful works. By insisting that the young cook Concepción "could become a true artist" (*E* 219; 223), both the text and the fictional Velázquez confront the central Byattian debate about exactly what art is, does, and can do. When Velázquez shows the two cooks his finished work, Concepción sees herself furiously frowning, immortalised in her ugliness. Yet when she has looked at it properly, she begins to laugh; the miracle occurs: "The momentary coincidence between image and woman vanished, as though the rage was still and eternal in the painting and the woman was released into time" (230).

This is the function of painting: to make present the world in such a way that the image of it remains eternal. This is Byatt's goal too, in language: "When I read I inhabit a world which is more real than the world in which I live, or perhaps I should say I am more alive in it. It is a language world. Language tries to capture and make permanent a moment in time which won't be captured."[39] As a reader, Byatt undoubtedly lives—intensely—in a language world, but this language world is constantly referring outside itself, testing its own limits, inter-rogating its own adequacy, and both creatively and anxiously calling up the non-verbal. Byatt *sees* paintings very well; she also knows how to make her readers see them through the prism of her carefully crafted, yet always infectiously passionate verbal descriptions. And she describes so very well because she does not seek to fashion a verbal analogue of the painting; rather, she wants to make the painting present as something sensationally perceived (and intellectually enjoyed), and she achieves this by precisely engaging the reader in fabulous voyages outside the text and outside the moment of reading.

NOTES

1. Nicholas Shrimpton, "Victorian Eco-Chamber," rev. of *Possession, Independent on Sunday* 4 March 1990: Review 18.

2. For some refreshing insights into her thoughts on her own and others' artistic practice, see Boyd Tonkin, "Antonia S. Byatt in Interview with Boyd Tonkin," *Anglistik* 10.2 (1999): 15–26.

3. Sylvia Bigliazzi, "'Art Work': A. S. Byatt vs. Henri Matisse, or the Metamorphoses of Writing," *Textus* 12 (1999): 193.

4. See, for instance, Paul Valéry's statement in "Autour de Corot": "Is not the first cause of a work of art a desire that it be talked about, even if this is only in a dialogue between the artist and himself?" *Oeuvres*, vol. 2 (Paris: Gallimard/Pléiade, 1960) 1307 (translated for this edition).

5. Jean-François Lyotard, *Discours/Figure* (Paris: Klincksieck, 1978) 10 (translated for this edition).

6. Louis Marin, *To Destroy Painting*, trans. Mette Hjort (Chicago: U of Chicago P, 1995) 105.

7. Tonkin 26.

8. Tonkin 23.

9. Tonkin 17.

10. John Gage, *Colour and Meaning: Art, Science and Symbolism* (London: Thames, 1999) 38.

11. Henri Matisse, "Notes of a Painter" [1908], *Matisse on Art*, ed. Jack Flam (Oxford: Phaidon, 1973) 35. A similar view was expressed by Cézanne in a letter to Camoin of 28 January 1902; see Paul Cézanne, *Letters*, ed. John Rewald (London: Cassirer, 1941) 218.

12. Jacques Derrida, *The Truth in Painting*, trans. Geoff Bennington and Ian McLeod (Chicago: U of Chicago P, 1987) 155.

13. See Peter Brunette and David Wills, "The Spatial Arts: an interview with Jacques Derrida," *Deconstruction and the Visual Arts*, ed. Peter Brunette and David Wills (Cambridge: Cambridge UP, 1994) 13.

14. Matisse, "Notes" 36.

15. Riffaterre defines an *ungrammaticality* as "a deviant grammar or lexicon (for instance, contradictory details)"; Michael Riffaterre, *Semiotics of Poetry* (1978; London: Methuen, 1980) 2.

16. Tonkin 17.

17. Mikel Dufrenne, "The Psychology of Reading," *Main Trends in Aesthetics and the Science of Art*, ed. Mikel Dufrenne (New York: Holmes, 1978) 129.

18. Umberto Eco et al, *Interpretation and Overinterpretation* (Cambridge: Cambridge UP, 1992) 50.

Judith Plotz

A Modern "Seer Blest": The Visionary Child in *The Virgin in the Garden*

Childhood is the great Romantic subject. Along with the artist, the child came in the Romantic period to be regarded as the normative human type.[1] That the child had been "set . . . in the midst" of us (to use a Scriptural phrase much beloved by nineteenth-century poets) by kindly Providence to be a source of saving authority was a Romantic article of faith.[2] Reverence for the saving wisdom and moral authority of the child, that "lively representation. . . of the ideal,"[3] that "perpetual Messiah,"[4] that "Mighty Prophet! Seer blest,"[5] pervades Romantic literature from Wordsworth's time until well into the twentieth century. An echo of this Romantic ideal haunts the pages of A. S. Byatt's *The Virgin in the Garden*, where the character of Marcus Potter emerges as a somewhat less blessed seer, an unmighty prophet whose gifts become afflictions and through whom Byatt illustrates and interrogates the late-Modern fate of the visionary child.

Of the wealth of Romantic tributes to the majesty of childhood, none is better known than that in Wordsworth's "Ode: Intimations of Immortality":

> Thou, whose exterior semblance doth belie
>   Thy Soul's immensity;
> Thou best Philosopher, who yet dost keep
> Thy heritage, thou Eye among the blind,
> That, deaf and silent, read'st the eternal deep,
> Haunted for ever by the eternal mind,—
>   Mighty Prophet! Seer blest!
>   On whom those truths do rest,
> Which we are toiling all our lives to find.[6]

As "A co-essential symbol of the life / Which God hath made a witness of Himself," the child can serve as source, guide, and goal to the adult.[7] From this "Type of the Divinity," Bronson Alcott claimed to derive his own spiritual renewal: "Baptismal waters from the Head above / These babes I foster daily are to me."[8] "The child is, was, and still shall be / The world's deliverer" because he is closer than the adult both to Nature and to God, and thus able to act as the "best instructor in the spells / And wiles of Nature" and as God's "little prophet and interpreter."[9] Such adulation is rooted in a perception of children as possessing certain gifts of consciousness—idealism, vision, holism, animism,[10] and self-sufficient isolation—which are the source of spiritual authority. A brief discussion of each of these gifts will help to define and illuminate the Romantic type to which Byatt's own child seer becomes a foil.

The Romantic tradition regards children as natural idealists in the sense that the Idea, whether defined simply as the thoughts of their own minds or more grandly as intimations of the spiritual force that sustains the world, approaches a truer reality beyond the physical realm. Blake's innocent chimney sweeper, for example, sees no contradiction between the physical shearing of Tom Dacre ("who cried when his head / That curl'd like a lamb's back, was shav'd") and the continued existence of his curls in the mind's eye ("Hush Tom! Never mind it, for when your head's bare / You know that the soot cannot spoil your white hair").[11] Coleridge likewise identifies childhood with the power of subduing the particular fact to the mental ideal, and his son Hartley's infantine idealism has become part of the folklore of Romanticism.[12]

A corollary to the Romantic view of the child's innate idealism is his imputed power of vision or faith. De Quincey finds in children a "closer communion with God," for "children have a specific power of contemplating the truth, which departs as they enter the world."[13] This type of vision is closely tied to another gift of consciousness, that of holism. Thinking synthetically rather than analytically, habitually grasping an overarching pattern or informing emotion before attending to particular parts, children are unifiers. Such is Coleridge's persistent theme: "In the child's mind there is nothing fragmentary; its numeration-table is truly Pythagorean,"[14] or again, "I saw in early youth, as in a dream, the birth of the planets; and my eyes beheld as *one* what the understanding afterwards divided into [many]."[15] With this all-embracing habit of mind, children become confident and creative non-specialists, whether they are prodigious polymaths such as Thomas Malkin and Marjory Fleming or ordinary "little children from 3 to 6 years old," who, Coleridge says, in their imitative play empathetically "exist in the form of others," yet easily return home to their true selves.[16]

Associated with this aptitude for wholeness is an animist habit of mind by which the child sees the universe as instinct with life. Wordsworth claims this habit both for the infant ("For him, in one dear Presence, there exists / A virtue which irradiates and exalts / Objects through widest intercourse of sense") and for the youth who feels "the sentiment of Being spread / O'er all that moves and all that seemeth still."[17] Whether benevolent or threatening, the natural world is perceived by the Romantic child as inherently animate and, as such, an appropriate analogue of his own life: "And the little ones danced and sported and laughed / And all the hills echoed."[18]

Perhaps the quality most admired in childhood by the Romantics is the infantine power of self-sufficient isolation. Children inhabit worlds of their own, and it is this solitude that liberates their genius. According to De Quincey: "God speaks to children . . . in dreams, and by the oracles that lurk in darkness. But in solitude, above all things . . . God holds 'communion undisturbed'" with them. Children are "privileged by nature and position" to enjoy what De Quincey hails as "that mighty silence" in which both self-discovery and the discovery of nature may take place.[19] In "To a Deaf and Dumb Little Girl," Hartley Coleridge praised the child's fortunate isolation, "her little being / Concentred in her solitary seeing— / . . . God must be with her in her solitude."[20]

The Romantic tradition regards these childish modes of thought as uniquely valuable—as what Alexander Smith called a "later revelation."[21] In their apparent vulnerability and ignorance, children exemplify Shelley's "Adonais" paradox of "a Power / Girt round with weakness."[22] Through their habits of perception, children are sources of strength, grace, and joy to the adults around them and to their own adult selves. Even though visionary or animist perceptions may be regarded either as delusions or, as Piaget interprets them, as transitory stages of psychological development, Romantic literature almost without exception imputes authority to the child's view of the world.

The figure of the child seer, however ironically diminished by his realistic twentieth-century setting, is prominently reanimated in A. S. Byatt's *The Virgin in the Garden*. As a testing of the literary and psychological legacy of Romanticism, the book does indeed offer the ideal context for the late-born visionary child. A consideration of multiple destinies in a dense scene of provincial life, *The Virgin in the Garden* is set in and around a Yorkshire school in the coronation year of 1953. The novel's central event is the production at a local country house of a verse drama written by Alexander Wedderburn, a young teacher at Blesford Ride School, celebrating the first Elizabeth, the Virgin–Queen in the garden of England. The book's main characters are six men and women—three contrasting couples—whose lives are touched, changed, and illuminated by the coronation pageantry. Elizabeth I presides over these six seekers as an emblem of human mutability transfigured by will into a fixed unitary pattern, "a Princess *semper eadem* and single" (*VG* 101).

This allusive tension between fixity and its costs, as Romantic as it is Elizabethan, teases the reader most poignantly in the silent form of Marcus Potter, a character that has so far attracted curiously little attention in criticism of *The Virgin in the Garden*. At sixteen, Marcus is the youngest child in the fiercely literary Potter family. Resolutely incommunicative and mathematically minded, Marcus is in many ways a stranger in the densely verbal universe the novel projects; perhaps, he must also seem alien and inaccessible to the literary critic. Yet, Marcus is also a visionary of sorts. According to Lucas Simmonds, not an unimpeachable source, he is "the seer," "the real thing. The miracle" (371; 405). Indeed, as a solitary visionary whose world becomes increasingly full of over-arching meaning, Marcus does fulfill the criteria for a Romantic seer—but with a difference.

Marcus enters the novel in a scene recalling the encounter in Wordsworth's "Resolution and Independence" in which the poet "by peculiar grace" meets "[b]eside a pool bare to the eye of heaven" a figure who "[s]tirred with his staff" the muddy waters for leeches.[23] In the opening pages of Byatt's novel, a young poet, Alexander, sees beside the Bilge Pond, rumored to be full of leeches, a "figure . . . bent awkwardly over it, stirring with a long stick" (25). Chapter 1, titled "That Far Field," positions Marcus not simply in a Wordsworthian "single field" but, by strategic misquotation both of Milton and of Roethke, manages to suggest that Marcus is in some sense a damaged blossom snatched by gloomy Dis from the "fair field" of Enna, and also one in desperate need of learning Roethke's lesson "not to fear infinity / The far field."[24]

The explicitly Wordsworthian echo is not fortuitous, for Marcus is afflicted with two kinds of visionary experiences, roughly equivalent to the two kinds of saving vision, the "Fallings from us, vanishings" and the "radiance which was once so bright" referred to in the *Immortality Ode*: "Which, be they what they may, / Are yet the fountain-light of all our day, / Are yet a master-light of all our seeing."[25]

Although Marcus's experiences are horrible to him—he certainly doesn't feel himself a blessed seer—they link him to the idealized child of Romantic tradition by making him aware how much the external world depends on the mind as its "lord and master"[26] and also how much the world can be seen as charged with brightness or with vivid menace.

The first kind of experience of a falling/vanishing, one that began as a childish game and became a compulsion, he calls "spreading himself." In such moments, Marcus has the sensation of leaving his body and diffusing his consciousness over a vast space:

He had played a game called spreading himself. This began with a deliberate extension of his field of vision, until by some sleight of perception he was looking out at once from the four field-corners. . . . It was not any sense of containing the things he saw. Rather, he surveyed them, from no vantage point, or all at once.

. . . Sometimes, for immeasurable instants he lost any sense of where he really was, of where the spread mind had its origin. He had to teach himself to find his body by fixing the mind to precise things, by shrinking the attention until it was momen-tarily located in one solid object. . . . he could in some spyglass way search out the crouching cold body, and with luck leap the mind across to it. (27)

That the situation is deeply Wordsworthian is apparent; it matches Wordsworth's note on the childhood experience behind the *Immortality Ode*: "Many times while going to school have I grasped at a wall or tree to recall myself from this abyss of idealism to the reality."[27] Although Byatt claims no expressly Wordsworthian lineage for her choice of the word "spreading" to describe Marcus's perceptions, the word is strategically present throughout the second book of *The Prelude*, "School Days," a book that carries the boy from early childhood to the age of sixteen. Wordsworth writes of feeling "a holy calm / . . . *overspread* my soul," of seeing "blessings *spread* around me like a sea," and intuiting "the sentiment of Being *spread* / O'er all that moves, and all the seemeth still."[28] In the 1805 *Prelude*, Wordsworth notes how the child's "mind *spreads* / Tenacious of the forms which it receives."[29] Wordsworth uses "spread" in a context of heightened visionary experience in order to suggest a beatific integration between the youth and all things. Marcus, however, the passive victim of *"being* spread," feels it as violation and alienation. Although the experience testifies to his power to separate the self as object from the self as subject (to borrow Crabb Robinson's borrowed formulation), Marcus finds no such meaning and certainly no comfort in it. Disorienting, uncontrollable, the "spreading" induces no holy calm but rather a kind of death: "He was now bitterly cold. . . . It always left him bitterly cold" (28).

Marcus's second sort of vision is a light hallucination or "photism." The term comes from William James's *The Varieties of Religious Experience* and springs readily to the lips of the voluble religio-scientist Lucas Simmonds, Marcus's biology master and friend of sorts. Always eager to give the boy's experiences a technical gloss, Simmonds expounds: "There's a technical term for it, Potter. Photisms. Experiences of floods of light and glory which frequently accompany moments of revelation. The phenomenon is known. . . . what you saw may have been more or less what Saul saw on the way to Damascus. What the shepherds saw in the fields at night" (126–27).[30] Unlike Saul and the shepherds, however, Marcus does not know what to make of his private illumination, which is far from being as comfortable as a comparison with Wordsworthian gleams and radiances might suggest. Though the light vision experienced by Marcus brings a sensation of complex completeness, suggested by controlled geometric forms and by psychic unity in concentrated terror, it suggests no particular meaning:

The light was busy. It could be seen gathering, running and increasing along the lines where it had been first manifest. Wild and linear on the railway tracks, flaming, linking, crossing on the tennis-court mesh, rising in bright intermittent streams of sparks from glossy laurel leaves and shorn blades of grass. It could also be seen moving where no object reflected, refracted or directed it. In loops, eddies, powerful direct streams, turbulence and long lines proceeding without let through stones, trees, earth, himself, what had been a condition of vision turned to an object of vision. . . . He was both saved (from bright blinding, from annihilation) and prevented (from losing himself in it) by a geometric figure which held as an image or more in that glare and play of light. He saw intersecting cones, stretching to infinity, containing the pouring and rushing. He saw that he was at the, or a, point of intersection, and that if it could not pass through it would shatter the fragile frame to make a way. He must hold together, but let it go through, like the burning glass with the gathered light of the sun. The rims flared and flared and flared. (120)

Both the "spreading" and the photisms are moments in which Marcus, in a telling phrase adapted from Hopkins's "Wreck of the Deutschland,"[31] is "stressed, distressed" in his mortality (120). He becomes the point of intersection between the finite and the infinite, the mortal and the immortal. Marcus, it is true, is only one site within this tightly patterned book of the union between the transient with the permanent: Alexander's play characterized Elizabeth I, the Virgo Astraea, as a divinized mortal, as "a stone that did not bleed" (101). Marcus's sister Stephanie admires the "Ode on a Grecian Urn" for "saying ambivalently that you could not do, and need not attempt, what it required you to do, see the unseen, realise the unreal, speak what was not" (78). A bedroom discussion of the living statue of Shakespeare's Hermione as "a resolution of the pains of life in Art" serves as the ironic prelude to Marcus's conception (86). However gratifying such a pattern of intersections between a mortal and immortal emblem may be in a formal work of art, Marcus's growing terror demonstrates that it is no model for a human life.

In addition to the spreading and the photisms, Marcus has other intimations of an overwhelming and all-encompassing pattern. In two formal realms, music and mathematics, he has gifts that appear unaccountable to his unmusical, innumerate family. Musically, he has perfect pitch, though he does no more than to play the viola "in an accurate expressionless way" (26). Mathematically, he had been a prodigy but has at sixteen fallen from the joyful childhood state in which he could once do instant mathematics by simply "seeing" the answer as a form rather than as a number:

I used to see—to imagine—a place. A kind of garden. And the forms, the mathematical *forms*, were about in the landscape and you would let the problem loose in the landscape and it would wander among the forms—leaving luminous trails. And then I saw the answer. . . . You see—it was important to see only obliquely—out of the edge of the eye—in the head—the *kind* of thing it was, the area it was in, but never to look directly, to look away on purpose, and wait for it to rise to form. When you'd waited, and it was *there* in its idea, you could draw the figure or even to say words to go with it. But it mustn't be fixed, or held down, or it . . . (63)

The power of figured thought, of *felt abstraction*, has vanished under the pressure for explanation from his father and a scrutinizing expert.

Allied to Marcus's openness to such formal visitations of ideal pattern is his susceptibility to psychological invasion. Vulnerability to the life of others shows itself in a talent for acting (a talent he seeks to hide): "Marcus had been a chilling and extraordinary Ophelia" whose performance made clear "that the play's events simply cracked and smashed the innocent consciousness" (26). Marcus is similarly susceptible to the coiled life in objects. In a brilliant chapter called "Meat," the gross rotundities of dead animal flesh in a butcher's shop, the "soft pale guts, hard giblets in glistening fat, red-veined golden-skinned clusters of eggs," the fresh liver with its "hot and bursting look" frighten him to the brink of unconsciousness (94). Such "spreading fear" of more and more parts of normal life makes it an ordeal for Marcus to eat, to walk downstairs, to turn on a tap, to flush a toilet, to read a page:

Every day something new became problematic and difficult. An early thing was books, always bad and now impossible. Print reared off the pages like snakes striking. His eye got entangled by the anomalous, like the letter *g*, and the peculiar disparity between its written and printed forms. Reading was unmanageable because he measured frequencies of *g*s, or sat and stared, mesmerised by one. Any word will look odd, stared at, as though it was incorrect or unreal or not a word. Now all words were like that. (118)

So charged with threatening life are ordinary objects—these rearing anomalous *g*s, this "hot and bursting" offal—that, in order to save himself from the excesses of the life "in that which moves and that which seemeth still,"[32] Marcus retreats as much as possible from all contact and reduces unavoidable interchanges to manageable form through geometry.

This isolation is Marcus's normal condition. Byatt creates an envelope of empty physical and psychological space around the boy. He is out of touch, in all ways, with his family. As Stephanie observes, "Marcus hates you—hates anyone—to touch him. Even as a baby, you couldn't cuddle him. He got asthma" (171). Although Winifred, his mother, feels inexpressible love for him, this love remains unexpressed either through gesture or word. Always, "She wanted to touch him, and did not" (89). "She held out her arms to Marcus, who avoided them" (28). Standing apart from her son, watching him as through a glass darkly, Winifred maintains a propitiatory silence: "About Marcus, she felt superstitiously that if she averted her attention from him, her eyes, her anxiety, her love, there was a chance he might get by. Might go unnoticed, either by Fate or his father" (85). His sisters—Frederica through insuperable self-absorption and Stephanie through engrossing circumstances—are almost as oblivious to Marcus as he is to them. A childhood photograph indicates their habitual relationship: "The two girls held hands, in velvet dresses with lace collars, and frowned. Marcus was alone in space, dwarfed by a huge, unrelated, beady-eyed teddy bear" (29).

Such distance from others is to Marcus's taste: "I want leaving alone," he tells Lucas Simmonds in a rare expression of desire (64). Habitually, in his free time, "Marcus courted vacancy" in his sanctuary, his "inviolable place, where no one came, the café of the Blesford Gaumont" (57), the local cinema. Indifferent to the films themselves, indeed more frightened than not at their "phantasmagoria" of images, "what he liked was the centre of this closed citadel, whose outer walls were blank and blind, whose doors were barred on the inside" (57). His other favorite place is the local sewage works, another formalized antithesis of the profusion of nature: "The sewage works was like a closed fort, iron-railed, windowless concrete boxes, artificial grass mounds. There was a human silence. All the sound was the discreetly humming wires, the scratching of rotor arms on deserted round tubs of gravel. . . . Recycled water, recycled liquid wastes, Lucas Simmonds had once told a class, were purer than spring water, quite sterile" (90).

Marcus's principal tool of isolation is ritualized geometry. Like Wordsworth, who turned to geometry to find a stable retreat from the uncertainties of moral philosophy and the political life, Marcus uses it to stay sane: "He learned early to be grateful for geometry, which afforded grip and passage where knots of turves and cakes of mud did not. Broken chalk lines, the demarcation of winter games crossing summer ones, circles, parallel tramlines, . . . were lines to creep along, a network of salvation" (27–28).

Ironically, however, ritualized geometry takes Marcus close to autism. He habitually withdraws into himself and makes self-protective patterns using any available materials: in the family sitting-room, he "began to work out a kind of mathematical pattern using knuckles and fingertips" (30); in science class, "He drew, on pieces of graph paper, a pattern of spirals moving through concentric diamonds. The point of this exercise was to avoid, yet indicate and deal with, the point at the centre where all the lines converged on infinity" (59). Any and every environment must be plotted to be subdued. Within the Gaumont Cinema, for example,

He had various techniques for avoiding thought. One was a soundless humming, a set of variations on a deliberately restricted number of notes in the middle range. Another was the analogous construction of rhythmic sequences with tapping and clutching of knuckles and thumbnails. Another was a kind of mathematical mapping of the Café and Soda Fountain. He would plot heights of pillars and distances between them, numbers of pink bulbs and creamy carpet roses, radii of light. (58–59)

Marcus acquired the technique of translating pain and anxiety into ordered shapes during bad spells of childhood asthma. In his pain, "Everything, inner and outer, [was] precisely defined in black outline against an encroaching haze. There was an extreme point where pain refined vision to mathematics,"

So that geometry was close to, and opposed to, the suffering animal. It intensified with pain, and yet the attention could, with effort, be deflected from pain to geometry. Geometry was immutable, orderly, and connected with extremity. He did not, in his mind, oppose pain and geometry: what was opposed to both was "normal life" where you took things easy as they came, things shiny, glossy, soft, hard, shifty, touchable, not needing mapping or ordering. (91–92)

Increasingly, however, "normal life" disappears into a labyrinth of "evasive rituals" which both order and derange his existence: "Waters, vertigo, figures, rhythms, the letter *g*, released him from worse imperatives. They conferred an ease of safety. He managed, too, to stop eating meat without taking up a position on vegetables. This was an evasion of the looming imperative that he should give up eating altogether" (119).

In his isolation, his seeming self-sufficiency, his private interior world, his visions of pure form, and his apprehension of a world charged with life, Marcus clearly resembles the Romantic wise child. He even goes through a Wordsworthian apprenticeship to visionary power, feeding his mind on vast shapes, "huge and mighty forms," instinct with power, "that do not live / Like living men."[33] Like Wordsworth, he seeks an isolated plain associated with Druids, and another "figured o'er with circles, lines, or mounds."[34] Like Wordsworth, he finds relief from anxiety in geometry and limited comfort from his sister. But the psychological and aesthetic framework within which Marcus exists makes his powers into a curse and terror to him, not, as hitherto in the Romantic tradition, a sign of elected strength. Whereas Romantic literature of childhood usually involves explicit authorial endorsement, Marcus's visionary experiences are always rendered from the boy's point of view only, a point of view of extreme isolation. Neither the narrator nor any of the other reliable characters intervene to explain. Nor can Marcus himself, caught in the clock-time chronology of the novel, place his visions within any context larger than the present. In a world without guiding authority, Marcus is a victim rather than an adept of vision.

Though "Marcus kept still and avoided thought" (58) as much as possible, all his evasions only lead him closer to one fearful explanation for everything: "I get frightened of things. . . . I worry for ages. About *things*. I must be sort of ill, I must" (124–25). Even here, however, he is not sure:

Marcus supposed that if one was properly mad one was not afraid of being mad. Mad people in films and books seemed to have in common a rock-bottom certainty that they were in the right. His own increasing anxiety about madness could perhaps be taken as a sign that he was sane. And madness in this literary household had overtones of raving, vision and poetry which were nothing to do with what was bothering him. (118)

"Allergic to poetry" (310), as he had been allergic to nature in his asthmatic childhood, Marcus has no words, neither religious nor literary, to fit around his experiences. His powers thus exist in a void of meaning that his disturbed and disturbing mentor, Lucas Simmonds, fills with pseudo-science, pseudo-religion, and questionable if genuine affection. Fascinated by what he takes to be Marcus's "special gifts of consciousness—that might extend the limits of human power" (61), Lucas takes Marcus in hand and attempts to manage his visions. Voluble where Marcus is silent, Lucas is above all an explainer. His "endless discourse" and "cheerful flow of talk" (149) reveal him as a great rambler in regions where vague religion, vaguer science, and compulsive pattern-making intersect. By placing Marcus's visions within his own larger scheme of the universe, a universe in which "Everything bristled with possible significance" (228), Lucas uses a vocabulary that is promiscuously assembled from religious, biological, botanical, geological, mythological, geographical, and alchemical sources, from "Freud, Frazer, Jung, the records of the Society for Psychic Research, Gerard's Herbal, J. W. Dunne, Gerald Heard. He used all these, the Red Guide to the North York-shire Moors, the Bible, his field guides of British flora and fauna, Mother Shipton, indifferently as a kind of eclectic *sortes Virgilianae*" (298). Lucas's central conviction is a Teilhardian belief that "the present Goal of Existence is the transference of Material Energy into Mental Energy" (147). Fighting anthropomorphism, Lucas refers to the transforming power of the Absolute Mind as "G." According to Lucas, "G" seeks agents such as Marcus to draw spirit down into the material realm. In his pamphlet, unread save by Marcus, entitled "The PAT-TERN and the PLAN," he describes the evolving pattern by which more dead matter is assimilated within the "Biosphere," Earth conceived as a living organism, which is "in its turn contained inside an even denser layer of Thought. . . . the Noussphere, the Earth-Mind" (146–47). Lucas is convinced that Marcus is a gifted visionary: "you were in the presence of a Power" (125), Lucas tells him. "G. believes in you," he insists. "I've been watching you for some considerable time and it's my considered opinion that He does. As an inlet for force or form" (62). Lucas sets up Marcus, this "seer," this "miracle," as a "kind of human dowsing twig, or divining rod" (234) to receive the impulses of the Noussphere through a series of experiments in telepathy and in active and passive vision. During Stephanie's wedding, Marcus becomes "a receiver, an antenna, an aerial. And after that, a transmitter" (261). As an antenna, he receives the mental image of grasses in a laboratory beaker on Lucas's workbench miles away; as a trans-mitter, he sends to Lucas, who sketches it, an image of the mouth of hell painted on the church wall. More troubling to Marcus than such telepathy is Lucas's insistence on "watching for signs" by charting any hint of pattern that comes during sleep or wakefulness. The recording both of dream signs from "hypna-gogic vision" (161) and of waking encounters transmute Marcus's world to

technicoloured phantasmagoria of carpets, bicycles, laurel bushes, weather cocks, policemen, angels, airmen, all of whom, blue-black, gilded, hyacinthine, glossy-spotted green, might have been heavenly messengers, infernal portents, symbols of the divine Pattern which, stared at, would yield to the naked eye, to his, Marcus's, stereoscopic visionary eye, their necessary internal structures or simple messages, pullulating with coded forms, molecular, genetic, thermodynamic, which, like burn-ing bush and God's hinder parts, would speak the keys to eternal truths by which he, Lucas Simmonds, Blesford, Calverley, England, and who knew what else, might be, would be, transfigured and illuminated. (162–63)

Finally, in order to actively solicit a contact with the absolute, Marcus and Lucas go to "Places of Power" (227), "places which traditionally and for good reasons had been felt to be meeting places between the earthly and unearthly" (228). The visits are disquieting and inconclusive. At Owgar's Howe, they whirl themselves into unconsciousness. At Whitby Abbey, their offering, held beneath a magnifying glass, is frighteningly consumed by sudden flames.

Lucas's involvement with Marcus is at once reassuring and threatening. The very act of speaking his vision to another person offers relief. Lucas's facile translations of the frightening experience into neat diagrams and verbal formulas serve to "neutralise" and "earth" Marcus's new experience (163). When Marcus reluctantly diagrams what he has seen, he feels immediate release:

On paper it looked like nothing. But the memory was still faintly dangerous.

"An infinity symbol," said Lucas. Marcus diffidently mentioned that it had seemed to indicate a burning glass. Also, Lucas said, an infinity symbol, a symbol of infinite energy passing through a point. They should, would use the symbol as a mantra, an object of joint contemplation and meditation.

Marcus looked at it silently. It looked diminished, as Lucas interrogated it. The whole thing was becoming diminished, safe to handle, wrapped in Lucas Simmonds's fluent words. Although Simmonds was paradoxically trying to unwrap it. With speech, it all receded, seeming, as it vanished, bright and desirable for the first time. (126–27)

The more Lucas chatters on about reaching the absolute, the safer Marcus feels: "'The first thing is to learn—which is hard, very hard—to *clear your mind . . .*' Marcus sat down. He folded his thin hands, one in the other, and bent his head submissively. Lucas's words, increasing in speed and number, fell gratefully, disturbing the unruffled surface of a mental pool only too often clear and empty" (149). Though Marcus radically distrusts language, he is content to pull over him Lucas's "word-work" as a blanket that "consoled and protected him if he did not think" (299). Also comforting is Lucas's superficial (and intermittent) normality as evinced by his sport car, his "bodily cheerfulness" (299), his jaunty idiom, his apparently purposive "sense of direction" (229), his near-perfect impersonation of the true school friend in a boy's school story, "cheery, normal . . . solicitous and gentle":

This Lucas provided huge sticky fruit cakes, cucumber and sardine sandwiches, toasted teacakes and chat to match. Barrow Minor's acne, VE's shocking O Level prospects, the bad moral influence of Edmund Wilkie, the laxness, in these latter days of his incipient fame, of Alexander Wedderburn. Cosseting, gossip and affection, he offered Marcus, honey, milk, apples and nuts, a kind of perpetual smiling beano which later extended into a dormitory feast. (164–65)

Yet the relationship is charged with menace. Although Marcus, completely uncritical intellectually, never finds Lucas's ideas especially peculiar, he is increasingly aware of the man's psychological frailty. Lucas's fear in response to the black-out at Owgar's Howe frightens Marcus, for his cheerful, commanding mentor has let him down. Still more is Marcus frightened by Lucas's terrible confessions at Whitby Abbey. "I'm so unhappy" (306), Lucas admits as prelude to an account of his earlier psychotic episode: "It began with the destroyer. In the Pacific, when I was serving on the destroyer. There was some trouble, with aerials and messages, there too, and a Tribunal, I was called before a Tribunal, and then in a white cell for a long time— . . . I had the idea they had me electronically tracked" (308).

Hearing reluctantly what he would rather not know, Marcus is also obliged to do what he has no wish to do. For the first and only time during their friendship, Lucas asks Marcus to touch him, sexually: "if only you could, if you could bring yourself—just to touch—I should be connected" (310–11). Repelled, but emotionally and morally constrained, Marcus does as he is asked and clasps Lucas's penis. Lucas has a sudden messy ejaculation. "'It doesn't matter,' Marcus said in an undertone. 'It doesn't matter, Lucas.' But it did matter. For a moment he himself had stirred in sympathy, and then Lucas had been convulsed and he was where he had always been, alone, out of touch, separate. He wiped his fingers on his handkerchief, his own trousers, anything. 'It does matter,' Lucas said. 'It's a disaster. It's the beginning of the end'" (311).

The failed sexual encounter, like the equivocal experiments in reaching the absolute, isolates each of them still further. Moreover, Lucas's behavior plunges Marcus into the terrible fear that Lucas might be insane. So long as Lucas seemed strong and confident, Marcus's own visions could be legitimized and explained; but with the collapse of Lucas's authority, Marcus is undermined: "If Lucas was mad, he, Marcus, was on his own with the things which initially had been almost too much for him, the geometry of water in plug-holes, the terror of staircases, the spreading, the fields of light. If Lucas was not quite mad, then it was at least a tenable hypothesis that they had aroused angry outside forces of some indeterminate nature" (340).

Eventually, however, there can be no doubt of Lucas's condition. Alexander comes upon him naked, his private parts decked with flowers, knee-deep in the ooze of the Bilge Pond, wielding a sharp butcher's knife with which he lacerates his thighs as he sings snatches of hymns. In this final breakdown, Lucas goes so unequivocally mad—"so classically, so grandly, so archetypally mad" (398)— that even the dullest of observers cannot fail to understand. Marcus, far from dull, understands, and, out of what may be loyalty or what may be kindred instability, he follows his friend into collapse, sinking into a state of apathy punctuated by bouts of screaming. The prognosis for his recovery is as uncertain as everything else about his uncertain visionary existence. *The Virgin in the Garden* does not pronounce a final judgment on the significance of the experience.

Such narrative reticence is particularly interesting since in an earlier work, *The Shadow of the Sun*, Byatt attributes the experience of photisms to Henry Severell, a novelist of genius, whose preeminence is acknowledged by all around him. Severell, like Marcus, has had "attacks of vision" (*SS* 58) since the age of seventeen; but unlike Marcus "he knew . . . that his visionary moments were a direct source of power" (59). In one such vision Severell sees light moving across a field:

And still the light poured, heavy, and white, and hot, into the valley before him and collected, molten and seething, on the corn beneath him; he could hear it thundering into the silence; and still he had to see, so that his cone was now an hourglass funnel, opening both ways, and the wide light all pressed and weighed in the point of intersection which was himself, and the gold figures, hieratic, with gold faces and swords of flame, walked in the sea of corn in ordered patterns, like reapers; he recognized them from before, and he knew that he had come to the end. They burst like dragon's teeth men, one by one, from the bright land; he knew they were not tangible, nor presences, nor differentiated one from the other; they were a way of seeing. . . . To see like this was to be alive. (80)

Henry Severell's literary genius certifies these experiences as revelations rather than delusions. His highly imaged consciousness of the vision in terms of "gold figures, hieratic" and "dragon-teeth men" links it to mythological patterns, as the ecstatic vocabulary makes this into a moment of high imagination. Such moments give him conscious insight into and a felt kinship with such figures as Blake, Coleridge, Böhme, and Henry More, whom he reveres as visionaries (59). Unlike the famous and self-aware Severell, however, Marcus is just a boy with no public status to give authority to his inner visions. Nor has he any symbol system except geometry in which to set forth his experiences. The description of the photisms in *The Virgin in the Garden* contains none of the details that make Severell's vision in *The Shadow of the Sun* resonate with meaning. There are no references to myth, to ecstasy, to objects in themselves beautiful made more beautiful. Severell's trained consciousness is able to impute the values of traditional mysticism to his experiences, but Marcus, the child of silence, has no words.

The result of the absence of authorized explanation is to isolate Marcus in his adolescent fear of madness and monstrosity. Rather than being a wisdom figure like the Wordsworthian child, this child-seer embodies the terrors and loneliness of childhood that are inseparable from the condition of not knowing oneself. Rather than being a source of saving vision, Marcus is almost destroyed by his special powers. He is saved for sanity and for use (if indeed he is saved) by the ordinary difficult affection and loyalty that link him to Lucas Simmonds.

The Virgin in the Garden offers the fullest, most realistic, and most equivocal treatment I know of the visionary child. The social testing of Marcus's experiences results in a much more guarded view of vision and the saving wisdom of childhood than is otherwise found in works in the Romantic tradition. It is the terror and pity of childhood, rather than its serene sagacity, that interests Byatt in this remarkable novel.

NOTES

1. See, for example, M. H. Abrams, *Natural Supernaturalism: Tradition and Revolution in Romantic Literature* (New York: Norton, 1971) 377–84; and Judith Plotz, "The Perpetual Messiah: Romanticism, Childhood, and the Paradoxes of Human Development," *Regulated Children/Liberated Children*, ed. Barbara Finkelstein (New York: Psychohistory P, 1980) 63–95.

2. The allusion to the Gospel of St. Matthew 18.2 figures as the epigraph of John Keble, *Lyra Innocentium: Thoughts in Verse on Christian Children, Their Ways and Their Privileges* (Oxford, 1846), and as the title of Wilfrid Meynell's child-loving anthology, *The Child Set in the Midst by Modern Poets* (London, 1892).

3. Friedrich von Schiller, *Naïve and Sentimental Poetry*, trans. Julius A. Elias (New York: Ungar, 1966) 87.

4. Ralph Waldo Emerson, "Nature," *Selections from Ralph Waldo Emerson*, ed. Stephen E. Whicher (Boston: Houghton, 1950) 53.

5. William Wordsworth, "Ode: Intimations of Immortality," *Wordsworth: Poetical Works*, ed. Thomas Hutchinson, rev. Ernest de Selincourt (London: Oxford UP, 1969) 461.

6. Wordsworth, *Poetical Works* 461.

7. Hartley Coleridge, "To Jeanette, Six Weeks Old," *The Complete Poetical Works of Hartley Coleridge* (London, 1851) 185.

8. A. Bronson Alcott, Sonnet 14, *Sonnets and Canzonets* (Boston, 1882) 69.

9. Elizabeth Rachel Chapman, Sonnets 27 and 6, *A Little Child's Wreath* (London, 1904) 55, 28.

10. Though the term is problematic, I use it in Piaget's restricted sense as simply "the tendency to regard objects as living and endowed with will." See Jean Piaget, *The Child's Conception of the World*, trans. John and Andrew Tomlinson (St. Albans: Paladin, 1973) 194.

11. William Blake, "The Chimney Sweeper," *The Poetry and Prose of William Blake*, ed. David V. Erdman (Garden City, NY: Doubleday, 1965) 10.

12. Cf. Samuel Taylor Coleridge, "To Thomas Poole," 16 October 1797, *Collected Letters of Samuel Taylor Coleridge*, ed. Earl Leslie Griggs, vol. 1 (Oxford: Clarendon, 1966) 210: "For from my early reading of Faery Tales & Genii &c &c—my mind had been habituated *to the Vast*—& I never regarded *my senses* in any way as the criteria of my belief. I regulated all my creeds by my conceptions not by my *sight*." In the notebooks, Coleridge reports his son Hartley, "speaking of some Tale & wild Fancy of his Brain," as saying: "'It is not yet, but it will be—for it *is*—& it cannot always stay *in* here' (*pressing one hand on his forehead and the other on his occiput)*—'and then *it will be*—because it is not nothing.'" *The Notebooks of Samuel Taylor Coleridge*, ed. Kathleen Coburn, vol. 3 (New York: Pantheon, 1956-) 3547.

13. Thomas De Quincey, "Suspiria de Profundis," *Confessions of an English Opium Eater and Other Writings*, ed. Grevel Lindop (Oxford: Oxford UP, 1996) 127.

14. Samuel Taylor Coleridge, "Opus Maximus," *Coleridge on Logic and Learning*, ed. Alice D. Snyder (New Haven: Yale UP, 1929) 127.

15. Samuel Taylor Coleridge, *Anima Poetae: From the Unpublished Notebooks of S. T. Coleridge*, ed. Ernest Hartley Coleridge (London, 1895) 77.

16. Samuel Taylor Coleridge, *Inquiring Spirit: A New Presentation of Coleridge from his Published and Unpublished Prose Writings*, ed. Kathleen Coburn (London: Routledge, 1951) 68.

17. William Wordsworth, *The Prelude* [1850], 2.238–40 and 2.401–2. This and all subsequent quotations from *The Prelude* are taken from *The Prelude 1799, 1805, 1850*, ed. Jonathan Wordsworth, M. H. Abrams, and Stephen Gill (New York: Norton, 1979).

18. William Blake, "Nurse's Song," *Poetry and Prose* 15.

19. De Quincey 114.

20. Hartley Coleridge, *Poetical Works* 179.

21. Qtd. in Matthew Russell, *Little Angels: A Book of Comfort for Mourning Mothers* (London: Burns and Oates, 1909) 78.

22. Percy Bysshe Shelley, "Adonais," *English Romantic Writers*, ed. David Perkins (New York: Harcourt Brace, 1967) 1051.

23. Wordsworth, "Resolution and Independence," *Poetical Works* 156.

24. Theodore Roethke, "The Far Field," *The Norton Anthology of Poetry*, ed. Alexander W. Allison et al., 3rd ed. (New York: Norton, 1983) 1122.

25. Wordsworth, *Poetical Works* 461–62.

26. Wordsworth, *Prelude* [1850] 12.222.

27. Qtd. in *English Romantic Writers* 279.

28. Wordsworth, *Prelude* [1850] 2.348–49, 2.395, 2.401–2 (*emphases added*).

29. Wordsworth, *Prelude* [1805] 2.253–54.

30. Lucas is paraphrasing William James's account in Lecture X of *The Varieties of Religious Experience* of "hallucinatory or pseudo-hallucinatory luminous phenomena, *photisms*, to use the term of the psychologists." See William James, *The Varieties of Religious Experience*, ed. Joseph Ratner (New York: University Books, 1963) 251. I am grateful to A. S. Byatt for this information.

31. Cf. Gerard Manley Hopkins, "The Wreck of the Deutschland," 1.5–6, *Poems and Prose of Gerard Manley Hopkins*, ed. W. H. Gardner (Harmondsworth: Penguin, 1953) 14.

32. Wordsworth, *Prelude* [1850] 2.402.

33. Wordsworth, *Prelude* [1850] 1.398–99.

34. Wordsworth, *Prelude* [1850] 13.338.

Alexa Alfer

Realism and Its Discontents:
The Virgin in the Garden and *Still Life*

In her 1979 survey of contemporary fiction, "People in Paper Houses," A. S.
Byatt ponders the "curiously symbiotic relationship between old realism and new
experiment" perceived to be at the heart of the English post-war novel (*PM* 170).
The conflict between literary experimentation and realist allegiances, with all its
connotations of avant-garde innovation and linguistic astuteness on the one hand,
and the socio-political impulse to return to a portrayal of "understandable characters in a reasonably straightforward style: no tricks, no experimental foolery" on
the other,[1] has become something of a commonplace in criticism of British
fiction between the end of the Second World War and the early to mid-1970s.
The debate is not a new one, of course. Mrs Woolf's earlier quibbles with Mr
Bennett are by now part of twentieth-century critical folklore.[2] In the immediate
post-war period, with modernism itself largely conventionalised, and in the face
of a radically transformed world order in which not just literature was feared to
have lost its bearings, the battle between literary experimentation and realist
formats of storytelling flared up with a renewed sense of urgency. Literary
practitioners themselves again fuelled the argument. C. P. Snow's influential
attacks on the experimental legacy of modernism[3] are matched in acerbity by B.
S. Johnson's characterisation of post-nineteenth-century realism as "anachronistic, invalid, irrelevant, and perverse."[4] If the works of a substantial number of
writers such as Iris Murdoch, Doris Lessing, Angus Wilson, or, a generation
later, Julian Barnes and Graham Swift, cast significant doubt on the notion of a
categorical opposition between "old realism and new experiment," literary criticism for its part nevertheless largely accepted and indeed perpetuated this dichotomy.[5] Its echoes continue to haunt scholars to the present day, as the debates

over the relative merits of postmodernism as an aesthetic and/or critical paradigm attest.[6]

Significantly, A. S. Byatt's focus in "People in Paper Houses" is on *symbiosis*, on productive rather than combative relations between the two poles of the storytelling debate. Her broader allegiances are, however, clear. Or are they? "If I have defended realism, or what I call 'self-conscious realism,'" Byatt writes elsewhere, "it is not because I believe it has any privileged relationship to truth, social or psychological, but because it leaves space for thinking minds as well as feeling bodies" (*PM* 4). At first sight, this is not such a far cry from the liberal-humanist mindset that underpins the classic case in favour of realism. Indeed, as Michael Westlake writes in a thoughtful though not entirely favourable review of *Still Life*, Byatt's fiction must appear, at one level at least, like an elaborate defence "of a certain kind of literary and philosophical faith," namely that of an epistemological humanism reaching back before, and at odds with "Continental theory" and post-structuralism in particular.[7] Overtly, Westlake continues, Byatt's project "owes much to considerations of realism, *coupled*," however, "with a suspicion that the narrative form as such must inevitably put that realism into question."[8] What Westlake is inclined to view as a potential (and potentially fatal) flaw in the fictional argument presented in *Still Life* reveals itself, on closer inspection, as a double intimation of the "curiously symbiotic relationship" not only between literary realism and experiment, but also between the creative and the critical imagination. As both writer and critic, A. S. Byatt is acutely aware of the formal and philosophical difficulties that have bedevilled the realist project from the outset. If she professes "a strong moral attachment to its values," such attachment is *always already*—and inextricably—bound up with "a formal need to comment on their [these values'] fictiveness" and a profound sense that all "models, literature and 'the tradition' are ambiguous and problematic goods" (*PM* 181).

Byatt's works present as much a continuation as a challenge to the traditions they engage with, and it is essentially *within* her fictions that the curious symbiosis of tradition and transformation, realism and experiment, storytelling and abstract thought unfolds its full potential. Internalising the theoretical puzzlements that have cast such long shadows over the twentieth-century novel, and actively reinscribing their discourses into the textual fabric of fiction itself, Byatt's novels and short stories productively worry about issues such as the vexed question of artistic representation, the relationship between perception and language, or the cultural constructions on which the novel itself is said to rest. In doing so, her fiction not least substantially complicates our notions of traditions of thought and storytelling as such—traditions the conceptual foundations of which her texts, by the same token, re-imagine, or, dare one say, *create* afresh at every narrative turn. If realism holds a particular claim to Byatt's literary allegiances in this project, it is her creative and ever-questioning experimentation *with* realist formats that not only marks her out as a highly innovative storyteller, but also renders her fictions valuable and important interventions in and contributions to the ongoing debates on our ways of worldmaking, both within and beyond the literary text.

"The problems of the 'real' in fiction, and the adequacy of words to describe it, have preoccupied me for the last twenty years," A. S. Byatt writes in the introduction to her 1991 collection of essays, *Passions of the Mind* (5). A decade on, Byatt's fictional output has diversified to an extent that might well call the continuing validity of this statement into question. In *Angels and Insects*, published in 1992, we are presented with suspiciously *un*problematic simulacra of the classic realist text; the five fairy stories that make up *The Djinn in the Nightingale's Eye* signal, if not a departure, then a considerable detour on the road towards a "self-conscious realism"; *Babel Tower*, the third in Byatt's projected tetralogy of condition-of-Britain novels begun in 1978 with *The Virgin in the Garden* and continued in 1985 with *Still Life*, allows the provocative and feverishly experimental atmosphere of its 1960s setting to strategically spill over into its own narrative structure, thus arguably paving the way for Byatt's most recent foray into fragmentation, *The Biographer's Tale*. And yet, if Byatt's writing—perhaps late-twentieth-century writing in general—has increasingly freed itself from the constraints imposed by the realism/experiment dichotomy, the variety of possible forms recovered and (re)invented in the process nevertheless reflects a continued and undiminished preoccupation with "the problems of the 'real' in fiction, and the adequacy of words to describe it." The old battle over whose "real," whose "words" may be gradually relinquishing its central place in our debates about the novel, its history and its future, but the question of "the relations between truth, lies and fiction"—ultimately a question of the nature of representation as such—remains as urgent as ever (*PM* 21).

During the early 1960s, Byatt says she learned from her encounter with Proust "that it was possible for a text to be supremely mimetic, . . . and at the same time to think about form, its own form, its own formation, about perceiving and inventing the world" (*PM* 22–23). What initially appears like the discovery of a mere—albeit exciting—possibility is transformed, in and through Byatt's own fiction, into an imperative inherent, or at the very least latent, in the "supremely mimetic" text itself. Two of Byatt's earlier novels, *The Virgin in the Garden* and *Still Life*, ponder this imperative from distinct and very specific angles. As "self-consciously realist novels about my own time and my own culture" (*PM* 22), they are among those of Byatt's writings that attest most fully to her habitual weighing of the nature of fiction and the problems of representational art.

"I wanted to write a historical novel," Byatt comments somewhat paradoxically on *The Virgin in the Garden*.[9] Set in 1950s Yorkshire, and deftly blending mid-twentieth-century realism with Renaissance allegory, *The Virgin in the Garden* is first and foremost a novel *about* history, a "time-novel" much in Thomas Mann's sense of the term: "It is a historical novel in so far as it aims to evoke the inner picture of a historical epoch. . . . But it also takes up pure time itself as its subject, a subject that it not only treats in terms of its hero[es]'s experiences, but explores in and through itself."[10] Later in her career, Byatt does, of course, go on to write historical novels that are more immediately recognisable as such. *The Virgin in the Garden* and its sequels, meanwhile, run as a thoughtful counterpoint to Byatt's more overtly historical fictions in that they explore the fractured historical sense of the post-war period alongside the concept of contemporaneity and the possibility (or, as the case may be, impossibility) of its representation. "'Contemporary' was in those days synonymous with 'modern' as it had not been before and is not now (1977)," the narrator comments at one point in the novel, momentarily arresting the 1953 action of the story with this uneasy intrusion of a voice—a narrative authority, moreover—from a specified future present (*VG* 242). The allusion to Stephen Spender's famous distinction between the *Modern* and the *Contemporary*, heavily biased as it is in favour of the modern, is not lost on the reader here.[11] Byatt's momentary emphasis may lie on the (discredited) contemporary in Spender's sense, but *The Virgin in the Garden* transforms Spender's dichotomy—a dichotomy ultimately between realism and modernism—into a complex interplay of competing temporal narratives in which memory and history alike form, dissolve, and reform again as part of a narrative structure that seeks to turn itself into a meditation on the history of modernity as such. As a narrative of temporal experience, as a narrative experience both *of* and *in* time, *The Virgin in the Garden* not only probes realism's much maligned "prior imagination of beginnings and ends"[12] as the condition of its own fragile presence as a text; it also struggles to make sense of a (literally) postmodern present that hovers uneasily between the overbearing and continuing presence of the monolithic Modern-ness of time just past and the desire for a recovered or, at the very least, recoverable self-presence in a future not quite yet within reach.

If *The Virgin in the Garden* ponders this dilemma in terms of speculations on the nature of time and historical knowledge in the context of provincial life in 1950s Britain, then its sequel, *Still Life,* doubles as an enquiry into the origins of representation as such. In the prologue to *The Virgin in the Garden*, three of Byatt's characters had come together at London's National Portrait Gallery to "hear Flora Robson do Queen Elizabeth" as part of an exhibition entitled *People, Past and Present* (9). On his approach to the Gallery, Alexander Wedderburn, in whose company we first enter the scene, "considered those words, once powerful, at present defunct, national and portrait. They were both to do with identity: the identity of a culture (place, language and history), the identity of an individual human being as an object for mimetic representation" (9). Once inside the gallery, Alexander finds himself face to face with the Darnley Portrait of Elizabeth I: "It was so clear, Alexander thought, that there had been someone real there to be portrayed. But she was like Shakespeare, a figure whose overabundant energy attracts dubiously mixed emotions, idolatry and iconoclasm, love and fear, and the accompanying need to diminish and reduce their strangeness and ordinariness by reductive myths and pointless 'explanations'" (13). At the time the novel is set, and on which the characters look back from a fifteen-year distance in the prologue, Alexander Wedderburn had been writing an Eliotesque verse-drama on the Virgin Queen, *Astraea*, performed in the year of the second Elizabeth's coronation and steeped in the complex dilemma of how to square the "then" with the "now"—of how to accommodate difference and the desire for historical continuity.

A few years on, in *Still Life*, Alexander is working on his second play, *The Yellow Chair*, based on Van Gogh's letters and paintings. If *Astraea* had sought to give dramatic form to T. S. Eliot's mythic dictum of the "dissociation of sensibility" and Alexander's own time's belated "nostalgia for a *paradis perdu* in which thought and language and things were naturally and indissolubly linked" (*PM* 9), he now "had trouble finding an appropriate language for the painter's obsessions with the illuminated material world" (*ST* 2). Once again, and with the benefit of considerable hindsight, Alexander's dilemma is reflected upon in *Still Life*'s prologue: "At first he had thought that he could write a plain, exact verse with no figurative language, in which a yellow chair was the thing itself, a yellow chair, as a round gold apple was an apple or a sunflower a sunflower. . . . But it couldn't be done. Language was against him, for a start. Metaphor lay coiled in the name sunflower, which not only turned towards but resembled the sun" (*ST* 2). In an essay entitled "Still Life / Nature morte," Byatt herself comments in remarkably similar terms on *Still Life*: The idea behind this novel, she writes, "was that it should be very bare, very down-to-earth, attempt to give the 'thing itself' without the infinitely extensible cross-referencing of *The Virgin* [*in the Garden*]" (*PM* 11). Most strikingly, however, it is midway through the novel itself that the narrator notes: "I had the idea, when I began this novel, that it would be a novel of naming and accuracy. I wanted to write a novel as Williams said a poem should be: no ideas but in things. I even thought of trying to write without figures of speech, but had to give up that plan, quite early" (*ST* 301).

Instead, *Still Life* has become a record of, and a complex fictional meditation upon, what the narrator recognises as the failure "to name without metaphor, to describe simply and clearly, to categorise and distinguish, one specimen from the other" (*PM* 11). As the rhetoric of this passage already suggests, *Still Life*'s weighing of the languages of representation reaches beyond considerations of the strictly literary; the seemingly irreducible difference/distance—as well as the occasional and unexpected kinship—between visual and verbal forms of perception and description are negotiated against the backdrop of scientific speculations on pre-linguistic cognition and the semantics of biological enquiry. All add layers of complex intertexts, rather than mere corroborating evidence, to the narrative. When young Marcus Potter, recovering from the nervous breakdown he suffered in the word-heavy world of *The Virgin in the Garden*, finds, in *Still Life*, respite and pleasure in the taxonomic study of grasses, "in listing and drawing" them, "simply *naming* the multitudinous things to be seen, for the sake of seeing them more clearly," he is supremely—and ironically—safe from Jean-Paul Sartre's as well as his own earlier "existential terror at the formless otherness of the root of a chestnut tree" and "would not have understood Sartre's sense that matter escapes our naming, bulges beyond it" (*ST* 300–1). The novel itself sides neither with Sartre nor with Marcus on this count. What it does do, however, is to recover from the names of Marcus's grasses—"differentiations, a taxonomy, Adamic names, muddled metaphors"—an image, or the Gestalt of an image "for the relation of words to things": temporary, local, unstable, "inventive, imprecise, denotative, practical, imagined" (*PM* 20).

"Form, as an element of human experience, must begin with the perception of difference," writes George Eliot in her "Notes on Form in Art."[13] What Byatt stresses in *Still Life* is that to articulate, to *know*, and to speak *of* this difference is to embrace the serpentine "processes of distinction and combination" that lie at the heart of language itself.[14] If metaphor emerges as an integral function of representational language in this novel, it also seems to share with non-literary figures of thought (taxonomy, a yellow chair, time past, time present) a more fundamental relationship to narrative fiction—one that can itself be said to take the form of metaphor and may provide a way into a productive reformulation of "the problems of the 'real' in fiction, and the adequacy of words to describe it."

In "Still Life / Nature morte," Byatt points to Paul Ricœur's philosophical work on metaphor as one of the intellectual cornerstones of her abandoned yet accomplished "novel of naming and accuracy" (*PM* 15). Over his long career as a philosopher, Ricœur has himself been a highly vocal and inspiring advocate of a mutually informative relationship between abstract thought and fiction, and Byatt's self-consciously "philosophical fictions" provide an interesting creative correlative to some of his positions. At the same time, Ricœur's insistence on fiction's capacity to take philosophy beyond its own perplexities also, and perhaps paradoxically, frees the literary imagination from some of *its* most puzzling impasses. One of Ricœur's most basic and exciting philosophical assumptions in this context is that there is a power to fictional narrative to redescribe a reality inaccessible to direct description. Interestingly, it is precisely in his studies on metaphor that such productive interrelation finds its grounds.

In *The Rule of Metaphor*, Ricœur does not so much philosophise about metaphor as recover the philosophical potential inherent in this figure of speech.[15] Conceiving of metaphor as a dialectical process of predicative displacement and assimilation at the level of the whole sentence, Ricœur shows how metaphor not only operates essentially discursively but can, and indeed should, be viewed as a model of discourse in its own right.[16] No longer "confined to a role of accompaniment, of illustration," metaphor "participates in the *invention* of meaning" at the level of the text as a whole.[17] First and foremost, however, the metaphorical statement emerges as supremely referential—albeit with a difference. In his introduction to the first volume of *Time and Narrative,* Ricœur argues that

the poetic function of language is not limited to the celebration of language for its own sake, at the expense of the referential function, which is predominant in descriptive discourse. [Rather,] the suspension of this direct, descriptive referential function is only the reverse side, or the negative condition, of a more covered over referential function of discourse, which is, so to speak, liberated by the suspending of the descriptive value of statements. In this way poetic discourse brings to language aspects, qualities, and values of reality that lack access to language that is directly descriptive and that can be spoken only by means of the complex interplay between the metaphorical utterance and the rule-governed transgression of the usual meanings of our words.[18]

This is not an appeal—in time-honoured humanist fashion—to a metaphysical "higher truth" or "reality" of poetic discourse. Neither metaphor nor the operations of mimesis, which Ricœur later recasts in the mould of metaphorical reference, pretend to any privileged relation to an external given; rather, they produce meaning, "redescribe" or "resignify" their referent, along a seamless hermeneutic circle of linguistic activity. Furthermore, both reference and its truth-values are inextricably language-bound in Ricœur's theory, enabling him to effectively counter what Michael Riffaterre, in a similar argument, has called the "representational fallacy."[19] In his essay on "Mimesis and Representation," Ricœur discusses the "representative fallacy" or "illusion" as allegedly stemming

from the impossible claim of uniting the interiority of a mental image in the mind and the exteriority of something real that would govern from the outside the play of the mental scene within a single entity or "representation." The illusory nature of this claim is said to be even clearer if one says that the interior presence and the exterior presence can be made present to each other through some process of adequation which would define the truth of the representation. Representation, accordingly, it is said, should be denounced as the reduplication of presence, as the re-presenting of presence.[20]

As a way of extricating "representation from the impasse to which it has been relegated, to return it to its field of play," Ricœur proposes a reconceptualisation of the complex notion of mimesis, a "mimetic opening to the closure of representation,"[21] which would also help to "dissolve the opposition between inside and outside, which itself arises from the representative illusion."[22]

Mimesis, or "the mimetic function of narrative," Ricœur argues, "poses a problem exactly parallel to the problem of metaphorical reference. It is, in fact, one particular application of the latter to the sphere of human action."[23] In *Time and Narrative*, Ricœur distinguishes between three stages or aspects of mimesis: mimesis$_1$ marks the point at which motives, goals and ethic qualities of human action become the immediate subject of narrative understanding. This first aspect of mimesis thus describes a state of *prefiguration*—what Mario Valdés calls the "pre-condition for textuality."[24] Mimesis$_2$, in its turn, denotes "the entry into the realm of the poetic composition," a stage Ricœur calls *configuration*.[25] This is the Aristotelian *mythos*, the configuration of the fable, the essence of emplotment. What finally emerges in mimesis$_3$ is a *new* configuration by means of the poetic *refiguration* of "the pre-understood order of action" (mimesis$_1$). It is here that fiction, according to Ricœur, "reveals its ability to transform and transfigure reality" itself,[26] and it is also here that "the mimetic function of the plot rejoins metaphorical reference."[27] Both operations partake in what Ricœur calls the "the paradox of productive reference," the paradox, that is, of reference *through* redescription: "only the image which does not already have its referent in reality is able to display a world. . . . *When*," by the same token, "the image *is made*, it is also able to remake the world."[28]

Marcus's list of names of grasses—"denotative, . . . imagined"—comes to mind again:

Alopecurus (Fox-tail)—from alopex, a fox, oura, a tail

Phalaris—canary grass—from phalos, shining

Gastridium—nit-grass—from gastridion, a little swelling

Aira—hair-grass—from aira, to destroy (darnel)

Arrhenatherum—oat like grass—arrhen, male, ather, an awn

Panicum—Panick-grass—from panis, bread

Anthoxanthum—vernal grass—anthos, a flower, xanthos, yellow

(*PM* 20; see *ST* 300).

All these names, Byatt writes, are "small metaphors—human perceptions, the nit, the little swelling, seeing the likeness in the difference of foxtail and haretail and grass." Even the double metaphors arising purely "out of etymological confusion"—Panick-grass—come to signify out of their very surplus of meaning: We see "the grass both quaking with fear and providing wheat-ears for bread." Above all, however, these names "are in their business a counter-image to Sartre's experience of namelessness," and they are so because they are mimetic icons, productively referential, giving local embodiment to the impossible, paradoxical "relation of words to things" to the precise extent that they allow us to perceive identity and difference not only between foxtail and grass, but also between word and thing, "simultaneously and dependent on each other" (*PM* 20; 15).

In the same summer as Marcus prepares for his Botany A-Levels, with grasses "his chosen area of special study," his sister Frederica "sat Finals at Cambridge and wrote orderly booklets, brimming with quotation and cross-referencing, on Tragedy, Literary Criticism, Dante and The English Moralists, who included, in those days, Plato, Aristotle, St Augustine and small slivers of Kant" (*ST* 298–99). We do not learn what Frederica makes of her Moralists, non-English to a man, but Paul Ricœur, for one, would have been interested.

Ricœur's *Time and Narrative* starts out with a dialogue between Augustine's *Confessions* and Aristotle's *Poetics*. What he extracts from his reading of these two texts are two interlinking sets of philosophical problems: Augustine's *distentio* and *intentio animi* on the one hand, and the Aristotelian plot on the other. According to Ricœur, the split or dissonance (*distentio*) the soul experiences when memory (of the past), attention (to the present) and expectation (of the future) strive towards a mutually intending relationship (*intentio*) finds its exact inversion in the Aristotelian *mythos*, where consonance is wrought from dissonance. What both Augustine and Aristotle share, and what makes them problematic in a philosophical sense, is the instability of the constructions they employ to overcome the dichotomies that lie at their respective centres. Taken together, however, they run in hopeful parallel to the paradox of metaphorical redescription. As we have already seen, "metaphorical redescription and *mimesis* are closely bound up with each other," and *Time and Narrative* brings the familiar argument forward to the point at which we can finally "exchange the two vocabularies and speak of the mimetic value of poetic discourse and the redescriptive power of narrative fiction."[29] What narrative essentially redescribes is, according to Ricœur, the experience of *time*.

Why does time require redescription through narrative? On the one hand, "The world unfolded by every narrative is always a temporal world." On the other, Augustine's *distentio* and *intentio* of time, and the resulting experience of dissonance-in-consonance, represent a basic philosophical paradox—a "secret," as Ricœur has it—that cannot be unveiled by the intellectual strategies of phenomenology alone. According to Ricœur, this "secret" requires a mimetic correspondence that can only be achieved through the act of narrative refiguration: "speculation on time is an inconclusive rumination to which narrative activity alone can respond. Not that this activity solves the aporias through substitution. If it does resolve them, it is in a poetical and not a theoretical sense of the word."[30]

Elizabeth Ermarth, in *Realism and Consensus in the English Novel*, identifies the "treatment of linear time" as "the central problem of realist fiction."[31] From a philosophical point of view, however, it may well be fiction itself that not only refigures the theoretical quandaries of time as such, but, in the very act of doing so, repositions itself along a hermeneutically conceived mimetic circle that takes it beyond linear pro/regression and one-dimensional descriptiveness into a refigured reality of its own making. What is at stake for Ricœur himself in the fundamental "reciprocity between narrativity and temporality" he proposes is indeed nothing less than a redescriptive refiguration of the real.[32]

Ricœur first explores his circle of time and narrative by way of an exploration of the narrative handling of time in historiography, and subsequently (in the second volume of *Time and Narrative*) through an enquiry into the experience of time and temporality conveyed through fictional narrative. The third and final volume of *Time and Narrative* terminates in a hermeneutic of the historical consciousness and recovers an inner link between fictional narrative and history that Ricœur calls "interwoven reference."[33] Such "interwoven" and again essentially *productive* reference denotes a process of two-fold transgression: fiction's entanglement in the realised potential of the past on the one hand, and history's eruption into the fiction of an unrealised potential of historical existence on the other. At the point of intersection of these two movements of transgression (T. S. Eliot's "still point"?), Ricœur recovers what he calls "human time"—a time in which the representation of time past through history merges with its fictional variations. In Ricœur's own words:

Historical intentionality only becomes effective by incorporating into its intended object the resources of fictionalization stemming from the narrative form of imagination, while the intentionality of fiction produces its effects of detecting and transforming acting and suffering only by symmetrically assuming the resources of historicization presented it by attempts to reconstruct the actual past. From these intimate exchanges between the historicization of the fictional narrative and the fictionalization of the historical narrative is born what we call human time, which is nothing other than narrated time.[34]

Here is another intimation of what Byatt, in the pages of this current volume, calls the indispensable "both–and" relationship at the heart of serious historical fiction. Back at "The National Portrait Gallery: 1968," however, the historical dramatist Alexander Wedderburn contemplates with little more than a faint sense of aesthetic amusement "the black circling curve of railings to which was tied a repeating series of pale reproductions of the Darnley Portrait of Elizabeth Tudor, faded coral, gold, white, arrogance, watchfulness, announcing 'People, Past and Present.'" On his way to St Martin's Place, "he had passed several recruiting posters for the First World War, pointing accusatory fingers at him, and a shop called 'I was Lord Kitchener's Valet,' full of reproduced bric-à-brac of the British Empire" (*VG* 9). American tourists clad in "English macintoshes, English tweed, English cashmere" complete the painful picture (10).

If Alexander's own historical sense differs from what he perceives as the "undirected and aimless" nature of modern parody (10), the difference seems to lie mainly in the degree of sophistication of the nostalgia that pervades the prologue to *The Virgin in the Garden*: "Alexander himself had considerable knowledge about the history of clothing, could place a shift of seam or change of cut in relation to tradition and the individual talent almost as well as he could a verse-form or a vocabulary. He watched his own clothes and his own poetry in the light of these delicate shifts of subdued innovation. But he was apprehensive that at this time there was no real life in either" (11). If the allusion to T. S. Eliot momentarily holds out the promise of a productive rather than reproductive relationship between past and present at the beginning of Byatt's "time-novel," Alexander seems resigned to the fact that, in 1968, the time for history as a living dialectic in Eliot's sense is long past.

Memory, the other form of retrospect anticipated in rather elaborate ways in the prologue to *The Virgin in the Garden*, hardly fares any better. At the gallery reading, Frederica is prompted to reminisce about the production of Alexander's play *Astrea* and the events of 1953:

"Funny, the Fifties. Everybody thinks of it as a kind of no-time, an unreal time, just now. But we were there, it was rather beautiful, the Play, and the coronation and all that."

"A false beginning," said Alexander.

"All the beginning there was," she said. "My beginning, anyway. That was what did happen." (15)

Significantly, it is only with the benefit of hindsight of her thirty-two-year-old self that Frederica can assert so confidently that "we were there," that that was indeed "what did happen." In 1953 itself, "reality for her was the future," and only when she "was old enough to equate the tenuous pastel hopes of 1953 with her own almost-adult knowledge that everything was a new beginning . . . did she come to feel nostalgia for what at the time she diagnosed boldly as blear illusion" (242).

"Time and art are twin architects of the forms which human beings use to define and thereby create what is real," Juliet Dusinberre reflects in her essay "Forms of Reality in A. S. Byatt's *The Virgin in the Garden*."[35] Byatt's characters certainly try their hands at both, but for all their attempts to come to grips with their own present as well as the several layers of time past that inform it, the sense of self-presence they so urgently seek eludes them. As (albeit fictional) human beings, they are as much caught up in self-emplotment as they are in the seemingly inescapable flux of time, and the way *The Virgin in the Garden* explores this deadlock provides an interesting link to Ricœur's three stages of mimesis. The novel's characters could be said to be permanently arrested at the second mimetic stage, that of configuration or re*present*ation in the literal sense of the word. If the novel as a whole succeeds in making the leap from representation to productive redescription (and, thus, along the mimetic circle, back to a refigured order of action in the pre/post-textual realm), it does so not least on account of an elaborate temporal structure that internalises what Ricœur called the "representational impasse" and essentially privileges the conscious (rather than merely conventional) use and *enactment of* the epic past tense over imperatives of representational immediacy. What is more, the characters' enactment of the first two stages of mimesis liberates the novel's broader narrative discourse in a rule-governed and essentially temporal shift in descriptive responsibility, thus suspending, so to speak, its directly referential function and releasing a new power of redescription that is new and powerful precisely because it is fictional.

Interviewing A. S. Byatt in 1983, Dusinberre observes with reference to *The Virgin in the Garden*: "You seem to suggest that things become real by moving into the past, and also that literature creates a reality more durable than lived experience." In reply, Byatt remarks: "When I read I inhabit a world which is more real than the world in which I live, or perhaps I should say I am more alive in it. It is a language world. Language tries to capture and make permanent a moment in time which won't be captured. . . . The present only becomes a real point in time when time has moved on and made it past."[36]

"Language worlds," their "reality," the way we live in them, and the way they come alive in the process of readerly inhabitation will continue to pose their own paradoxes, retain their own secrets. No amount of self-referential experimentation, nor the stubborn insistence on the seemingly self-evident correspondence between the world that surrounds us and the names we bestow on it, will finally unravel them. What we can do, however, is to continue to tell each other stories that speak of these paradoxes, stories that remember and articulate, in and through themselves, "the problems of the 'real' in fiction" and the quest for "the adequacy of words to describe it." The inherited forms and values of realism are not the worst models we could choose in this endeavour, although they are certainly not the only ones. If anything, A. S. Byatt's experiments with realist formats and her fictional redescriptions of their theoretical dilemmas show how realism, far from being epistemologically naive, is—and probably always has been—a potentially profoundly self-conscious mode of storytelling, productively worried about its philosophical as well as aesthetic premises and centrally concerned not so much, nor so simply, with the "faithful representation of reality" as with the problems and pitfalls of our desire for such representations and the always essentially textual strategies we employ in pursuit of them. As Dusinberre writes of *The Virgin in the Garden*:

Its very existence as a verbal artifact declares what its naturalistic characters are forced to deny, that the real exists through the mediation of the unreal verbal form, which makes durable in words the human capacity for enduring things. The novel offers no consolation except that it is, like the world it creates, there. The recorded moment of time is made real by being imagined. In questioning the power of images and literary forms, the novel defines itself as a form of reality.[37]

NOTES

1. Kingsley Amis, qtd. in Blake Morrison, *The Movement: English Poetry and Fiction of the 1950s* (Oxford: Oxford UP, 1980) 299.

2. Virginia Woolf, "Mr Bennett and Mrs Brown" [1924], *A Woman's Essays*, ed. Rachel Bowlby (Harmondsworth: Penguin, 1992) 69–87.

3. See, for example, C. P. Snow, "Preface," *The Realists: Portraits of Eight Novelists* (London: Macmillan, 1978) 7–10; and "Challenge to the Intellect," *Times Literary Supplement* (15 Aug. 1958): 6.

4. B. S. Johnson, "Introduction," *Aren't You Rather Young to be Writing Your Memoirs* (London: Collins, 1974) 13–14.

5. An extremely useful alternative account of the—in this case *productive*—tension between experimental and traditional writing is provided by Andrzej Gasiorek, *Post-War British Fiction: Realism and After* (London: Arnold, 1995).

6. See, for example, Alison Lee, *Realism and Power: Postmodern British Fiction* (London: Routledge, 1990).

7. Michael Westlake, "The Hard Idea of Truth," *PN Review* 15.4 (1989): 33.

8. Westlake 35 (emphasis added).

9. A. S. Byatt, qtd. in Olga Kenyon, *Women Novelists Today: A Survey of English Writing in the Seventies and Eighties* (Brighton: Harvester, 1988) 75.

10. Thomas Mann, "Einführung in den *Zauberberg*," *Der Zauberberg* (Frankfurt am Main: Fischer, 1950) xxiii [translated for this edition].

11. See Stephen Spender, "Moderns and Contemporaries," *The Idea of the Modern in Literature and the Arts*, ed. Irving Howe (New York: Horizon, 1967) 43–49.

12. Leo Bersani, "Realism and the Fear of Desire" [1969], *Realism*, ed. Lillian Furst (London: Longman, 1992) 241.

13. George Eliot, "Notes on Form in Art," *Selected Essays, Poems and Other Writings*, ed. A. S. Byatt and Nicholas Warren (Harmondsworth: Penguin, 1990) 232.

14. Eliot 232.

15. Paul Ricœur, *The Rule of Metaphor: Multi-Disciplinary Studies of the Creation of Meaning in Language*, trans. Robert Czerny with Kathleen McLaughlin and John Costello (London: Routledge, 1978).

16. See Paul Ricœur, "Metaphor and the Main Problem of Hermeneutics," *Reflection and Imagination: A Ricœur Reader*, ed. Mario J. Valdés (New York: Harvester, 1991) 303–19.

17. Paul Ricœur, "The Function of Fiction in Shaping Reality," *Reflection and Imagination* 123.

18. Paul Ricœur, *Time and Narrative*, trans. Kathleen McLaughlin and David Pellauer, vol. 1 (Chicago: U of Chicago P, 1984) xi.

19. Michael Riffaterre, "Intertextual Representation: On Mimesis as Interpretive Discourse," *Diacritics* 11.1 (Sept. 1984): 158.

20. Paul Ricœur, "Mimesis and Representation," *Reflection and Imagination* 137.

21. Ricœur, "Mimesis" 137.

22. Ricœur, "Mimesis" 151.

23. Ricœur, *Time and Narrative* xi.

24. Mario J. Valdés, "Paul Ricœur's Post-Structuralist Hermeneutics," *Reflection and Imagination* 28.

25. Ricœur, *Time and Narrative* xi.

26. Ricœur, "The Function of Fiction" 129.

27. Ricœur, *Time and Narrative* xi.

28. Ricœur, "The Function of Fiction" 129 (emphasis added).

29. Ricœur, *Time and Narrative* xi.

30. Ricœur, *Time and Narrative* 6.

31. Elizabeth Deeds Ermarth, *Realism and Consensus in the English Novel* (Princeton: Princeton UP, 1983) xii.

32. Ricœur, *Time and Narrative* 3.

33. Ricœur, *Time and Narrative* 77–82.

34. Paul Ricœur, *Time and Narrative*, trans. Kathleen Blarney and David Pellauer, vol. 3 (Chicago: U of Chicago P, 1988) 101–2.

35. Juliet Dusinberre, "Forms of Reality in A. S. Byatt's *The Virgin in the Garden*," *Critique: Studies in Modern Fiction* 24 (Fall 1982): 56.

36. A. S. Byatt, interview with Juliet Dusinberre, *Women Writers Talking*, ed. Janet Todd (New York: Holmes, 1983) 184–85.

37. Dusinberre, "Forms of Reality" 61.

Michael J. Noble

A Tower of Tongues:
Babel Tower and the Art of Memory

Also through here passes a spiral stairway, which sinks abysmally and soars upwards to remote distances. In the hallway there is a mirror which faithfully duplicates all appearances. Men usually infer from this mirror that the Library is not infinite (if it really were, why this illusory duplication?); I prefer to dream that its polished surfaces represent and promise the infinite. . . .

(Jorge Luis Borges, "The Library of Babel")

To think of contemporary literature and contemporary literary theory is to think of a fantastic edifice, a tower containing impossible, contradictory corridors and staircases, a skyscraper whose various levels encompass entire cities, an artificial mountain of information subject to a storm of natural and metaphoric winds. If this structure is the utopian skycity of modernism, it is also a Gothic cathedral and the Acropolis of Athens. Its architects follow the labyrinthine design of Jorge Luis Borges's "Library of Babel"; they model the geometric cities of Doris Lessing's *Re: Colonised Planet 5, Shikasta*. This construct is the tower of Umberto Eco's *The Name of the Rose* and the courtyard square in Italo Calvino's *Castle of Crossed Destinies*. With regard to the twentieth century, it is important to remember that *deconstruction* implies a flourishing and ambitious *construction*, however paired it may be with the already inscribed and much-touted *destruction* foreshadowed by such structure, and foretold ad nauseam by contemporary critics.

A. S. Byatt's *Babel Tower* is replete with actual and fictitious architectures, with buildings as metaphors but also as mediums for the organization and structure of memory. In "Memory and the Making of Fiction," Byatt characterizes her writing, and *Babel Tower* in particular, as consisting of "large static structures of mnemonics to put things into, to remember their relations."[1] Pondering Proust, Joyce, Mann, and Woolf, and looking at the ways in which these writers "weave significant personal memories, recognitions, and epiphanies into a texture of language and thought,"[2] Byatt underscores the schematic and highly constructed nature of the relationship between memory and fiction. Referring back to medieval and Elizabethan memory theaters, she thus summons an unusual tradition for contextualizing the mnemonic structures of a work of fiction.

The tradition of Elizabethan memory theater is indebted to classical sources. Frances Yates summarizes the "general principles of the mnemonic" from Quintilian's *Institutio oratoria,* which enumerates a system of *loci* (or places) that become the sites of memory storage and retrieval:[3] "In order to form a series of places in memory, . . . a building is to be remembered, as spacious and varied a one as possible, the forecourt, the living room, bedrooms, and parlours, not omitting statues and other ornaments."[4] Once the building has been constructed in the mind, the orator fills it with the *imagines* (or images) that will be used to remember a speech. In the *Ad Herennium*, which offers the most complete account of the art of memory, the locus is a stage and the image a dramatic scene from *Iphigenia*.[5] Largely inheriting their conception of the classical art of memory through the *Ad Herennium*, Elizabethan thinkers contrived highly complex memory theaters using Tudor architecture as the *loci* for a wide variety of Christian, Cabalist, and occult imagery. The image of the Tower of Babel was quite common. Yates convincingly demonstrates, for example, how Robert Fludd uses the five doors of Shakespeare's *Globe Theatre* as the framework for one of the most encyclopedic memory treatises of the era.[6] The door in the upper left corner of Fludd's theater depicts the Tower of Babel—possibly, speculates Yates, as an allegory for the confusion that will be overcome by the art of memory.[7]

A. S. Byatt's express interest in Yates's research—even the fictionalized presence of "Dr Frances Yates" in the prologue to *The Virgin in the Garden* (12)—manifests a similar ambition. Her *Babel Tower,* with its "structures of mnemonics," which frequently allude to and revisit earlier memory theaters, likewise gives order to chaos, if not perhaps to overcome confusion, then to counterbalance it, to stave it off and artfully render it so that it may be at least partially understood.

In *Babel Tower*, the traditional art of memory is applied neither anachronistically to the twentieth-century setting of the novel nor naively to the medium of literature. To consider the *doors* of Byatt's own memory treatise, for instance, is to consider them both as mnemonic devices, like the doors of Fludd's *Theatrum Orbi*, and as literary figures—effectively synthesizing several arts—not only the arts of memory and *belles lettres*, but also architecture itself and several of the visual arts. Although there are many types of *doors* in *Babel Tower,* Richard Todd, in his analysis of the novel, finds that "*Babel Tower* offers three openings that correspond to the three main strands of its story, prefaced by a fourth that provides a kind of continuo."[8] These openings occur as the tentative introductions of a narrator acknowledging a variety of possible beginnings. The words, "It might begin" (*BT* 1), envelope the initial set of images—the beginning that Todd refers to as the "continuo"—in possibilities of sight, sound, and color as a thrush feasts on snails, cracking their shells upon a stone (1). In another beginning, the narrator paints the mind of a poet: "Or it might begin with Hugh Pink. . . . His thoughts buzz round him like a cloud of insects, of varying colours, sizes and liveliness" (2). The novel starts over yet again when a cleric answers a telephone call: "Or it might begin in the crypt of St. Simeon's Church" (4). Finally, the novel might also begin with the first chapter of *Babbletower*, the novel-within-the-novel written by one of *Babel Tower*'s characters: "Or it might begin with the beginning of the book that was to cause so much trouble, but was then only scribbled heaps of notes, and a swarm of scenes, imagined and re-imagined" (10). With regard to Byatt's mnemonics, however, we might identify at least five different openings of the kind Todd describes, five doors corresponding to the work's various strands.

THE ALTAR

The number five had a very practical application in the context of the memory arts, related to the five fingers of the hand.[9] Each of the fingers would be associated with an imagined or remembered place. Hence, grouping memory places in sets of five was a common practice. The number also held numerological, even magical significance—especially in the work of Fludd, in which five different doors of five different colors open onto the stage of his *Theatrum Orbi* as five memory *loci*.[10] Similarly in Byatt, each of the novel's introductions provides a distinct locus (each in a distinct *color*). The first such locus (Todd's *continuo*) precedes even the primary narratives and highlights the page itself as the site of memory.

The *imagines* of this rhetorical space occur visually in the typography as well as in the highly visual connotations and denotations of its language. Imitating the "pure white" and "shining black" of the snail shells described in the passage, the lines of the black words on the page stripe the bifurcated spirals of the shell's turret (1). By using language as a plastic medium to represent graphically the same image signified in the text, the page-as-locus masquerades as the embodiment of the idea. This first door of this contemporary memory theater is the shaped song of the thrush. It is a *carmen figuratum* like George Herbert's poem "The Altar," alluded to in the function of one of the thrush's stones as an "anvil or altar" (1).[11] And just as the thrush uses a stone as his anvil, Byatt uses this locus as an anvil upon which to temper the images of her novel. The anvil rises from the chaotic ruins of Babel that serve as the backdrop and foundation from which a new construction emerges.

As in Fludd's iconography, the images of this particular locus retain certain "talismanic" or "magically operative" resonances.[12] Byatt's narrator describes engravings in many of the languages of Babel: "Characters are carved on the stones. Maybe runes, maybe cuneiform, maybe ideograms of a bird's eye or a creature walking, or pricking spears and hatchets" (1). The talismans become magically operative in their invocation of previous systems, forgotten languages, and ruined civilizations. For example, the stone with the bird's eye (p)recalls the thrush "looking with his sideways stare, for his secret prey in the grass" (1). The stone with "a creature walking" (p)refigures another of the multiple entrances into the text, that of the poet, Hugh Pink, walking through Laidley Woods (2). The hatchets foretell an ending as well as a beginning—in one of Frederica Potter's attempts to leave her husband Nigel, he throws a hatchet at her, wounding her in the leg, effectively ending their marriage and freeing Frederica to live a new life.

Apart from the ideograms on the stones, the narrator also comments on the "coiled remains" of fossilized shells (1). She commingles these organic structures with alphabets "carved" upon the stones: "Here are broken alphabets. . . . Round the stones are the broken shells, helical whorls like empty ears in which no hammer beats on no anvil" (1). In addition to repeating the word *broken* to associate the alphabets with the shells, Byatt also repeats the image of the anvil. In its first occurrence, the anvil served as a mechanical device for the thrush to break open his meal. When the same word reoccurs in the comparison of the "helical whorls" to "empty ears," it represents the *incus*, a small bone in the ear, while still retaining a resonance of its first utterance. Completing the design, a third usage of *anvil* merges the two denotations of the word so that the activities of listening and of hammering become conjoined: "The thrush appears to be listening to the earth" (1).

There is a decidedly verbal and even literary application to the mnemonic created by this first beginning. The image of the thrush constructs symmetrical patterns of aural and visual images that will recur, in different and ever more elaborate incarnations, again and again over the course of the novel: "He [the thrush] stabs, he pierces, he carries the shell with its soft centre to his stone. He lifts the shell, he cracks it down. He repeats. He repeats. He extracts the bruised flesh, he sips, he juggles, he swallows. His throat ripples. He sings" (1). Echoing a passage from later in the novel—a quotation from Samuel Beckett's *Waiting for Godot* in which Vladimir and Estragon discuss rustling leaves, voices, and feathers—the author–persona employs a pre-existing architecture (in this case, a particular cadence) to house a personal iconography. The Beckett passage reads:

Vladimir: Rather they whisper.
Estragon: They rustle.
V.   They murmur.
E.   They rustle.
Silence
V.   What do they say?
E.   They talk about their lives.

V. To have lived is not enough for them.

E. They have to talk about it. (qtd. in *BT* 386–87)

Frederica places this passage from *Waiting for Godot* into her own novel, a project she calls *Laminations*. By mimicking the cadence of the Beckett dialogue with its short sentences and repetitions, the description of the thrush foreshadows the other text's significance while storing it as a memory image—much like the ideograms on the stone, with their talismanic invocations of the novel's narrative threads.

This first door into *Babel Tower* painstakingly situates a microcosmic stage upon which the entire novel plays itself out. Its precision resembles the minuscule edifices of a crystal snow-globe admired by a tailor in Byatt's short story, "The Glass Coffin": "he stared in wonder at this beautiful model and could not begin to imagine what fine tools or instruments had carved and wrought it" (*DNE* 13). In *Babel Tower*, a beautiful model of the organic snail shell repeats itself in hundreds of artful, minutely detailed transformations.

A CREATURE WALKING

Hugh Pink's walk through Laidley Woods is another beginning to *Babel Tower*. As he walks, he composes a poem, and, in his mind, he inscribes his thoughts upon the landscape. In the beginning, these thoughts are disorganized—they "buzz" around him like insects—but, as he moves onward, he gives them order and form in "a rich red honeycomb of a poem about a pomegranate" (2). Yates points out that the classical guidelines for creating potent *imagines* emphasize firing the emotions through "striking and unusual images."[13] These may be "beautiful or hideous, comic or obscene," and they often include *imagines agentes*—active, human images "wearing crowns or purple cloaks, bloodstained or smeared with paint, of human figures dramatically engaged in some activity."[14] For Hugh, the pomegranate assumes a similar dramatic power; he thinks "of the blooded pink jelly of pomegranates, of the word, pomegranate, round and spicy" (2). When Hugh adds the Persephone myth to create an *imagine agente*, he is aware of the "automatic power" of the myth and "thinks of Persephone as he used to imagine her when he was a boy" (2). He overwrites the images he *sees* with those he *remembers*, creating a palimpsest in which the existing text is not erased, although another and paradoxically older one is imprinted over its surface: "As he thinks, his eyes take in the woods, brambles and saplings, flaming spindle-berries and gleaming holly leaves. He thinks that he will remember Persephone and holly, and suddenly sees that the soft quadruple rosy seed of the spindle is not unlike the packed seeds of the pomegranate" (2). Hugh literally *sees* the spindles of the holly berries with their vibrant colors, but he also *sees* a connection to the pomegranate, a connection that will form the basis of this memory image and of the poem he composes.

In addition to the holly, Laidley Woods holds many other memory images. The avenue of yews reminds Hugh of his days as a student, and he "will remember the trees for the images in his mind's eye, and the images for the trees" (3). Seemingly, the narrative style in this passage could be characterized as stream-of-consciousness. The use of images to convey psychological responses and the apparent use of random association might certainly suggest such a technique. Byatt's emphasis, however, is on memory and creation rather than consciousness (or rather on consciousness as memory). Although Byatt presents everything through Hugh's thoughts, she revises and critiques the classic stream-of-consciousness approach. The link between the dark trees and the dark corridors of Hugh's youth does *not* express an uninterrupted free flow of thought. On the contrary, Byatt presents it as a deliberate act of consciousness, as a *reconstruction* of the past. The metaphor is not only natural but artificial, and it relates to an act in the future. Hugh *will* remember the trees for the images and vice versa. Likewise, he *will* remember Persephone through the image of the holly, and he *will* remember a particular image of Persephone from his youth. He places these in the future so that he can recollect them when he writes his poem.

Continuing his walk, Hugh adds another human figure to the palimpsest: his onetime friend Frederica. At first he does not recognize her—she is "in the wrong clothes, in the wrong place, at the wrong time" (3). As he finally recognizes Frederica, certain details emerge spontaneously, details he had previously inscribed upon his image of this woman. Addressing her, "He is about to add her old surname, and stops. He knows she is married. He remembers the buzz of furious gossip and chatter at the time of this marriage" (3). Frederica's marriage quickly becomes connected to the myth of Persephone already inscribed upon the landscape. Because it is autumn, the time when Persephone would have newly rejoined her husband Pluto, the image of Frederica on the other side of a stile becomes an image of Persephone at the limits of the Underworld. Hugh remembers some of the gossip: "It was put about that this man [Frederica's husband] kept her more or less locked up, more or less incommunicado, in a moated grange, would you believe, in the country, in outer darkness" (3). Frederica, as Persephone estranged from the natural world, the world of Demeter, becomes a part of the mnemonic Hugh constructs. Persephone and Pluto finally merge with Frederica and her husband Nigel into a composite *imagine agente* in Hugh's poem:

> Pomegranate-taste is almost
> No taste, and so surprising. She savours
> The absence, she swallows
> The dark little spheres in their jelly.
> Her throat ripples. Her palate
> Considers, remembers
> The taste of earth and water, faintly sweet.
>
> (76–77)

In Hugh's "Pomegranate," the seeds retain their function as a memory image. The woman's palate *remembers* the "taste of earth and water," and the Pluto-figure of the poem beguiles the Persephone-figure with this taste. Similarly, Frederica symbolically chooses the remembrance of her sister's death over her own life. It is the "absence" that the woman relishes, the absence of her sister and her own vitality. Frederica's mourning also alludes to Demeter, whom Hugh represents through images of dryness and dust (77). This allusion is prefigured in his childhood misunderstanding of pomegranates, when he had imagined the seeds to be dry (2).

In *The Book of Memory*, Mary Carruthers argues that medieval scholars approached their memorization and reading of sacred texts through the metaphor of eating. She cites Hugh of St. Victor, who walks through the "forest" of scripture and whose "ideas (*sententias*) like so many sweetest fruits, we pick as we read and chew [*ruminamus*] as we consider them."[15] Unlike Hugh Pink, Hugh of St. Victor reads rather than composes, but the images of walking through a wooded landscape and of chewing/ruminating clearly resonate. Carruthers compares this devouring of sacred texts with the mirror imagery used by Gregory the Great (Pope Gregory I) when he quotes Augustine: "Holy Scripture . . . presents a kind of mirror to the eyes of the mind, that our inner face may be seen in it. There truly we learn our own ugliness, there our own beauty."[16] Carruthers refers to the reflection given by this textual mirror as a "memory phantasm" that "is both a 'likeness' (*simulacrum*) and one's 'gut-level response' to it (*intentio*)."[17] Reading transforms the memory contained in the text into a personal memory. Eating the text and seeing oneself reflected in the text occasion the "re-creation" that Carruthers describes as the metamorphic process of memory.[18]

In "Memory and the Making of Fiction," Byatt writes about the memory phantasms of Marcel Proust's *Remembrance of Things Past*. She looks at "Proust's first account of the discovery of involuntary memory" to see "how he places metaphors of death and haunting."[19] Like Hugh of St. Victor, Proust's narrator uses the imagery of a walk in the forest to illustrate the recovery of memory. Proust alludes to Celtic beliefs about the souls of the dead being "held captive in some inferior being, in an animal, in a plant, in some inanimate object."[20] These souls remain in this state until "we happen to pass by the tree or to obtain possession of the object which forms their prison. Then they start and tremble, they call us by our name, and as soon as we have recognised their voice the spell is broken. . . . And so it is with our own past."[21] Stressing the correlation that Proust's narrator makes between the souls of the dead and "our own past," Byatt cites Freud's theories of ancestor-worship and argues that memories of ancestors "persist as icons, as hauntings, in our minds."[22] She relates the breaking of the spell described by Proust's narrator to the "magic tasting" he experiences when, as an adult, his mother gives him a madeleine cake with his tea, and the taste returns him to his childhood: "this new sensation . . . had on me the effect which love has of filling me with a precious essence; or rather this essence was not in me, it *was* me."[23] The essence that fills him, as if surrendered by a found object, is the essence of his "own past"—"it *was* me." The past tense underscores his recovery of childhood, and what he *was* is consumed and becomes a part of him. Byatt distinguishes this Proustian "involuntary recall" from other memory experiences, experiences like that of Hugh Pink, where the memory "presented itself immediately to be *recognized* as a memory, at the time of being an experience."[24] Thus, Hugh's knowledge that he *will* remember Persephone in the holly berries is also the premonition of a future memory, a deliberate act of storage suggested by the "rich red honeycomb" of the poem he will write (2).

Honeycombs abound in Byatt's creative and critical work. Recalling a visit to Arbury Hall where George Eliot was born and raised, Byatt describes its architecture as "white honeycombs of Gothic tracery" with "scurrying servants in honeycombs of corridors."[25] Carruthers finds the honeycomb to be one of the most ubiquitous images of memory in both classical and medieval culture. She cites Longinus, Quintilian, Seneca, and many others who liken the orator to a "bee producing honey":[26] "It seems to me that this association of bee-cells and honey with books whose wisdom is to be packed into the compartments, *cellae,* or *loci* of an ordered memory carries over also to the metaphors that liken books and memory to fields and meadows . . . full of flowers, which the reader must cull and digest in order to store the *cella* of his memory."[27] Discovering such *cellae* in the Gothic structures of Arbury Hall, Byatt cites Eliot's observation that the architecture preserves "the spirit of the old English baronet."[28] In another context, Byatt compares Eliot's memories of the Hall to the hauntings in Proust. Characterizing Proust as a "devoted reader of Eliot," she relates epiphanic moments of special knowledge or insight to moments of memory.[29] Her comparison centers on the "'glittering' quality of certain experiences" and the "glittering visions" seen by such poets as Wordsworth.[30] Proust's account of Celtic animism, for example, causes the objects to "start and tremble" when they have been recognized.[31] And in *Daniel Deronda*, Eliot writes of the "sounds and accents that haunt" familiar landscapes.[32] The physicality of these stored memories and the sensuality of their recollection Byatt relates to the "corporeal similitudes" written of by Thomas Aquinas.[33] Yates describes in more detail how Aquinas "corporealised in memory" his own *Summa,* "like a Gothic cathedral full of images on its ordered places."[34] It is the corporeal nature of memory that Byatt relates back to the hauntings in Proust, noting that they "are also facts as well as metaphors" because they have reality in some object or taste[35]—such as that of the tea and cake, or of the pomegranate's taste of earth and water.

ST. SIMEON'S CHURCH

Yet another door onto the stage of *Babel Tower* portrays Daniel Orton, Frederica's brother-in-law, in the crypt of St. Simeon's Church—a church that once had "gaudy nineteenth-century stained glass," depicting, among other biblical narratives, "the tongues of fire descending at Whitsuntide" (6–7). This image of the Pentecostal fire recurs throughout the novel—in Jude Mason's *Babbletower*, for example, and in Gerard Wijnnobel's thoughts and remembrances of his grandfather. One of Wijnnobel's grandfather's favorite disputes was "whether or not the Tongues of Flame which descended on the apostles in the Upper Room at Pentecost had caused them to be able to speak, amongst the unknown tongues in which they babbled, a version, a fragmentary part, of the original Tongue" (191). The Tongues of Flame thus function as a doubly coded mnemonic that corporealizes not only the confusion of tongues but also the pre-Babel, original tongue.

During the Second World War, enemy bombing had shattered St. Simeon's windows. One of the members of the church's congregation then gathered the pieces of broken glass, but "he was not able, or even willing, to reconstitute the narratives as they had been" (7). Instead, he composed "a coloured mosaic of purple and gold constellations, of rivers of grass green and blood red, of hummocks of burned amber and clouded, smoke-stained, once clear glass. It was too sad, he told the Vicar, to put the pictures together all smashed, with gaping holes" (7). If fire had initially destroyed the window and had exploded the "tongues of fire" into fragments, the "once clear glass" must remain, in its contemporary reincarnation, "smoke-stained," quite literally capturing and incorporating the memory of its deconstruction.

The new windows frame a confused composite of the old Bible stories; the introduction of chaos into the mnemonic does not, however, destroy its beauty or its memory function. Rather, it illustrates and remembers the relation of language to reality and to itself. In "Memory and the Making of Fiction," Byatt writes: "My own [memory] structures are rather like abstract paintings—a rising series of increasingly acute triangles in complementary colours may represent one text in construction, a series of concentric spirals, or even a double helix, another."[36] Byatt likens her use of geometry in these abstract paintings to the role of the image in Elizabethan memory theater. In talking about the "geometric icon[s]" that she creates, she remembers having an "almost eidetic memory" in her youth.[37] She knew "geometrically" where things she had read or written were located on the page. The new, abstract stained glass at St. Simeon's likewise employs geometry to create memory icons. The glazier's use of these geometric fragments laminates chaos with order.

In addition to the fractured iconography of St. Simeon's windows, the architecture of the church's crypt can also be linked to the art of memory. The narrator describes the crypt as "dark and solid" with "three telephones, set round the base of a pillar, in plywood cubicles soundproofed with a honeycomb of egg-boxes" (4). Like Hugh's "rich red honeycomb," the honeycomb in the crypt, much like the crypt itself, denotes containment and storage. In Daniel Orton's cubicle, there is a jug of anemones whose *open* blossoms reveal "a white and a dark crimson with a centre full of soft black spikes and black powder" and whose *unopened* blossoms conceal "bright inside colours hidden under fur, steel-blue and soft pink-grey" (5). Carruthers explains how medieval scholars would use a "florilegium," an early version of the commonplace book, to "record the contents of their memory" or their *sophismata*.[38] In this same tradition, Frederica compiles her *Laminations,* which is "like any student's commonplace book" and which contains her favorite passages from literary works such as *Waiting for Godot, Howard's End*, and "Ode: Intimations of Immortality" (387). These selected texts are like the "bright inside colours" of the closed anemones in Daniel's cubicle, and their placement within Frederica's commonplace book both contains them and keeps them private. Similarly, the novel encloses and preserves various mnemonics. Fragmented narratives—like the shattered glass at St. Simeon's— are reconfigured and pieced together, intricately designed like honeycomb or like "a series of concentric spirals, or even a double helix."[39]

BABBLETOWER

Intricacy of design also characterizes a fourth beginning or door, offered with the same statement of possibility. This story "might begin" with the novel written by Jude Mason. *Babbletower* opens with a chapter entitled "Of the Foundation of Babbletower," yet the foundation presented here is not that of the tower itself but the founding of the colony that subsequently moves into the pre-existing structure of La Tour Bruyarde. La Tour Bruyarde, a *noisy* and *querulous* tower, doubles as the background locus against which the images of *Babbletower* are cast. It consists of "layer upon layer of dwellings . . . one corridor upon another, a Baroque balcony abutting a Gothic cloister, a series of classical windows, in elegantly diminishing proportions as they rose higher, under an unfinished thatched roof that might have suited a mediaeval byre" (26).

The plot of Mason's *Babbletower* advances at intervals throughout *Babel Tower*, organizing itself around the architecture of La Tour Bruyarde. *Babbletower* guides the reader through the living quarters, through schools and great halls, but also through several different theaters. When the revolutionary protagonist, Culvert, addresses his followers, he assembles them in the "Theatre of Tongues" (62). Other theaters include the Theatre of Speech, the Theatre of Mime, the Theatre of Cruelty, and the Theatre of Sacrifice. Culvert's designation of specific rooms as the sites for social performance as well as his elaborate and symbolic ornamentation of these rooms once again attests to the significance of classical and Renaissance memory arts upon the function of Byatt's text. On a frieze in the Theatre of Tongues, tongues of flame become "part of a lively depiction of hell-fire, . . . borne out by the presence of a soot-black demon over the south door, brandishing eight arms each holding a wailing infant" (62). Thus, the iconographic talismans carved upon the stones in the novel's initial beginning have their counterparts in the graphics used to illustrate the different theaters. The friezes become, in turn, additional sites for recording knowledge.

What distinguishes the memory theater that Byatt presents as La Tour Bruyarde from earlier memory systems employing the Tower of Babel is Byatt's emphasis on *babble*. If, as Yates suggests, the tower in Robert Fludd's system represents the confusion that is to be overcome,[40] Byatt's twentieth-century Tower of Babel embraces this confusion. La Tour Bruyarde uses Babel as a locus to bring together both order and chaos. Michel Serres, in *Genesis*, writes:

> We draw up plans . . . we even conceive a general theory of systems, a kind of general, universal system for reaching the sky. Let us call this whole endeavor the constructivist model. Now then, it ends in *noise*, in the foreign noise of external languages . . . Babel is not a failure, it is at that very moment when the tower is dismantled that we begin to understand without concepts. Here and there, Babel is unified, a few great stretches of bare wall appear and remain, colossal cathedrals, half-swamped in the rubble, monumental temples overrun by the jungle.[41]

Babel no longer (or not only) serves as the stage for folly. If the constructivist model has been demolished, it has only been done halfway. Its cathedrals are only half-buried. As a stage for memory, the Tower of Babel does not accomplish the grand aspirations of Elizabethan memory theater to encompass all knowledge or to create a "universal system for reaching the sky." But, in the composite failure of the years—in the Baroque balcony, the Gothic cloister, the classical windows and the mediaeval byre—there are significant connections to be remembered. "Here and there, Babel is unified."

A FIFTH DOOR

Byatt's *Babel Tower* is third in a proposed tetralogy. The prologues of the first two novels, *The Virgin in the Garden* and *Still Life*, comprise yet another memory theater, staging not only the ideas and events of their respective novels, but the ideas and events of the entire tetralogy. The prologue to *The Virgin in the Garden* takes place in 1968, sixteen years after the events presented in the body of the novel. Although the three published novels of the tetralogy are more or less chronological, *Babel Tower* only takes the reader through to 1967. The prologue to *Still Life*, however, occurs in 1980, placing itself far beyond the events of the tetralogy thus far.

The prologues foreground remembered ideas and personal intellectual history—not just events of plot. In the prologue to *The Virgin in the Garden*, Alexander Wedderburn meets Frederica and Daniel at the National Portrait Gallery for a performance by Dame Flora Robson as Queen Elizabeth I. Seated before the stage, Alexander remembers the inspirations for his own 1953 play about the Queen. Similarly, as Frederica listens to Dame Flora recite one of the Queen's lyrics, *A Song betweene the Queen's Majestie and Englande*, she recalls a line from Shakespeare: "Memory tugged. Come over the born, Bessy. Frederica got excited" (15). The effect of this lyric, especially in its context as a line performed upon a stage, demonstrates how literature itself serves a mnemonic function—how Frederica remembers through Shakespeare and how Alexander remembers through Spencer.

In addition to the *mise en scène* presenting Dame Flora Robson as Queen Elizabeth, there are numerous other stagings in the prologues to both *The Virgin in the Garden* and *Still Life*. Returning to the National Portrait Gallery after a considerable absence, Alexander associates the redecoration of the museum with a "stagey richness," observing "alcoves for Tudor icons" in the manner of memory *loci* for particular *imagines* (*VG* 9–10). Other kinds of memory images serve as *imagines agentes*. Frederica is transformed into Britomart, the female knight of chastity from Spenser's *Faerie Queene*: "Frederica, in a kind of brief knitted corselet of dark grey wool with a glitter in it, and boots with a metallic sheen, *was* Britomart, her hair cut into a kind of bronze helmet, more space-age, maybe, than Renaissance" (12–13; emphasis added). Other *imagines agentes* include individuals present at the performance, people whose proper names represent their ideas and research. Roy Strong, then Director of the National Gallery, serves as a proxy for Elizabethan iconography, and Frances Yates is described as a "contemplatively vague figure . . . whose writings on the images of Elizabeth Tudor as Virgo-Astraea had, as it turned out, signally changed the whole shape of his [Alexander's] own life" (12).

Many of the mnemonics in these prologues, however, do not reveal their meanings until the later novels. In the prologue to *The Virgin in the Garden*, a man approaches Frederica as she climbs the steps to the National Portrait Gallery. He will not reappear until *Babel Tower*. This large man, "foreshortened from above, consisted of a wide expanse of glossy black PVC raincoat, crisping out round a bulky body, and a heavy mass of straight blond hair, with a sheen like cool butter" (11). He is Paul Ottokar, and he wears the same raincoat in this brief and anonymous *future* appearance as he does in *Babel Tower*, a raincoat that the reader may or may not remember. He is also the twin of the man who will be Frederica's lover. Byatt explains the function of the twin brothers as memory images in "Memory and the Making of Fiction." She ties them to "the theme of pairs of men, starting with Kafka's two 'assistants' in *The Castle* who were connected by a student in my extra-mural class with twins and with testicles, and ending with newly invented identical twin brothers . . . who are in their turn connected with Nietzsche's Apollo and Dionysus."[42] The links between these various pairs are created by memory as well as by reason. As Byatt emphasizes, "I have tied my memory tightly."[43] This tying corresponds to one of her "most basic metaphors" for "interlocking systems of mnemonics."[44] She speaks of a "fishing net, with links of various sizes, in which icons are caught in the mesh and drawn up, placed in the links, into consciousness—they come up through the dark, gleaming like ghosts or fish or sparks, and are held together by the links."[45] Similarly, the links between *The Castle*, the student in her extra-mural class, and her reading of Nietzsche are mnemonic in nature. The icons resonate with each other because they are all pairs. The testicles, in particular, are images that she borrows from Yates. Later in the essay, she refers to Yates's description of "memorising a ram with large testicles to remind lawyers of their opponent and his witnesses (testes)."[46] Although John and Paul Ottokar do not appear at Frederica's divorce trial as witnesses, a private investigator testifies to their sexual entanglements with her. This testimony about the twins witnesses against Frederica's morality and suitability as a mother. When Paul Ottokar accosts Frederica on the steps of the National Portrait Gallery, it is a symbol of the threat that still follows her as a woman. When observed by Alexander, it becomes a performance of that threat.

In *Babel Tower*, there is no prologue set in the future, only the multiple beginnings of the thrush hammering the snail shells, of Hugh Pink walking through Laidley Woods, of Daniel in the crypt at St. Simeon's, and of the opening chapter of *Babbletower*. These multiple beginnings reinvent the more traditional realizations of memory theater in the first two novels. Thus, Byatt layers various mnemonics one upon another. Her *Babel Tower* is built from these various layerings, and over the course of the novel, the layers are not integrated. There is not one pinnacle of conclusion for all of the various theaters contained within the tower; rather, there are several conclusions, just as there are several beginnings. Each conclusion has a separate atmosphere and place, a separate memory locus. In one ending, Frederica renews her relationship with John Ottokar. In another, there is the announcement that the censors will no longer suppress the publication of *Babbletower*. Yet another, this time final, ending is provided by the closing paragraphs of *Babbletower*, in which the tower is abandoned and its inhabitants are left in a heap of bones. This heap of bones returns the reader to the fallen stones presented in the opening (also originary) mnemonic of the novel: "So the three old men began to walk away across the valley, looking back from time to time at the Tower, and the grim mound at its foot, until it was so far away, that its human origin could not be distinguished, and it looked like a chance heap of rocks, sprouting green here and there, with what might be shells or pebbles clustered palely at its foot" (617).

NOTES

1. A. S. Byatt, "Memory and the Making of Fiction," *Memory*, ed. Patricia Fara and Karalyn Patterson (Cambridge: Cambridge UP, 1998) 66.

2. Byatt, "Memory" 49.

3. Frances A. Yates, *The Art of Memory* (Chicago: U of Chicago P, 1966) 3.

4. Yates 3.

5. Yates 14.

6. Yates 326.

7. Yates 326–27.

8. Richard Todd, *A. S. Byatt* (Plymouth: Northcote House, 1997) 12.

9. Yates 108.

10. Yates 332.

11. As Yates observes, the image of the anvil is commonly found in Renaissance memory

treatises (107)—its presence in *Babel Tower* signals Byatt's participation in and exploration of the memory arts.

12. Yates 334.

13. Yates 10.

14. Yates 10.

15. Qtd. in Mary Carruthers, *The Book of Memory: A Study of Memory in Medieval Culture*, Cambridge Studies in Medieval Literature (Cambridge: Cambridge UP, 1990) 164–65.

16. Qtd. in Carruthers 168–69.

17. Carruthers 169.

18. Carruthers 169.

19. Byatt, "Memory" 52.

20. Marcel Proust, *Swann's Way*, trans. C. K. Scott Moncrieff and Terence Kilmartin (1913; New York: Vintage, 1981) 47.

21. Proust 47.

22. Byatt, "Memory" 53.

23. Proust 48.

24. Byatt, "Memory" 48.

25. A. S. Byatt, "A. S. Byatt on Angels and Insects: The Architectural Origins of a Provocative Film," *Architectural Digest* 53.4 (1996): 104.

26. Carruthers 37.

27. Carruthers 38.

28. George Eliot, qtd. in Byatt, "Architectural Origins" 100.

29. Byatt, "Memory" 52.

30. Byatt, "Memory" 47, 57.

31. Proust 47.

32. George Eliot, *Daniel Deronda* (1876; London: Penguin, 1995) 22.

33. Qtd. in Byatt, "Memory" 70.

34. Yates 79.

35. Byatt, "Memory" 52.

36. Byatt, "Memory" 66.

37. Byatt, "Memory" 66.

38. Carruthers 174.

39. Byatt, "Memory" 66.

40. Yates 326–27.

41. Michel Serres, *Genesis*, trans. Geneviève James and James Nielson (Ann Arbor: U of Michigan P, 1995) 123–24.

42. Byatt, "Memory" 49.

43. Byatt, "Memory" 49.

44. Byatt, "Memory" 64.

45. Byatt, "Memory" 65.

46. Byatt, "Memory" 66.

Kuno Schuhmann

In Search of Self and Self-Fulfilment: Themes and Strategies in A. S. Byatt's Early Novels

> In a way, your stories convey the sense of becoming who one is. It is that need you sense, to become who you are.
>
> (Boyd Tonkin[1])

The early works of famous writers have a special kind of attraction. Do the first attempts reveal a personality that may be more carefully hidden in later texts?[2] Does the first shaping of themes throw additional light on the later novels?[3]

In view of this general interest it is surprising that in Byatt's case the early novels have so far not met with the critics' detailed attention. This may well have to do with their publishing history. After their first printing (*Shadow of a Sun* in 1964 and *The Game* in 1967), both novels were unavailable for some time. A first reprint of *The Game* had been undertaken by Penguin in 1983, but it was only in the wake of *Possession*'s Booker success in 1990 that both novels were reissued in close succession (the first novel in 1991, now under the originally intended title *The Shadow of the Sun*, the second in 1992).

For the following considerations biographical aspects are of little concern. Undoubtedly, Byatt's experience as a Cambridge student and the specific relationship to her sister Margaret Drabble have left traces in her fiction.[4] But it is more important to see how this material was refined and shaped.

Although my attention is focused also by the knowledge of Byatt's later novels, a specific comparison must be saved for a later occasion. Even in these early works, a hallmark of Byatt's writing, the tight interweaving of narrative strategies and theoretical disquisitions, is apparent.

As first attempts, their achievement is not so much in solving as in probing thematic and structural problems and the possibilities of an original approach.

Hence the title of my essay. Both novels are quests also in that they show a young author's search for her own identity and for possible ways of realising her artistic desires and ambitions.

As to my own approach, I am old-fashioned enough to adhere to Helen Gardner's conviction that "The critic's function . . . is to assist his readers to find the values which he believes the work to have."[5] In particular, I hope to show that Byatt's early novels give embryonic shape to concepts that unfolded their whole potential with the student movement of 1968 and are still with us at the beginning of a new century. The most important of them is "self-fulfilment," an ambiguous term. As an ideological concept, it takes for granted the existence of a Self and demands the gratification of individual desires irrespective of communal concerns. In its more objective meaning it insists on the development of an identity— that is, the considered unfolding of individual characteristics as a prerequisite for a life dedicated to some matter of general import.

The ideological note is dominant in the term "self-actualising" as used in Anthony Clare's review of Alain de Botton's *The Consolations of Philosophy,* where Clare says of de Botton's presentation of Socrates: "At times, he sounds like one of those bearded, rangy self-actualising Californian psychotherapy gurus who declare that the wise man can lose nothing if he has invested everything in himself, and progress consists in, among other things, making a friend of yourself."[6]

Byatt herself distinguishes between the two meanings and connects them with Iris Murdoch's well-known deliberations on sincerity and truth: "'Sincerity' might, I suppose, be translated as 'self-consistency' or 'truth to oneself.' Iris Murdoch finds it inadequate. What we need, she says, in a sentence that electrified and electrifies me, is 'the hard idea of truth' as opposed to 'the facile idea of sincerity'" (*PM* 24).[7]

THE SHADOW OF THE SUN

At first sight, Byatt's first novel tells a simple story. Anna is the undistinguished daughter of the eminent writer Henry Severell and his wife Caroline who is entirely devoted to the well-being of her husband. We follow Anna from home and school through university to the threshold of a home shared with a married man.

Kelly has noted how convincingly the heroine has been endowed with the characteristics of her age. "Byatt has given her all the awkwardness of adolescence."[8] At appropriate moments her clumsiness is emphasised (*SS* 10, 11), and the signs of the concomitant conflict of generations, based on differing value systems as well as on prejudice and immaturity, are also included. For example, Anna knows how much her mother would appreciate seeing her properly dressed, "and she had magnified this piece of ordinary politeness into a kind of elaborate social torture contrived by her mother to humiliate her" (12).

And yet, this is no novel of adolescence. Byatt makes her heroine speak out against this type of novel in unmistakable words: "I tell you what, I *hate* adolescent novels, they're so boring. I tell you what, they're not interesting, they're not important, and neither am I, they're all about nothing, and so am I" (93). Indeed, Byatt has spared her heroine the indignity of existing in a novel of this type by making it in equal parts also the story of Anna's artist father. Both stories share the problem of identity and the quest for the essentials of life. Henry Severell, at his age, has of course found his identity as a man and as a writer. He knows how to find corroborations of his self-assuredness.

Self-fulfilment in Henry's case is not the gratification of any personal predilections but the realisation of his creative urge. The necessary state of creativity is not achieved without effort—a certain ritual, even. To the outward observer this takes the form of aimless walkabouts in the landscape adjoining his home, "fits of really strange behaviour," as his wife calls them (8). They make him enter into a visionary experience of landscape gaining material and energy for his creative work. What Byatt unfolds here is a gradual progress via several stages to a loss of personal identity, a merging with nature in which natural objects keep their characteristics while the observing wanderer becomes "unrecognizable" (61) and is transformed into a "grotesque figure" (63), combining human and animal qualities with "the civilized voice . . . the scarecrow wildness of his face" blurring the boundaries between man and animal existence (88).

What finally counts for Henry are not the social relationships of real life providing for the well-being of individuals but the discovery of patterns allowing him to position the figures in his novels. He writes about people without understanding or liking them in real life (173). He takes possession of people and their surroundings as copy for his books and subjects them to the same treatment as he does his fictional characters (184–85).

As an artist, Henry is a singular case and cannot be emulated. It is part of Anna's dilemma that she, as the daughter of such a father, not only tries, in her early stages, to live up to his example and "be creative," but that she is also encouraged by him in her attempts because he cannot imagine a child of his being fundamentally different from himself.

Anna's life at Cambridge includes a night scene culminating in an epiphany that invites comparison with Henry's visionary spells. Standing alone on a bridge, Anna thinks that this occasion of being left to herself—it is long past the closing time of colleges—will give her an opportunity to act from herself and from a knowledge of herself: "This will change me, Anna thought . . . I must put all of myself into seeing" (237). And she remembers Henry's visionary kind of seeing and is "looking . . . for what he would have seen" (238). But it comes as no surprise, at least not to the attentive reader, that this act of will does not produce the desired effect. In the end, Anna must admit that she has not been "stirred out of herself"—she is "going to have to go on just as I am. I shall not change" (238–39).

For Anna, this is the discovery of her self. It will make her, at a later stage, refuse the offer of a comfortable life as a member of the landed gentry and wife of her fellow student Peter Hughes-Winterson; such an existence would have been as alien to her as the dedicated and isolated life of an artist. But it does not follow that her decision to live together with another man, who has been her lover for some time and is the father of her unborn child, brings her to self-fulfilment. Rather, it is just another intermediate stage in her young life, an open ending that has "the unfinished quality of real life."[9]

Oliver Canning, Anna's lover and mentor, a university teacher and an ardent critic of her father's work, offers her a way of life that is the exact antithesis of her father's liberalism. For he propagates a concept of education that is not based on the development of specific individual endowments in accordance with social requirements. He insists that the elite should be adapted to intellectual standards and cultural techniques. University education for average people he considers a sheer waste (81). His advice to them (and he considers Anna to be one of them) is to become useful members of society by accepting reality and following more practical ways of life. "Reality. A combination of one's own limitations and, in some form or other, the eternal kitchen sink" (135). He helps Anna to achieve what she could not learn from her father: "connecting the self with the world of things."[10] What makes his philosophy persuasive is its adherence to common sense and that it opens an insight into one's own nature, albeit a disappointing one because it may imply a confrontation with one's own shortcomings.

Anna's decision to join her life with Oliver's indicates that she is now ready to face up to her self. It is a sign of emancipation from her parents. For her mother has offered her own way of life as an exemplary one for all wives. When Margaret, Oliver's wife, complains about the daily chores of a housewife as being trivial and unsatisfying, Caroline answers: "I think of it as an art of living, . . . and somebody must do these things" (46).

And at the beginning of the novel Caroline had been characterised as "a sacrificially devoted wife herself" (7). Obviously, she has carried to an extreme the acceptance of the basic realities of (family) life and its obligations. She seems to have lost her personal self in the role of a wife. And it is this commitment that entitles her to elaborate on the concept of self-fulfilment. The narrative occasion is Margaret's cry for help in a marriage wrecked by the relationship between Oliver and Anna. But Caroline's judgement, addressed to her husband, is of more general import:

"People," she went on, probing, "won't grow up and accept life as it is. They can't cope with the fact that marriage can be boring, that it isn't all love and companionship, it can't be, not if a man is worth anything. They get bored, they say they aren't fulfilled and shout for help. They should learn to sacrifice themselves. Where would you be, for instance, if I was always trying to talk to you, or 'fulfilling myself' instead of coping with the bank and the grocer and the telephone? I don't suppose I find these any more fulfilling than anyone else might. But they have to be dealt with." (173)

What Caroline speaks out against is exactly that "self-actualising" that I have characterised in my introductory remarks—a selfish attitude based on vague desires and sentimental illusions. Kelly's interpretation of these remarks as indicative of "Caroline's own unhappiness"[11] seems to me a simplification of Byatt's subtle approach to the complexities of social (and especially married) life.

It is true that the narrator does not share or even confirm Caroline's attitude. For her assertion that sacrifices must be made is qualified by the comment: "Or so it was assumed" (49), revealing the ideological nature of this attitude. And at a later stage her attitude in these matters is called "reluctant realism" (98)—an indication of her own reservations. And indeed, she has not completely sacrificed her own interests, although she has put them last. For example, her passion for singing survives as a regularly enacted daydream: "When alone she had a private life in which she sang Mozart at Glyndebourne" (172), and even Henry is not allowed to interrupt it.

He, however, has his own qualms, as "he believed that it was not enough to live a life for someone else" (173). Yet, when he vents his unease, Caroline laughs him off "with genuine contentment" (176).

This is hardly the picture of an unhappy marriage, although it is dominated by the man's interests. Caroline has submitted to Henry's single-mindedness as a creative writer to a degree that is detrimental less to herself—at least, she finds some satisfaction in the arrangement—than to her children, first of all to Anna. Caroline's choices take account of Henry's needs and to some extent of her own. It is neither "self-actualising" in the ideological sense nor is it "self-fulfilment"— there is no indication that Caroline has ever searched for and shaped a self of her own. It is, as it were, a selfless actualising, enforced by social conventions, a paradigm hardly to be copied by others, least of all by her own daughter, who belongs to a generation with a different self-image.

How far, then, has Byatt succeeded in her first published attempt at fiction? It would be easy to point out details where the narrative strategies do not work as smoothly as more mature craftsmanship would make them. In some places, the narrator finds it necessary to elucidate the meaning of the dialogues. Some of the characters still retain vestiges of stereotypes. This is, at certain stages of her development, even true of Anna, owing perhaps to a simple realism that makes her, to use Iris Murdoch's categories, sincere but not true.

But it cannot be doubted that Byatt has done justice to her themes. In themselves, both stories, that of a non-artistic adolescent girl and that of a mature artist's problematic existence, are fascinating studies of character. By putting a considerable distance between herself and Anna, Byatt has successfully resisted the temptation of every young novelist to write a "me-novel." As she says herself in the introduction to the 1991 reprint of the novel: "I didn't want to write a 'me-novel' as we scornfully labelled them then, literary sophisticates, inexperienced human beings."[12]

Even so, she had to write from experiences available to her, which were those of a young girl and woman. On the other hand, she invented an adult figure resembling herself in some parts: "Henry Severell is partly . . . my secret self."[13] In this she seems to have followed "the sense of becoming who one is," mentioned by Boyd Tonkin, incorporating in Henry her own desires and interests, her knowledge of romantic poetry, and her pursuit of critical studies as well as creative writing.

And yet, one closes the book with some unease. In my opinion this has to do with a structural problem. In combining the two stories Byatt united two contradictory concepts: emancipation and dedication, the search for self and self-fulfilment on the one hand, and the oblivion of self for the sake of creativity on the other. Between them, they create a strong friction that would—in the hands of a more experienced writer—have yielded its full narrative potential. At this stage of her life, A. S. Byatt herself seems to have been at a point of intersection of two opposing desires: to get away from her past self and to find her future self. For the incorporation of one, Anna, she could use her own memory, reliving the uncertainties and anxieties of a young girl. The delineation of the other she could not back up with experience. She had to depend on her imagination to *pre*live the concerns of a mature writer. Under these conditions, the synthesis of imagination and experience could not succeed. The novel's potential exceeded the writer's resources.

At the same time, this novel reaches far beyond the usual scope of a beginner. It probes the traditional forms of narrative without imitating modernism's provocations. It is a first proof of what later becomes a basic attitude of Byatt's—what she herself has called "self-conscious realism" (*PM* 4)—a realism, as Michael Westlake puts it, that is always coupled "with a suspicion that the narrative form as such must inevitably put that realism into question."[14]

Anna's story is undoubtedly an example of a rather simple realism. But in connecting it with Henry's story, especially with the careful delineation of his visionary walks, Byatt surmounts the usual limits of realistic strategies. She transfers to the novel what has traditionally been regarded the domain of the poet. Also, the romantic concept of the artist—out of touch with daily life and oblivious to the needs of others—which Henry claims for himself is strictly qualified and called into question by the limitations it imposes on his wife and his daughter. Byatt's first novel is the ambitious and promising attempt of a young writer to refuse the easy satisfaction of "the facile idea of sincerity" and to try to find an adequate narrative form for "the hard idea of truth." It is a search for a self-fulfilment unhampered by conventions and ideologies.

THE GAME

A remark by one of the characters in this novel sounds like an exposition of one of its central concerns: "We talk a lot about living fully, but the last thing we want to do is live anything through" (*G* 234). Even so, this is not discussed as frequently in the novel as one might expect. As an Oxford don, Cassandra, who makes the remark, has a tendency towards generalisations that are not always borne out by concrete fact. And yet this remark is of use for the analysis of this novel, For it allows us to distinguish again between the ideological proposition, "living fully" or "self-actualization," which Cassandra seems to regard as a generally accepted concept, and the idea of "living through," which demands of those who pursue it a readiness to accept suffering and perhaps failure.

Compared to its predecessor, this novel is more complex and no longer the work of a beginner. Instead of following a central character's search for self, it concentrates on various irritations of identity.[15] Aspects of the growth and the shaping of identity are included by means of flashbacks. Attention is given to the uncertain boundaries between opposite terms, such as critical and creative work, art and life, factual and imaginative deliberations, and so on. The main characters come closer to what Byatt later admired in George Eliot, "who wished to make her ideas 'thoroughly incarnate' in particular individuals" (*PM* 51).

Like the first novel, this one has to do with family relations, different positions *in* and ways *of* life, and correlated critical and creative activities distributed between the sisters Cassandra and Julia Corbett. But creativity and imagination are no longer considered the exclusive domain of fictional writing, restricting critical activities to facts and analysis. Cassandra, the Oxford scholar, maintains: "Even in my work—the discovery of facts isn't enough. One has to imagine them" (82). The novel conjoins these two major activities, which have become another hallmark of the writer A. S. Byatt.

It is the dilemma of the Corbett sisters that the close bond they enjoyed as children becomes an impediment to the development of separate adult identities. In their childhood game, which gives the novel its title, they played first with a pack of cards and then with clay figures at devising increasingly elaborate stories after the example of the Brontë children. Their first separation, which comes when Cassandra goes up to Oxford, does not immediately lead to their estrangement. The turn of the tide comes when Julia, in Cassandra's absence, becomes intimate with Simon Moffitt, with whom Cassandra had started a precarious relationship at Oxford. By an effort of will, Cassandra, who has inherited from her Quaker father a tendency towards self-denial and moral severity, manages "to uncreate him [Simon] in her mind" (113) and to detach herself from Julia. From then on, she leads the retired and dedicated life of an Oxford don, while Simon, who has developed a professional interest in snakes, disappears on a research expedition to South America.

Meanwhile Julia has married Thor Eskelund, a Quaker social worker from Norway. She has a daughter and a lover and becomes a successful novelist, finding apparent self-fulfilment in what she has always longed for, "a real life of my own" (119). Cassandra's desires are more complicated. Overtly, she suppresses all longings for self-fulfilment outside her professional existence. But her dreams still reveal what she had once expected—that a gradual deepening of her acquaintance with Simon would have enabled her "to share normal things with him" and to admit them (and him) into her own, "her other world" (112). The embrace, which had now become impossible, could still have happened then (125).

It is part of the complexity of this novel that characteristics are not evenly distributed. The two sisters are ambiguous characters. At first sight, Julia is the more realistic of the two. Indeed, her general attitude reminds one of Oliver Canning in *The Shadow of the Sun*. Like him, she accepts her ordinariness and makes good use of her limited possibilities. But Cassandra, though out of touch with the realities of daily life, is also realistic, if only in her theoretical assessment of reality. She accepts certain manifestations of egoism as a necessary part of social reality: "We all diminish each other. We all impinge on each other. It's natural" (80). Julia, in contrast, sees her independent writer's life threatened by the existence of her family, a personal destiny decreed by ill will and lack of sympathy.

All the central characters of this novel experience social life as an infringement of their potential for self-fulfilment, and all of them try to escape its narrow range—Simon by becoming an explorer in foreign parts; Thor by accepting a life of piety and missionary work; Cassandra by constructing her own imaginary world; and Julia by disposing of the identities of others whenever it suits her narrative purposes.

It is Simon who expresses a view of reality that sets a standard for this novel, although the others hesitate to accept it: "Our picture of reality is never fixed but can always be elaborated and made more accurate. And this changes us" (25).[16] Accordingly, no one in this novel can attempt to teach reality as Oliver Canning had done in *The Shadow of the Sun*. They all find themselves in a life-long process of trial and error adapting themselves to ever-changing conditions. This excludes permanent self-fulfilment. It also allows for "the contingency of events" in which Jane Campbell sees a distinguishing feature of this novel.[17]

Two elements of plot provide the occasions for establishing and elucidating these connections. One is a family reunion of the Corbetts at the deathbed of the father, where the two sisters reconsider their past, try to bridge the gulf that has divided them, and agree on more pleasant relations in the future. The other element is Simon's return to Britain and his appearance on a television programme that is viewed by the sisters and gives them a chance to exchange their impressions. And, finally, for the first time in her career, Byatt invents a novel to be included in her own novel—according to Campbell, another indication of her respect for contingency.[18]

A television programme in which a herpetologist reports on his researches is, of course, expected to be an objective documentary.[19] Instead, from the very first announcement, Byatt casts doubt on the enterprise of unproblematic representation—because the announcer has the "superlatively normal face of a girl whose cultured voice above her cultured pearls quavered" (10). The artificial pearls point to the cultured voice as equally artificial, both oddly contrasting with the nature documentary that is to follow.

These suspicions are confirmed by the producer's statement that people "like on the telly . . . something that reproduces a reality they recognize" (192). This, however, would hardly explain why people should be interested in the exploration of a reality hitherto unknown to them.

The statement sounds like a self-fulfilling prophecy that excludes all qualifying aspects—for example, the effect, as witnessed by Simon, that civilisation has on the inhabitants of newly explored regions. We "erode their basic dignity . . . We ignore differences—radical differences" (105). And Simon also notes the effect of talk shows on their performers: "They make one feel savaged. Food for thought" (200).

That the producer's view of his own medium is a superficial one is confirmed by Cassandra's reflections on the same subject. Watching Simon's series on his observations of snakes and Julia's participation on the panel of a television debate on art and life, she comes to think about the effects that television, as a new medium, may have on the possibilities of presenting a factual or a fictive reality—a problem that has from then on had Byatt's repeated attention. As a literary scholar, Cassandra has been familiar with textual strategies only. These can reimagine the past so that it can appear as present, without, however, suppressing completely and lastingly the distance between past and present.

This attitude seems to be irrelevant, indeed positively detrimental, to a television documentary presenting something as real and present. It does not invite any reflections on the manner of its presentation. Only after deliberately stepping out of the magic circle can the viewer discover television's necessarily illusionist nature. For what it really presents is a past moment in the existence of an object that has necessarily changed since the moment when its picture was taken. It follows that what the viewer sees is not the object as it really is, now, but what it was in the past. What is presented as real has become unreal.

Therefore, the difference between "telling" in a book and "tellying" on the screen is not in their respective closeness to reality but in their different uses of illusion. While the one creates a momentary illusion, suspending the reader's disbelief, the other one depends on constant illusion.

Once this has been admitted, all restraints are abandoned and imagination can be reinstated in its own right. This allows Cassandra to imagine Simon as he may be now. However, the result of this is just another subjective picture. Because now the identity of the person imagining sets a new barrier. To overcome it would mean to achieve complete identification with the other. But that way, as Cassandra knows very well, lies madness—the continuous identification with another identity.

And there is even another relation in which the medium proves deceptive. Cassandra had taken it for granted that the voice she heard on television was Simon's. Now she learns from him that the real speaker was his cameraman, Anthony Miller, who was later devoured by piranhas. Again, nothing is what it seems. Television communications become highly suspicious. The allegedly true picture is an image of past appearances, a recorded voice does not belong to the person depicted. Identities become questionable.

No wonder then that Cassandra finds it increasingly difficult to correlate details into a meaningful whole. "I connect and connect, meaninglessly, J's 'sense of release,' his [Simon's] rebirth platitude, the hostility of the objects round me, and my need for release from them" (170).[20] Her increasing madness seems to be accelerated by the distorted and misleading messages she receives from television.

Sense perception had already played an important part in *The Shadow of the Sun*. There, Henry had a special gift of imaginative vision that revealed the essence of things. Anna's failure to compete with him, on the other hand, illustrated the restrictions of normal ways of seeing. In both cases subjective qualities were decisive. In *The Game*, however, Byatt has concentrated on the qualities of the object. Here, the viewer is in a different situation, encountering not the object itself but a version prefabricated by the medium of representation. The process itself may resemble that in *The Shadow of the Sun*—things seen are transformed by the imagination. But a "vision" that starts from a distorted version of reality can never achieve a reliable insight. The viewer cannot completely escape the power of the prefabricated object.

In incorporating these considerations, Byatt's novel indicates not so much the aesthetic limitations of television documentaries, but the ambiguous influence of such products of the culture industry. While they may supply to the general consumer an easy satisfaction and a compensation for desires unfulfilled in real life, the more seriously minded recipients will find in these superficial pictures of reality impediments on the way to self and self-fulfilment.

It is one of the ironies of this novel that Julia, endowed with very little imagination, if any at all, should be a novelist, while the highly imaginative Cassandra restricts herself to keeping a journal. It says something for Julia that she is proud of keeping within the limits of her talents: "We must know our own limitations: this was a theme she often wrote on" (74). And with direct concern to her narratives: "She claimed no more than the virtues of an accurate recorder" (141). Cassandra, on the other hand, knows that "mere recording . . . is valueless" (82). And she knows very well by what subtle processes reality is transferred into fiction: "If we *imagine* our experience we transmute it—rearrange it, meditate on it, light it differently, change it, relate it to the rest of the world" (81)—an adequate description also of Byatt's techniques.

By following the successive stages of Julia's literary production, Byatt has left no doubt that all this is the result of an increasingly dubious craftsmanship. In her early novels, Julia had depicted the daily lives of housewives, embellished with "an element of romantic fantasy" (57). Later on, this element disappeared, and she concentrated in a more general way on what "the novel can explore"— women's boredom (139). All that was the product of fancy. New possibilities seem to become available through irritating changes in her own domestic life. As her daughter Deborah smugly comments: "Well at least you've got some real difficulties to write a real book about, for a change" (160).

A real book is exactly what Julia wants to write at this stage: "And I meant to try and write a *real* book—a complicated book—not about myself" (160–61). For her, a real book can, however, not be realised in terms of the domestic novel. It requires an effort to overcome the limitations she had so far acknowledged, in order to see "in the reality that restricted one—the nevertheless shining and extensive possibility" (164). In this, the driving force is not literary but personal ambition. The intrusion of new household members had made her lose "With her privacy . . . her sense of identity" (163). The real book is thought of as a compensation for this loss. When it is finished, Julia recognises that "she had achieved a new sense of identity to act from" (205).

This is completely different from the artistic self-fulfilment that—according to Byatt in another connection—"seems to provide an alternative to the communal and is something to do with connecting the self with the world of things."[21] To achieve the hoped-for cathartic effect, Julia has subjected the world to her own personal desires. And she has succeeded at the expense of others, particularly of Cassandra. On her, the effect is fatal. She has to endure what Julia, for her part, had self-pityingly complained about: that with her privacy her identity has been destroyed.

For Julia's novel *A Sense of Glory*, the story of an Oxford lady don and her colleagues, with all their whims of behaviour and the minutiae of dressing, can be easily decoded as an accurate (Julia's *forte*!) and rather ruthless portrayal of Cassandra and her surroundings. In her egotism, Julia has not anticipated what this would do to her sister. While Julia believes her permanently imprisoned, far from reality, in the ivory tower of scholarship, Cassandra comes to realise that by being exposed to the public she has been deprived of her freedom and reduced to the status of an object. She "does a little more than simply see me, and that little is intolerable" (276). The invasion of Cassandra's privacy has enabled Julia to present to the public an exact and inescapable likeness. And Cassandra knows that the exposure of her self, based on the total seizure of all her characteristic features, can never be revoked. It has the finality of a destructive satire. Cassandra is well aware that from then on she and Simon can only fill in the blueprint of their lives as devised by Julia. Of course, a more detached observer would have doubted that the constraint exerted on a fictive person should be able, like black magic, to doom a person in real life. But in a state that she herself calls madness, Cassandra becomes inextricably involved. She finds it impossible to resist the compulsion of a prefabricated future life and sees her only escape in committing suicide.

Comparing *The Game* to *The Shadow of the Sun*, one can see Byatt's second novel as another attempt at grappling with the problematic relation between artist and society. Henry Severell, oblivious to anything but his creative work, ignores the rights of others and maims them inadvertently in real life. Julia Corbett, by transporting others into her fictions, deprives them of their individual existence and cannot even claim any literary merit as mitigating circumstances. What, in the first case, was artistic egotism has turned into undisguised personal egoism in the second case.

This implies yet another dimension, and again it is Byatt herself who has paved the way from text to context. In *Unruly Times*, her study of Wordsworth and Coleridge, first published in 1970, three years after *The Game*, she discusses, among other things, various romantic concepts of the poet: on the one hand, Wordsworth's "self-contained poetic 'self'" (*UT* 43), and on the other Keats's concept of *negative capability*, the selflessness of the poet, "the poetical Charac- ter itself [which] is not itself,"[22] with the well-known illustrating references to Shakespeare.

It seems to me that Keats's ideal, paraphrased by Walter Jackson Bate as temporarily "negating one's own ego," maintained against the temptations of "an egoistic assertion of one's own identity,"[23] is the pivot around which Byatt's considerations revolve, still covertly in the early novels, and more openly in her later fiction.

Accordingly, Henry Severell could be described as a "self-contained poetic 'self'" of the Wordsworthian type. And in Julia Corbett's self-assertion one might hear Hazlitt's strictures on Wordsworth for "an obtrusion of the poet's personal feelings, interests, defences, and the danger of losing that 'high and permanent interest beyond ourselves' to which arts should aim" (qtd. in *UT* 235). By marking the extremes—Henry's celebration of his poetic self and Julia's succumbing to her personal self—Byatt has firmly established a field of force that allows her to test the validity of more complex considerations developed in her later fiction. And in Deborah Corbett, critical, open-minded, and resistant to easy temptation, the reader receives a promise that not all has been said and done. Indeed, she reappears as Frederica in *The Virgin in the Garden*.

NOTES

1. Boyd Tonkin, "Antonia S. Byatt in Interview with Boyd Tonkin," *Anglistik* 10.2 (1999): 24.

2. "What seem the most autobiographical aspects of her work, which are her depictions of relationships between fathers and daughters and between sisters." Richard Todd, *A. S. Byatt* (Plymouth: Northcote House, 1997) 8.

3. "While Byatt's art has certainly matured over the past 30 years, her preoccupation with the artist, the imagination, and the impossibility of love and the inevitability of loss has remained constant." Kathleen Coyne Kelly, *A. S. Byatt* (New York: Twayne Publishers, 1996) 14.

4. For this latter aspect see Joanne V. Creighton, "Sisterly Symbiosis: Margaret Drabble's *The Waterfall* and A. S. Byatt's *The Game*," *Mosaic: A Journal for the Interdisciplinary Study of Literature* 20 (1987): 15–29.

5. Helen Gardner, *The Business of Criticism* (Oxford: Clarendon, 1959) 7. Compare A. S. Byatt on present-day tasks of literary criticism: "What one needs, far from a very, very complex theory and a very, very difficult language, is a way of talking to people about reading. You know, delighting people in reading so that they will go back and actually do a few more bits of reading particularly from the past" (Tonkin 18).

6. Anthony Clare, rev. of *The Consolations of Philosophy*, by Alain de Botton, *Literary Review* (April 2000): 44.

7. See Iris Murdoch, "Against Dryness" [1961], *The Novel Today*, ed. Malcolm Bradbury, 2nd ed. (London: Fontana, 1990) 15–24.

8. Kelly 19.

9. Kelly 24.

10. Tonkin 25.

11. Kelly 22.

12. A. S. Byatt, "Introduction," *SS* viii.

13. Byatt, "Introduction" x.

14. Michael Westlake, "The Hard Idea of Truth," *PN Review* 15.4 (1989): 35; here qtd. from Alexa Alfer, "The Fiction of A. S. Byatt," *Anglistik* 10.2 (1999): 39.

15. This is also indicated by an abundance of "self"-composita such as "self-protection" (*G* 58), "self-indulgence" (58, 90), "self-conscious" (67), "self-effacement" (87), "self-denial" (87), "self-aggrandizement" (228), etc.

16. For a detailed discussion of Byatt's negotiations of realism in the context of postmodern theories, see Alfer 27–40.

17. Jane Campbell, "The Hunger of the Imagination in A. S. Byatt's *The Game*," *Critique: Studies in Modern Fiction* 29 (1988): 160.

18. Campbell 160.

19. For a detailed discussion of the image of the snake in this and other narratives of Byatt, see Annegret Maack, "Metamorphosen der Schlange: Zu A. S. Byatts Bildersprache," *Anglistik* 10.2 (1999): 68–78.

20. The obvious allusions are to the epigraph of E. M. Forster's *Howards End* (1910) and to T. S. Eliot's *The Waste Land* (1922): "On Margate Sands. / I can connect / Nothing with nothing." T. S. Eliot, *Selected Poems* (Harmondsworth: Penguin, 1948) 60. Later than Byatt, Bernard Kops used these lines as the central motif of his novel *On Margate Sands* (London: Secker & Warburg, 1978).

21. Tonkin 25.

22. *The Letters of John Keats*, ed. Hyder Rollins, vol. 1 (Cambridge: Cambridge UP, 1958) 386–87.

23. Walter Jackson Bate, *John Keats* (Cambridge, MA: Harvard UP, 1964) 249.

Jackie Buxton

"What's love got to do with it?": Postmodernism and *Possession*

The postmodern reply to the modern consists of recognizing that the past, since it cannot really be destroyed, because its destruction leads to silence, must be revisited: but with irony, not innocently. I think of the postmodern attitude as that of a man who loves a very cultivated woman and knows he cannot say to her, "I love you madly," because he knows that she knows (and that she knows that he knows) that these words have already been written by Barbara Cartland. Still, there is a solution. He can say, "As Barbara Cartland would put it, I love you madly." At this point, having avoided false innocence, having said clearly that it is no longer possible to speak innocently, he will nevertheless have said what he wanted to say to the woman: that he loves her, but he loves her in an age of lost innocence. If the woman goes along with this, she will have received a declaration of love all the same. Neither of the two speakers will feel innocent, both will have accepted the challenge of the past, of the already said, which cannot be eliminated; both will consciously and with pleasure play the game of irony. . . . But both will have succeeded, once again, in speaking of love.

(Umberto Eco, Postscript to *The Name of the Rose*)

The year 1990 saw the publication of an academic novel that became a surprise best-seller; within three months, it had carried off the Booker Prize and the Irish Times–Aer Lingus International Fiction Award. By mid-January 1991, it was into its eighth print run and was being lauded as the season's runaway success. The book was *Possession*, a title that uncannily prophesied its readerly effect.

Unabashedly subtitled *A Romance*, *Possession* concerns the illicit passion of two Victorian poets, and the contemporary scholars who discover, and subsequently map, their relationship. As weighty as any of its Victorian antecedents, *Possession* encompasses two centuries and a good many of the generic forms of literary history. In five-hundred-plus pages, the reader is presented with substantial examples of memoirs, fairy tales, academic essays, diaries and journals, public and private correspondence, and of course, poetry—over 1600 lines of it, in fact. Clearly, *Possession* is no ordinary novel. Reviewers are unanimous in their praise, and virtually unanimous in their implicit or explicit tagging of the novel as postmodernist. Highly forthcoming in their approval, they are less forthright in outlining the reasons for this postmodern classification. Perhaps this is so self-evident as not to require explanation? Even the most cursory of literary surveys on the subject, however, shows that *postmodernism* is by no means an uncontested category. Whether constituted in literary, artistic, architectural, social, political, economic, or epistemological terms, postmodernism boasts no lack of commentators. No doubt, were these reviewers questioned, their responses to the question of what postmodernism is would run the length of the definitive spectrum. What is more interesting to me is the repeated descriptive attribution to *Possession* of that single term. Thus, it is not my intention to throw another definition of postmodernism into the theoretical arena (although that will probably be inevitable); rather, I want to examine those aspects of the novel that may have led to its postmodern categorization and the political and aesthetic consequences of that critical understanding. My concern is less with what postmodernism *is* than with what its proponents and detractors claim that it *does*. How might the debate settle on and around *Possession*, and, more importantly, how does *Possession* quite self-consciously *activate* this debate? What's love got to do with it? Everything, it seems.

While reviewers applaud *Possession* as a virtuoso performance of academic erudition, nineteenth-century ventriloquism, comedy, passion, and narrative allure, they are divided in terms of an explicit identification of its literary placement. Drawing attention to *Possession*'s generic pastiche, its self-conscious interrogation of literary and historical Truth, and a plot that resembles a corridor of mirrors, many critics employ the language of postmodernism, if not the label itself. To Hulbert, for example, Byatt "mixes up styles, genres, voices in good postmodern manner" to produce "old-fashioned mystery, comedy, and romance tricked out in newfangled, self-reflexive style."[1] Others are more definite in their categorization, although some confusion remains as to what kind of postmodern tag best classifies the text. *Possession* is variously cast as "postmodern romance,"[2] "postmodern gothic,"[3] or as belonging to "that genre of ingenious books" known as "postmodern literary thrillers."[4] What is perhaps most strikingly common to all reviewers' responses is the reliance on comparative texts to illuminate *Possession*'s textual strategies. Interestingly enough, the names that crop up with extraordinary regularity are those most often cited in postmodern literary criticism: Vladimir Nabokov, Jorge Luis Borges, John Fowles, Umberto

Eco, D. M. Thomas, and David Lodge. While the precise classification of *Possession* seems undecided, the broad category under which it falls is quite clear: postmodernist fiction. How then might the general characteristics of postmodernism inform an examination of the novel?[5]

A POSTMODERN POSSESSION OF THE PAST

Possession opens in the London Library, where Roland Michell, a rather dull English postgraduate, is researching the work of the famous Victorian poet, Randolph Henry Ash. His discovery—and subsequent theft—of two passionate letters by Ash to an unknown woman constitutes the basis of the mystery that drives the novel. Certain clues in Ash's letters lead Roland to the less known Victorian poet, Christabel LaMotte, and the contemporary feminist scholar whose work is concerned with her, Maud Bailey. Together, Roland and Maud track down yet more letters confirming an unsuspected romance between the married Ash and the reclusive LaMotte, and, in the process, they establish one of their own. They are both aided and hounded in their quest by a bevy of rival academics eager to discover the full story of the Victorian poets' liaison. In the weaving of this intricate, heavily literary plot, Byatt mercilessly parodies contemporary academia, employs a pastiche of styles and forms, and exploits the popular narrative models of romance and gothic and detective fiction. By mixing ontological worlds in an epistemological quest, she self-consciously plays with the competing meanings of both *possession* and *romance*. *Possession* also exhibits a postmodern obsession with "the question of how we can come to know the past today."[6] The American academic, Mortimer Cropper, seeks to own the past by accumulating its material artifacts; Beatrice Nest seeks to protect the past by guarding its inhabitants' privacy; Roland and Maud's method is not that of biographical pilgrimage, but the discovery of the past through its textual monuments, "the twists and turns of [its] syntax" (*POb* 25).[7] Their endeavors raise the novel's implicit questions: is the past the possession of scholars or blood descendants, of those who physically hold its remnants or those who 'truly care' about their meanings? *Possession* is thus an academic novel in both senses of the word.

Byatt is not only intimately acquainted with the nineteenth-century world of letters, but also with the trends and discourses that characterize late-twentieth-century academia, and her parodic representations of various scholarly types can be very amusing. There is Beatrice Nest, the reluctant editor of Ash's wife's journals and the victim of changing critical interests, as described by James Blackadder, Roland's graduate supervisor: "Poor old Beatrice began by wanting to show how self-denying and supportive Ellen Ash was and she messed around looking up every recipe for gooseberry jam . . . for *twenty-five years*, can you believe it, and woke up to find that no one wanted self-denial and dedication any more, they wanted proof that Ellen was raging with rebellion and pain and untapped talent" (36). There is Blackadder himself, the footnote-fettered editor of

Ash's poetry and plays, and the victim of his New Critical mentor's pedagogic ministrations: "Leavis did to Blackadder what he did to serious students: he showed him the terrible, the magnificent importance and urgency of English literature and simultaneously deprived him of any confidence in his own capacity to contribute to or change it" (32). There is Maud's fellow psychoanalytic feminist critic, Leonora Stern, an exuberant bisexual whose loud personality is in total contrast to Maud's reserved English coolness. For Byatt, Leonora is the epitome of the new feminist criticism, insisting as she does on seeing everything LaMotte wrote as a metaphor for feminine sexuality.[8] Byatt's imitation of this kind of enquiry is so exaggerated that it only confirms Leonora's satiric status:

When I last wrote I mentioned I might write something on water and milk and amniotic fluid in *Melusina*—why is water always seen as the female? . . . I could extend it to the *Drowned City*—With special reference to non-genital imagery for female sexuality—we need to get away from the cunt as well as from the phallus— the drowned women in the city might represent the totality of the female body as an erogenous zone if the circumambient fluid were seen as an undifferentiated eroti- cism, and this might be possible to connect to the erotic totality of the woman / dragon stirring the waters of the large marble bath, or *submerging her person* in it as LaM. tellingly describes her. (154)

Given this kind of intensely intellectualized sexuality, Maud's comment to Roland on the meaning of their mutual desire for a clean, white bed in an empty room is indeed telling: "Maybe we're symptomatic of whole flocks of exhausted scholars and theorists" (291).

Byatt reserves her most biting satire for the academic representatives of sexual and material possessiveness: Fergus Wolff and Mortimer Cropper. A child of poststructuralism, Fergus engages in some convolutedly erudite scholarship. When he first appears in the novel, his current textual project faces him with "the challenge" of "deconstruct[ing] something that had apparently already decon- structed itself" (37). His lupine insincerity is indicated by the Harlequin-ro- mance-like language with which he lures Maud to his bed: "You are the most beautiful thing I have ever seen or dreamed about. I want you, I need you, can't you feel it, it's irresistible" (64). Cropper exemplifies the personal, scholarly stake in the construction of one's literary object, and his biography of Ash bears the marks of his own self-aggrandizement (268). His interest in Ash is implicitly necrophiliac and ghoulish; he wants to imprison his artifacts in the airless glass mausoleum of the Stant Collection, and his grave-robbing expedition pulsates with sexual undertones (535–36). Cropper is a pornographic voyeur, both liter- ally and symbolically. Lacking the time required to win access to the correspond- ence by means of his chequebook, he laments the lost chance to subject those letters to the erotic embrace of his "black box" desire (415). The most telling indictment of Cropper, however, is the locale in which he is first found furtively photographing Ash memorabilia. A lengthy description of his environs builds to an image of his enthroned activities. Cropper is presented—not to put too fine a point on it—*on the crapper*. In contrast to Cropper's interest in dead relics is Roland and Maud's shared sense of the vitality of this textualized passion: "They were alive" claims Roland in an attempt to explain his theft of the letters (56). Before long, Maud too is infected by the sense of urgency in the relationship between two long-dead poets whose work, she agrees, "stayed alive, when I'd been taught and examined everything else" (62).

It is therefore highly appropriate that *Possession* begins with the description of a book at once funereal and alive—a book concerned with seeking "historical fact in the poetic metaphors of myth and legend" (5), with finding fact in fiction. Certainly, *Possession* is a detective story, but it is a detective story concerned with reading. The novel is bursting with addressors and addressees, textual authors and consumers, and fictions within fictions. Its detectives are literary analysts, but these intrepid textual sleuths are dealing not with the cause-and-effect rationalization of a recent event (customarily a murder), but with a "crime scene" from which they are distanced by a century or more. Roland and Maud's "case" is primarily historiographic in nature; by means of historical and fictional documents they not only reconstruct and track their 'villains', but they also rewrite literary history. Thus, to rework a term of Linda Hutcheon's, the novel is a historiographic (detective) metafiction, one in which "possession" acts as both *arche* and *telos*, question and solution. Although the possibility of a death is implicitly raised (that of the poets' child), the mystery resides not in the conventional detection of the perpetrators of a murder but, rather, in tracing the trajectory of the crime itself: passion. In this inversion of the genre, the criminals—Ash and LaMotte—are discovered at the outset; the narrative progression is in detecting the exact details of their illicit exploits.[9]

On the Ash/LaMotte trail, all of the contemporary scholars' analytical skills are brought to the fore. Increasingly, they discover interconnections in the Victorians' poetry that provide fresh evidence of their liaison, which is hardly surprising since "literary critics make natural detectives" (258). Just as Maud is led to the original correspondence by a supposedly insignificant poem of LaMotte's, so a seemingly casual reference in her longer poem, *Melusina*, begins to read "like a classic literary clue" (258). It is a self-conscious choice on Byatt's part and a relationship on which she is quite willing to comment: "I felt I could write a literary detective story that needn't be quite so papery [as Eco's *Name of the Rose*], because once I'd written the poetry the scholars were actually doing the kind of detection that one really does with poems, which is finding out their meaning . . . what the poet was really concentrating on. The poems I wrote contain various clues to the detective-story plot."[10] Although Maud and Roland are generally successful in their use of a poetic treasure map, not all of the clues that they discover lead to the correct interpretation. LaMotte's painfully Dickinsonian poem on the subject of spilt milk is a case in point (411–13). It is understandable that they conclude that the poet's child was still-born in the light of such lines as "It came all so still / The little Thing—/ And would not stay—/ Our Questioning—" (412). So, although Byatt introduces some helpful clues, she is clearly not averse to the introduction of a red herring either. What is perhaps the most subversive inflection to the conventional object of detection is the revelation of Maud's direct genealogical descent from the woman she has been investigating. When she realizes that the myth of her own origins is maternally centered, her earlier comment acquires a retrospective irony: "You know the theory that the classic detective story arose with the classic adultery novel—everyone wanted to know who was the Father, what was the origin, what is the secret?" (258).

Possession is full of such self-reflexive comments on the fictive nature of readerly—and writerly—constructs. Indeed, the novel is prefaced with an authorizing statement of deception. One aspect of the novel's subtitle is outlined in the epigraph by Nathaniel Hawthorne. Instead of a mimetic fiction of "minute fidelity" to the "ordinary course of man's experience," we will presumably be presented with a created truth "of the writer's own choosing," offered by way of the latitude inherent to the Romance form.[11] The second epigraph from Browning's "Mr Sludge, 'the Medium'" promises even more postmodernist delights. The satirical tone of the poem arises from the self-confessed suggestion that Sludge's abilities are rooted in sleight of hand rather than in authentic spiritual communication with the world of the dead. This medium–conjurer argues, however, that his trade is simply that of all (literary) artists; he offers the pleasurable fruits of the past by means of a few useful falsehoods. Quoting the common exclamations of admiration for the production of "such solid fabric out of air," Sludge exposes their unacknowledged implications in a more accurate restatement: "How many lies did it require to make / The portly truth you here present us with?"[12] Thus, Sludge's preface contains both an implicit proclamation of the constructedness of the fiction that follows and multi-layered ironies surrounding its own 'authorizing' status. Presumably, the "helpful lies" of Robert Browning and Emily Dickinson inform the "portly truths" of Randolph Henry Ash and Christabel LaMotte. And this is only the beginning of Byatt's manipulation of the notions of "truth" and "fiction."

THE SUBJECT OF (LITERARY) HISTORY

Possession contains many self-conscious moments, either in references to other fictions or in implicit or explicit postmodern gestures. Just as Roland is indeed the *childe* of his poet-mentor, so it is no accident that Maud, often described as "icily regular, splendidly null" and emotionally sequestered like "The Lady of Shalott" (550), is housed atop Tennyson Tower (45). By Byatt's own admission, Eco's *Name of the Rose* inspired the writing of *Possession*, and the novel is strewn with allusions to the poetry of Wordsworth, Coleridge, Tennyson, Robert Browning, Donne, and Herbert, and the novels of Dickens, Woolf, and George Eliot. The most important postmodernist hat-tipping is to

Fowles' *French Lieutenant's Woman*, another text that considers the Victorian age alongside (and through) the contemporary one. When Chapter 15 opens with "The man and the woman sat opposite each other in the railway carriage" (297), the reader might presume that the couple is Roland and Maud returning from their Yorkshire expedition. In fact, it is Randolph and Christabel embarking on *theirs*. In an unusual break from the twentieth-century locale in which the story has been conducted to this point, Byatt presents an omniscient time capsule: the crucial tryst-"elopement" by the two Victorians. Or is it omniscient? The poets are introduced through the speculations of a "hypothetical observer" who studiously documents their appearance and demeanor in an attempt to discern their relationship (298). Implicitly, the reader (and the writer) is that observer, projected into the novel as a fellow traveler. Although certainly not as emphatically authorial as Fowles's intrusion, the situation, description, and tone of this episode echoes Fowles's embodied entrance to his own fiction. If the revelation of the consummation of Ash and LaMotte's relationship is a knowing one, then the consummation of their modern-day counterparts' relationship is equally self-conscious: "with infinite gentle delays and delicate diversions and variations of indirect assault Roland finally, *to use an outdated phrase*, entered and took possession of all her white coolness" (550; emphasis added).[13]

The twentieth-century scholars' activities are marked by an awareness of their contemporary condition, that they are studying art in an "age of mechanical reproduction." So, when Roland and Maud visit Bethany, the scrupulously restored former home of LaMotte and Blanche Glover, they are unable to distinguish the real from its referent. Maud refers to the house as a "simulacrum," while Roland comments that "It would have looked older. When it was younger." Both recognize it as "a postmodern quotation" (230). Similarly, Cropper's carefully orchestrated and illustrated lecture is indicative of his perverse admiration for the hyperreal. The finale of his high-tech (self-)performance is "a product of his passion": a hologram of Ash's snuff box "floating in the church like a miraculously levitated object" (417). In an effort to foil the self-interested scheme behind Cropper's scandalous *exposé*, Blackadder and Leonora employ an equally public medium: they appear on national television to defend and *to sell* their poets to the masses. Leonora's pep-talk with Blackadder prior to going on air is a hilarious comment on the perceived philistinism of contemporary appetites:

"I guess we've got *three minutes* to make out the importance of all this stuff to the great greedy public and that don't include illustrations. No, you've got to make out your Mr Ash to be the sexiest property in town. You've got to get them by the balls, Professor. Make 'em cry. . . . *One* thing you'll get said in the time, and that's your lot, Professor."

"I see that. Mmn. One thing—"

"One *sexy* thing, Professor." (434–35)

But *is* it philistinism, or merely a comment on the novel's own narrative strategies? In *Possession*, Victorian poets (and poetry) are presented as "the sexiest property in town." Glossily packaged as a romance, *Possession* has been sold to "the great greedy public," and, what is more, *that public has bought it.*

If the novel calls into question such notions as originality and truth, then the idea of an authentic, centered, Cartesian self is also given a postmodern twist. While Mortimer Cropper's ubiquitous appearances in his lectures and writings on Ash suggest an over-inflated sense of self, there is a very Freudian point in his self-examinations beyond which he will not go (118). Blackadder's subjectivity is so inextricable from that of his subject that even he questions his own originality. Blackadder is not the only one to be *subject-ed* to the influence of the Victorians. After reading Blanche Glover's account of "the prowler" at her and Christabel's door, Roland groups Maud in their seclusion and likens himself to Randolph Ash, "an intruder into their female fastnesses" (65). Maud's self-possession—her Christabel-like fear of love as a loss of freedom—reveals a highly personal stake in the preservation of a poetic subject uncontaminated by romantic assignations: "Part of her was still dismayed that Christabel LaMotte should have given in to whatever urgings or promptings Ash may have used. She preferred her own original vision of proud and particular independence, as Christabel, in the letters, had given some reason to think she did herself" (268). It is her own sense of self that she protects. But Maud and Roland are too well-educated to support anything as romantic as the notion of a coherent self: "Narcissism, the unstable self, the fractured ego, Maud thought, who am I? A matrix for a susurration of texts and codes? It was both a pleasant and an unpleasant idea, this requirement that she think of herself as intermittent and partial" (273). An "old-fashioned textual critic" Roland may feel, but he is nevertheless fully "trained in the post-structuralist deconstruction of the subject" (56, 13). Consequently, he has "learned to see himself, theoretically, as a crossing-place for a number of systems, all loosely connected. He had been trained to see his idea of his 'self' as an illusion, to be replaced by a discontinuous machinery and electrical message-network of various desires, ideological beliefs and responses, language-forms and hormones and pheromones. Mostly he liked this" (459).[14]

Their subjectivities, however, become increasingly intertwined with those of Ash and LaMotte, as the gulf between the past and the present rapidly diminishes with the novel's progression. As the Hawthorne epigraph promises, this Romance "connect[s] a bygone time with the very present that is flitting away from us." That bygone time constantly interrupts the present diegesis of the novel as Byatt weaves the contemporary and the historical into one immediate textual present. The borders between then and now, fiction and reality, are continually undermined. LaMotte and Ash—two fictional characters—are given historical weight through their interaction with non-fictional figures: Coleridge, George Crabbe, Ruskin, Éduard Manet, and George Frederic Watts, while Maud and Roland are "filled out" through reference to the poetic fictions of Tennyson and

Browning. The former instance is what one may expect of the historical novel; the irony lies in the question of accessibility. With two notable exceptions, the world of Ash and LaMotte is a wholly removed one, only accessible through its surviving documents, yet it is presented as more vital and immediate than the constrained world that Roland and Maud (and we) occupy. The sterility of their existence is blatantly indicated by the nature of Roland and Val's love-making. Completely unstimulated by Val's declarations of love and desire, Roland can only achieve an erection by contemplating an image that is "half-fantasy, half-photogravure"—*an image of Ellen Ash* (141). When Maud and Roland join forces, however, their relationship is increasingly charged with the "kick galvanic" of Victorian passion (297). The text seems to suggest that Victorian fictions are somehow dictating contemporary realities. There is one other crucial postmodernist gesture in the relationship between these two intercon-nected worlds: the conclusion of Maud and Roland's historiographic journey. Armed with every piece of documentation they are ever likely to gain, the scholars assume that they have discovered the truth that lies at the heart of the lovers' tragic relationship and have firmly established the ownership of the locket of hair stowed in Ash's pocket watch. That they are utterly wrong in their interpretation only ironically underscores the constructed, fallible nature of the historical enterprise and the impossibility of discovering any ultimate Truth.

It is the pursuit of this "truth" that constitutes the investigative plot that drives the novel, but detective fiction is not the only narrative model in operation in the text. Romance, in both its "high" and "low" forms, is the "significant other" in evidence in *Possession*'s complex plot structure. Neither model, however, has a consistent priority. Thus, the quest form of Roland and Maud's discreet private-eye sleuthing transmutes into the classic stampede of an academic "cops and robbers." LaMotte and Ash's passion may bear the hallmarks of tragic romance, but the moderns experience a conclusion not unlike that of Shakespearean com-edy, a conventional ending of which they are quite cognizant (524). The Ash–LaMotte romance is also all-consuming in more ways than one; as Maud and Roland map its progression, it progressively maps them. Expressing a desire to see "something new," something "without layers of meaning," Roland proposes a picnic at the Boggle Hole: "Perhaps we could take a day off from *them*, get out of their story, go and look at something for ourselves" (291).[15] *They* may not know it, but we discover in the following chapter that it *is* a part of the poets' story, for Ash and LaMotte also visited the beach on a similarly perfect day a century earlier (311). Clearly, there is no escape; Maud and Roland are imprisoned in a plot that both is, and is not, their own. It is an observation that Roland himself makes late in the novel. Recognizing that he is in "a Romance, a vulgar and a high Romance simultaneously" (460), he feels the frightening attraction of that narra-tive model: "Roland thought, partly with precise postmodernist pleasure, and partly with a real element of superstitious dread, that he and Maud were being driven by a plot or fate that seemed, at least possibly, to be not their plot or fate but that of those others" (456). Roland's pleasure stems from his participation in a "postmodernist mirror-game"; his dread stems from his belief that the game has "got out of hand" (456). To act in accordance with this narrative compulsion is somehow to compromise or to surrender one's integrity, Roland dispassionately theorizes: "'Falling in love' characteristically, combs the appearances of the world, and of the particular lover's history, out of a random tangle and into a coherent plot. Roland was troubled by the idea that the opposite may be true. Finding themselves in a plot, they might suppose it appropriate to behave as though it was that sort of plot" (456). Consolation, however, is at hand. They may be plot-entrapped, but at least that plot is of a safely variable nature: "In any case, since Blackadder and Leonora and Cropper had come, it had changed from Quest, a good romantic form, into Chase and Race, two other equally valid ones" (460).

BYATT'S PURSUIT OF POSTMODERNISM

But how postmodernist is *Possession, really*? Is the relationship between the past and the present an instance of postmodernist intertextuality or "merely" the result of a well-crafted fiction? Is the novel truly self-reflexive or simply self-conscious? Is there a difference? I would argue that there is. While Maud and Roland exhibit a scholarly postmodernist sensibility, the text itself exhibits a strong suspicion of that epistemic condition, even a condemnation of it. For all its postmodern gestures, *Possession* is first and foremost a "straight" narrative, a realistic fiction. Although Fergus Wolff and Beatrice Nest may *recall* Dickensian characters, although Christabel LaMotte and Randolph Ash *echo* Emily Dickinson and Robert Browning, although Roland and Maud *seem* to be reincarnations of their respective poets, these allusions are implicit rather that explicitly metafictional ones. The contemporary scholars might reflect on their theoretically unstable subjectivity, their textualized status as a nexus of competing discursive formations, but they do so as fully rounded fictional characters. Never once in the novel is their fictionality, or the fictionality of either temporal locale, called into question. *Possession* is in many ways a Victorian novel, for it replicates the realism of its forebears in capturing the nineteenth-century ethos. In another sense, *Possession* is a nineteenth-century novel because that is where its real passion—and its author's passion—lies. One world is obviously given ideological priority in this text, and it is the Victorian one, this literary Golden Age from which the present one is construed as a falling away. In comparison to the engaged Victorian poets, the contemporary academics appear not only anemic, but also decidedly repressed. A comment of Byatt's is indeed illuminating in this respect:

This is part of the whole joke of the novel: the dead are actually much more alive and vital than the living. . . . The poor moderns are always asking themselves so many questions about whether their actions are real and whether what they say can be thought to be true, given that language always tells lies, that they become rather papery and are miserably aware of this, and this is part of the comedy.[16]

In *Possession*, Byatt honors the Victorians, but she also unashamedly celebrates Romance in both its "high" and its "vulgar" forms. Part of Maud's and
Roland's problem is their very unwillingness to become passionately involved,
and not just in a romantic sense. These emotional incapacities, it is suggested, are
the result of their education: a sexualized knowledge so devoid of passion that it
has only produced a kind of sexual exhaustion. Here is the omniscient narrator on
the paradoxical nature of this all-too-knowing age:

They were children of a time and culture that mistrusted love, "in love," romantic
love, romance *in toto*, and which nevertheless in revenge proliferated sexual language, linguistic sexuality, analysis, dissection, deconstruction, exposure. They were
theoretically knowing: they knew about phallocracy and penisneid, punctuation,
puncturing and penetration, and polymorphous and polysemous perversity, orality,
good and bad breasts, clitoral tumescence, vesicle persecution, the fluids, the solids,
the metaphors for these, the systems of desire and damage, infantile greed and
oppression and transgression, the iconography of the cervix and the imagery of the
expanding and contracting Body, desired, attacked, consumed, feared. (458)

Faced with such distrustful knowledge, Roland and Maud conduct their burgeoning romance in silence because, tellingly, "Speech, the kind of speech they knew,
would have undone it" (459). As the academics' relationship strengthens, however, their faith in the theories in which they have been trained wavers. Alone
together at Thomason Foss, they make some personal admissions that are most
informative. Maud muses on the frequency with which sexuality is identified in
and by our culture, and continues:

We know all sorts of other things, too—about how there isn't a unitary ego—how
we're made up of conflicting, interacting systems of things—and I suppose we
believe that? . . . We never say the word Love, do we—we know it's a suspect
ideological construct—especially Romantic Love—so we have to make a real effort
of imagination to know what it felt like to be them. (290)

Roland agrees. Responding, he mourns the loss of "Mystery" in such knowledge
and suggests the destructive nature of such investigations: "And desire, that we
look into so carefully—I think that all the *looking-into* has some very odd effects
on the desire" (290). Since this discussion informs their professed longing for a
clean white bed—a moment of connection between the two scholars—I suspect a
strong authorial investment in these "revolutionary" revelations. Byatt, it seems,
is using postmodernism—or, at least, post-structuralism—against itself.[17]
    According to Hutcheon, postmodern fiction makes explicit the conventionally
veiled processes of narrative representation; historiographic metafiction fore-
grounds the textual—and therefore, constructed—nature of the means by which
we approach the past, today. The modern scholars' access to the past is certainly
documentary in nature. The Victorians are tracked "like any other dead soul"
(*POb* 37) through bio/bibliographical texts and surviving archival material. The

only way that *they* can know history is through its inscription. While the conclusions reached by the grouped academics at the end of *Possession* (retrospectively) underline the impossibility of any totalizing knowledge, the reader's experience is exactly the opposite. Transgressing the boundaries of historical knowledge, the true facts are proffered in an omniscient authorial *deus ex machina*. "There are things that happen and leave no discernible trace," we are told at the beginning of the postscript; "Two people met, on a hot May day, and never later mentioned their meeting. *This is how it was*" (552; emphasis added). We discover that Ash did meet his daughter, and that the lock of hair in his pocket watch is not Christabel's but hers. Essentially, we are presented with privileged information about events that Roland et al. will never know.[18] The postscript is clearly a playful sideswipe at postmodern historicism, for it concerns things that "are not spoken or written of, though it would be very wrong to say that subsequent events go on indifferently, all the same, as though such things had never been" (552). What Byatt presents here is not a textual construction, but a living human being, a materiality as opposed to a discursive trace. Maia Thomasine Bailey is something of the past that is not merely an inscription, but is emphatically corporeal, an undeniable product of her parents' (literary) liaison.

Although Maud's and Roland's interest in the outcome of the poets' affair is somewhat voyeuristic, it is mitigated by the intention that informs it (and the romance that their investigation breeds). In contrast to their rival academics, it is implied that only Roland and Maud can make the effort to imaginatively "know" how Ash and LaMotte felt. Their will to knowledge stems not from professional greed but from "something more primitive": "narrative curiosity" (259). Presumably, their obsession with discovering the truth becomes the reader's obsession as well. And in the three "transgressive" time capsules that punctuate the novel, our narrative curiosity is satisfied. "Coherence and closure are deep human desires that are presently unfashionable," thinks Roland in the midst of his postmodernist musings (456). Implicitly, the conclusion to *Possession* is therefore an unfashionable one. Poignant though it may be, the ending is fundamentally a happy one: Ash meets his daughter in an idyllic summer setting, and she repeatedly asserts that she is "extraordinarily" content (554). Byatt herself is an enthusiastic advocate for the plenitude offered by traditional forms. Referring to a contemporary "narrative hunger," she defends both the well-made plot and the satisfactions of all-encompassing narrative closure:

I haven't used the plot naïvely. . . . But it has given me intense pleasure. I love those Victorian novels in which, when you come to the end, you're told the whole history of every character from the end of the story until their dying day. I love that kind of thing, it makes me very happy. I don't see why we shouldn't have it: it's not wicked, as we were told in the sixties, it's just pleasant. Everybody knows it's fiction, but then everybody knows the whole thing is fiction.[19]

Given the authorial investment in Roland's emerging poetic sensibility, Byatt is also an advocate of traditional conceptions of readerly and writerly practice (not to mention a Romantic conception of the Imagination). On his return from Brittany, Roland begins to make lists of words, words that resist "arrangement into the sentences of literary criticism or theory" (467). He subsequently learns that Ash's artistic message is a crucial one: the "important thing" is "the language of poetry" (513). Roland's realization is accompanied by the narrator's self-conscious meditation on the intense pleasures of reading. Proclaiming the visceral nature of this involvement, the narrator invokes a readerly erotics of "acute sensuous alertness" (511). A variety of reading strategies is outlined—formalist, structuralist, subjective, and so on—but "impersonal readings" constitute the privileged form (512). T. S. Eliot is alive and well, it seems. Rereading Ash's poem, Roland experiences this impersonality, and the result is akin to that of a modernist epiphany. A deconstructionist, Roland has been trained in the theories of linguistic indeterminacy: "He had been taught that language was essentially inadequate, that it could never speak what was there, that it only spoke itself" (513). His altered interest is therefore an implicit indictment of the centrality of that post-structuralist tenet. It is also significantly focused on the death-mask image of the man who inspired it, Randolph Ash: "He could and could not say that the mask and the man were dead. *What had happened to him was that the ways in which it* could *be said had become more interesting than the idea that it could not"* (513; emphasis added). Roland's aesthetic narrative "reward," then, suggests the ideological component to Byatt's project: a rejection of criticism—or at least certain kinds of criticism—in favor of an outright celebration of the creative poetic sensibility, of the imagination, and, most important, of the "power and delight of words" (511).

A POSTMODERN SEDUCTION?

What then is Byatt's relationship to postmodernism, considering the modernist-inflected concerns that dominate the latter half of the novel? And is there not in that very question an unacknowledged criterion of postmodernist commitment? Undoubtedly there is. But it seems to me that postmodernist usage need not necessarily indicate a wholesale celebration of postmodernism per se. Of all the current theorizations of postmodernism, it is Hutcheon's that I find most compelling since it maintains a relational tension between aestheticism and ideological critique, an acknowledgment of the political impulse that unites aesthetic characteristics with worldly concerns. Moreover, although *The Politics of Postmodernism* does not broach the subject of self-referential critique, the logic of Hutcheon's argument for postmodernism's complicitous critique of dominant ideologies and narrative modes does suggest the possibility of a postmodernist challenge to postmodernism itself.[20]

I take Hutcheon's political impulse to mean a politics of *resistance. Possession*, however, is hardly a subversive text; indeed, its ideology is a heterosexual, humanist one. We *can* know everything, the novel seems to imply, but Byatt remains (coyly?) silent on the exact details of the purportedly lesbian nature of

Blanche Glover's relationship with Christabel LaMotte. Blanche is the one Victorian character whose story is *not* told. If Blackadder and Beatrice Nest are the protective, custodial "parents" of the Victorian poets, then Roland and Maud are the poets' heirs. Roland, however, becomes the aesthetic, creative heir to Randolph Ash, while Maud remains "merely" the biological heir to Christabel LaMotte. There is also, of course, the privileging of the romantic world of the Victorians, a priority that leads one reviewer to wonder "if there is not a repressed Byatt, more robustly reactionary than she knows, longing to burst out and declare that traditional country life is best, and the modern world is scruffy and smutty, and what a girl needs is a strong, handsome man to look after her."[21] I believe that Jenkyns is accurate in tone if not in content; I fail to see where, exactly, he finds a celebration of "country life" in the novel; the modern world is not smutty, but deprived of romance; and LaMotte's independent, feminist perspective is too sympathetically drawn to make of her a wilting romantic heroine. Nevertheless, *Possession* does reflect the ideology of the conventional romance narrative: Roland meets Maud, they court, kiss, make love, and presumably live happily ever after. But *is* Love the "suspect ideological construct" that Maud perceives it to be? Obviously not for Byatt, who makes it clear that Roland and Maud's romance is a productive, liberating affair.

No doubt the criticism could be leveled that I have offered an overly simplistic reading of postmodernism, but it is a critique that is in part enacted in this essay. Responding to reviewers' designations, I have attempted to outline those aspects of the novel that could be considered to be postmodernist. *Possession*'s postmodernism in one light, however, is its modernism in another; the construction is a critical, interpretative one rather than a given of the text. Perhaps, then, postmodernism is best considered as a style; there *are* discernible characteristics of postmodernism, but because those characteristics are historically non-specific— Sterne's *Tristram Shandy* is an example—postmodernism is a literary device rather than an inevitable product of postmodernity. If *Possession* is a postmodernist text, then it is one that is deeply suspicious of "postmodernism," whether it is construed as an aesthetic practice or as a historical condition. *Possession* may not celebrate the postmodern, but what it *does* do as a literary text is to seduce the reader into the consumption of Victorian poetry (or its simulacrum!). *Possession*, as both title and concept, quite literally describes the text's allure. Solicited by an initial suggestion of illicit love, the reader's attention is maintained by the lure of a soluble romantic mystery. *Possession* may not, *à la* Roland Barthes, shift bliss to the sumptuous ranks of the signifier, but on one level it does present something of an erotics of reading (albeit a heterosexually inflected one)—a readerly seduction that Barthes refers to as "the pleasure of the text."[22] Given Byatt's reference to the moderns' misery as the joke of the novel, hers is as tongue-in-cheek a contribution to the postmodernism debate as the Eco quotation with which I prefaced this essay: in an age of "false innocence" and mistrustful cynicism, Byatt has nevertheless succeeded "once again, in speaking of love."[23] Ultimately, I suspect that *Possession* will be denied access to the canon of postmodernist texts for the very reasons outlined: the novel offers modernist ideology in postmodernist guise. What is most interesting is that, at this historical moment, *Possession* is deemed to inhabit that category; it is an identification that only supports my belief that postmodernism is more of a constructed "reality" than a quantifiable materiality.

NOTES

1. Ann Hulbert, "The Great Ventriloquist," rev. of *Possession, New Republic* (7 Jan. 1991): 47.

2. Thomas D'Evelyn, "A Book About Books," rev. of *Possession, Christian Science Monitor* (16 Nov. 1990): 13.

3. Liz Heron, "Fiction," rev. of *Possession, Times Educational Supplement* (6 Apr. 1990): 26.

4. Judith Thurman, "A Reader's Companion," rev. of *Possession, New Yorker* (19 Nov. 1990): 151.

5. Despite the definitional debates surrounding the term, postmodern theorists will not disagree that postmodernism exhibits or embodies the following: parody, irony, self-reflexivity, indeterminacy, a refusal of traditional borders, and a self-conscious querying of subjectivity, "Truth," History, and totalizing narratives/knowledges.

6. Linda Hutcheon, *The Politics of Postmodernism* (London: Routledge, 1989) 47.

7. Roland has "never been much interested in Randolph Henry Ash's vanished body" (24), while Maud feels a positive discomfort at physical proximity to her distant ancestor: "I very rarely feel any curiosity about Christabel's life—it's funny—I even feel a sort of squeamishness about things she might have touched, or places she might have been—it's the *language* that matters, isn't it, it's what went on in her mind" (62). Of course, their cerebral responses are ironically telling in terms of subsequent events.

8. It is a view that is undermined by the scholars' discovery that Christabel's poetic landscape has a geographic rather than a metaphysical basis: *Melusina* is primarily influenced by Christabel's wanderings in Yorkshire over the period of her affair with Ash (289).

9. In this respect, it could also be argued that Byatt's generic inversion is, in fact, two-fold. As the narrative progresses, it appears that Ash and LaMotte—the supposed criminals—increasingly become the victims of the contemporary detectives' quest for the truth.

10. Eleanor Wachtel, interview with A. S. Byatt, *Writers and Company* (Toronto: Knopf, 1993) 81.

11. Nathaniel Hawthorne, preface, *The House of the Seven Gables: An Authoritative Text, Backgrounds and Sources, Essays in Criticism*, ed. Seymour L. Gross (New York: Norton, 1967) 1.

12. Robert Browning, "Mr Sludge, 'the Medium,'" *Dramatis Personae*, ed. F. B. Pinion (London: Collins, 1969) 158.

13. The combination of coy Harlequin-romance phrasing and an admittedly archaic usage leads one to suspect that Byatt's tone can only be tongue-in-cheek here. It is indeed ironically appropriate that, in a text so concerned with romance, this is the final—*and only*—use of *possession* in a sexual sense.

14. Byatt introduces a negative tenor to both these self-conceptions—an issue that I address in the latter half of this essay. Each self-construction bears the seeds of its deconstruction. Maud's textualized subjectivity is problematized by her subsequent musings on

materiality and history: "There was the question of the awkward body. The skin, the breath, the eyes, the hair, their history, which did seem to exist" (273); Roland's "learned" sense of self is something that he is content with. *Mostly.*

15. Even at this point, however, there is an implicit allusion to the Victorians' presence in the intertextual transposition of Charles Smithson from *The French Lieutenant's Woman.* When they arrive at the beach, there is a fossil-collecting young man "with a hammer and a sack busy chipping away at the rock-face" (292).

16. Wachtel 82–83.

17. Considering Hutcheon's identification of postmodernism as complicity with, and critique of, dominant ideologies and narrative modes (4), I wonder if she would characterize *Possession* as *doubly* metafictional? Does its complicity and critique of postmodernism itself make it *post*-postmodern?

18. It could be argued that this information is essential in establishing the partiality of the moderns' knowledge, and therefore is part of a postmodernist comment on the impossibility of (historical) Truth. But an undeniable (and paradoxical) consequence of this narrative necessity is that the truth is *not* withheld from the reader.

19. Wachtel 88.

20. Hutcheon 4.

21. Richard Jenkyns, "Disinterring Buried Lives," rev. of *Possession, Times Literary Supplement* (2 Mar. 1990): 214.

22. Roland Barthes, *The Pleasure of the Text*, trans. Richard Miller (New York: Hill, 1975).

23. Umberto Eco, *Postscript to The Name of the Rose*, trans. William Weaver (San Diego: Harcourt, 1984) 67–68.

Jean-Louis Chevalier

Conclusion in *Possession*

When one considers conclusions from a general aesthetic viewpoint, there is perhaps no apter phrase, no more telling text, than the Latin maxim, *Finis coronat opus*—the end crowns the work—which may be understood to mean that perfection is not attainable without completion.

Now, if one deals with conclusions from a moral angle, an assertion from the French fabulist immediately comes to mind, *En toutes choses il faut considérer la fin*, with its emphasis upon examination and reflection as prerequisites to action.

And if one looks into the uses of language for a suggestive approach to the word and idea of *conclusion*, and how these combine with other words and ideas in common usage, one finds English more vividly figurative, imaginative, and thought-provoking than French. Granted that it is possible, and indeed frequent in both languages, to *draw a conclusion*, to *come to a conclusion,* or to *reach a conclusion*—phrases that all imply an act of volition—it is only in English that volition proves dynamic and urgent enough to move one to *jump to a conclusion* without seeming worse than hasty. It may denote recklessness, it may be rash, overbold, and misleading in terms of the stern discipline of intellectual training and the rationale of careful thinking out—as a phrase, nonetheless, it connotes determination and resolve in the jumper, and a power of attraction, a magnetic pull, in that which has the jumper stake his all and jump. Conclusions are more compelling, and often dramatic, when it becomes conceivable to *jump* to them— all the more so as they are not only jumped to but also jumped with, so to speak, in English, in battles of words and ideas—as is expressed in another fine phrase, to *try to conclusions*, meaning to fight. This is done with friend or foe and is a noble or ignoble form of contest or disputation as the case may be, but one entailing triumph or defeat and, always, a measure of finality.

This is what I shall attempt, as a first move, a first double move, in a dubious battle with *Possession*, a work fraught with conclusions ceaselessly and urgently tried to by various drawers, comers, reachers, and jumpers, which will make me study *Possession* as a *consideration of ends and ending*. This will lead me to a view of the aesthetics of conclusion, and my third part will approach *Possession* as both a *crown* and a *coronation*.

Possession is the story of a *theft*, heralded in the verse epigraph of Chapter 1, where it is equated with *dispossession:* "Until the tricksy hero Herakles / Came to his dispossession and the theft" (*POa* 1), writes Randolph Henry Ash, the great English poet, in 1861. Now, Ash is both the subject of the nineteenth-century story and the object of the twentieth-century story in *Possession*, a two-storied *Romance*, which makes sense in various times and places but full sense only in the fullness of time and space, *sub specie aeternitatis—et poesis*. However, the perpetrator of the initial dispossession and theft in *Possession* is not Herakles, but a young scholar of 1986, Dr Roland Michell, who does not steal "the fruit of gold" from "the Hesperidean grove" as a set task (1), but two of Ash's manuscripts from the London Library, when he is "seized by a strange and uncharacteristic impulse of his own" (8). In other words, *Possession*, as a story, starts with the poet of a heroic dispossession and theft being made the *corpus delicti* of an unheroic theft and dispossession. In other words again, *Possession* is basically a story of words: a famous poem of stealth by a famous poet, and unknown manuscripts stolen by an unknown scholar, all amount to words of the self-same poet, words public and words private, words poetic and domestic, or not quite domestic, not homely, but comely, attentive, assiduous, and seductive.

What do words mean? What do they wish to mean? What do they mean without wishing? And how to read them? These are the questions at the back of Roland's mind when he goes to the London Library "looking for sources for Ash's *Garden of Proserpina*" in "Ash's own copy of Vico's *Principj di una Scienza Nuova*" and discovers "leaf after leaf" of notes in Ash's own hand (2), which seem to have escaped the notice of all Ash specialists, and very numerous they are throughout the world. Among Ash's papers are two draughts of the same letter to an unknown lady: "Dear Madam, / Since our extraordinary conversation I have thought of nothing else. . . . Did you not find it as strange as I did, that we should so immediately understand each other so well? . . . I am sure you understand" (5–6). Whereupon the demon of conclusion pounces upon Roland, author of a doctoral dissertation on the "Presentation of Historical 'Evidence' in the Poems of Randolph Henry Ash" (9), and a very good "old-fashioned textual critic, not a biographer" (50):

Roland was first profoundly shocked by these writings, and then, in his scholarly capacity, thrilled. His mind busied itself automatically with dating and placing this unachieved dialogue with an unidentified woman. . . . He had no idea who she might be. Christina Rossetti? He thought not. . . . Had the correspondence continued? If it had, where was it, what jewels of information about Ash's "ignored, arcane, deviously perspicuous meanings" might not be revealed by it? Scholarship might have to reassess all sorts of certainties. On the other hand, had the correspondence ever in fact started? Or had Ash finally floundered in his inability to express his sense of urgency? It was this urgency above all that moved and shocked Roland. . . . He read the letters again. (6–8)

Roland had come into the London Library an honest man in search of erudite sources, and ironically he leaves stricken with conclusion-seeking. The passion is not uncommon among scholars, most of whom may be said to thrive on conclusion-seeking, indiscriminatingly if innocuously more often than not, but not criminally as a rule. This aspect of the disease will be dealt with later. What should engage our attention for the time being is Roland's self-explanation for his act.

On the one hand, the pilfered letters obviously mean "an amazing discovery . . . a solid discovery" (19) and "he must try to find out" who the lady was (21). The investigation must be made for the sake of scholarship—although not his special branch of scholarship, for "What Roland liked was his knowledge of the movements of Ash's mind, stalked through the twists and turns of his syntax, suddenly sharp and clear in an unexpected epithet" (20)—and also for the solace of self-esteem, because "he saw himself as a failure and felt vaguely responsible for this" (11).

But those are only external, academic reasons, easy to draw, to come to, to reach, and even to jump to, and they have mainly to do with Roland's conception of his job and his image of himself in his job. The more profound ones, those we have to try to, concern the letters themselves in so far as they are "Urgent, unfinished. Shocking. . . . these dead letters troubled him, physically even, because they were only beginnings" (20–21)—an explanation that is taken up again when Roland finds someone with whom to share his secret:

"I see," she said. "They're alive."
  "They don't have ends."
  "No. They're beginnings." (56)

This is the true incentive, and Roland pinched the letters "Because they were alive. They seemed *urgent*—I felt I had to do something. It was an impulse. Quick as a flash. . . . I don't think they're *mine*, or anything. . . . They seemed private. I'm not explaining very well. . . . It was something *personal*. . . . I wanted them to be a secret. Private. And do the work" (50). To "do the work" is to conclude, and the whole of *Possession* is both its trying and trial, often called, at first, in an exorcising way, "a wild goose chase" by the two people who undertake it. For Roland does not "do the work" single-handedly. He is soon joined in the venture by Dr Maud Bailey, another scholar of distinction, whose academic attainments complete his own, bringing their partnership to full strength, after Roland has discovered that the addressee, if not the recipient, of Ash's letters may have been Christabel LaMotte, another poet, who is to Maud what Ash is to him:

"I knew one little poem by her [Christabel LaMotte] when I was very small, and it became a kind of touchstone. . . . I just liked the rhythm. Anyway, when I started my work on thresholds it came back to me and so did she." . . . .

He hesitated. "They [Ash's poems] were what stayed alive, when I'd been taught and examined everything else."

Maud smiled then. "Exactly. That's it. What could survive our education." (53–55)

The whys and the hows of the conclusion–quest require full attention. To Roland and to Maud, the works of Randolph Henry Ash and of Christabel LaMotte have always been alive. Similarly. Specifically. Unrelatedly. Once and for all, Roland has made Ash his poet, and Maud has made Christabel hers—or, more truly, Ash has made Roland his student, and Christabel has made Maud hers. There has been in each case an act of recognition, followed by an act of foundation, which may be what vocation means—a sense and certainty of fitness—or else election—a sense and certainty of choice. And so Roland worked on "evidence" in the works of Ash, while Maud worked on "liminality" in the works of LaMotte, each in his or her own sphere. They did not know each other, nor did they know of one another. And while Roland had never read a line or even heard of LaMotte, a so-called minor poet, Maud, who could hardly ignore Ash, the greatest Victorian poet, rejected his works on account of "All that cosmic masculinity. . . . All that ponderous obfuscation. Everything she [Christabel] wasn't" (42).

Now they come upon an unfinished and perhaps never sent letter in which Ash tells a woman how well she understands his poetry, and they have some ground to assume that the woman may have been Christabel. This they immediately turn into a hypothesis, that is to say a supposition made as a basis for reasoning and a starting-point for investigation. And in fact they do reason and investigate, because it is their speciality as textual critics to bring out the meaning of a text when they find one; and because they have a personal interest, Roland in Evidence and Maud in Thresholds. These are intellectual inducements. But Roland and Maud also reason and investigate because "beginnings" are "alive," or, what amounts to the same thing, "beginnings" must have "ends" or be abortions; and because the letters are "urgent" and they themselves are "shocked" by that very urgency, and avowedly moved by its appeal. Emotion works on them as by magic, and backs up and promotes intellectual eagerness, till they can no longer tell the one from the other, nor separate themselves from an apparently endless quest in which every arduously obtained answer involves further interrogation. This is their primrose conclusion path from dispossession to possession.

One cannot enter, for lack of time, into the details of their extensive chase, which has to be performed cautiously, on account of many academics and institutions having official, hierarchical, and rival interests in the matter, and of their detaining and controlling most of the material that must be re-examined for still unrecognised but now telling proofs. But the chase also has to be carried out in the open, more or less, whenever laymen outside academe must be approached for the material they may own, or do own, without realising how important it may be, or actually is. Accessible and inaccessible documents alike are to be inspected without their keepers and trustees suspecting exactly the reason why Roland and Maud are attracted to them, which is no easy task, seeing how inquisitive, intuitive, and possessive they all are. Hence the elaboration of tactics of gradual insinuation or surprise incursion, and a dissimulation of real interest and evasion of direct questions.

Let us take the one example of Ash's wife's journal, which may offer hidden clues to a percipient investigator as to the very existence and nature of the relationship between Ash and Miss LaMotte. These diaries should have been edited years ago by Dr Beatrice Nest, in whose hands they are still placed. Roland knows her very well, Maud does not, in consequence of which they devise different techniques of approach. Roland uses a direct approach: "I've come up against something—I wondered if you could help. Do you happen to know if Ellen Ash says anything anywhere about Christabel LaMotte?" (117). But he has to prevaricate when asked a direct question: "'Just anything really. . . . I just wondered. . . . I don't know. . . . Do you think I could *see* what she said? It might be—' he rejected 'important'—'it might be of interest to me. I've never read *Melusina*. There seems to be a revival of interest in it'" (117–18). And when Professor Cropper, the hated American rival of Roland's despotic chief, Professor Blackadder, turns up at the wrong moment and cross-examines him, Roland's denegations sound very feeble, while Beatrice Nest innocently betrays him:

"Glad to see you, Michell. Making progress? What did you want to know?"
  His clearcut face was composed of pure curiosity.
  "Just checking on Ash's reading of some poems."
  "Ah yes. Which poems?"
  "Roland was enquiring about Christabel LaMotte. I couldn't remember anything . . . but there turned out to be a minor reference . . ." . . .
  "Christabel LaMotte," said Cropper, musing. . . . "Was Ash, do you think, interested in her?"
  "Only very marginally. I'm just checking. Routinely." (119–20)

Maud, on the other hand, opts for obliqueness: "Maud had constructed a sort of questionnaire about Victorian wives, under headings, and worked her way slowly round to the question, which did interest her, of the nature of the reason for Ellen's writing" (219)—and when, after a lot of quibbling, she finds important documents that have inexplicably escaped destruction 120 years ago, and the attention of her fellow scholars for several decades, she has again to resort to dissembling:

Maud closed her face and dropped her eyelids on what must be a glitter of pouncing. She said, trying to make her voice indifferent, "This looks like it. Any more? This looks like the *second* letter she mentions. Is the first one there?" . . . .

Maud sat, holding this sheet of paper, in an agony of indecision. What Evidence had Ellen kept? And of what? . . . How could she make copies of precisely *these* documents without alerting Beatrice, and with Beatrice, surely, Cropper and Blackadder? A kind of imperious will in her tapped at her like a hammer, and was interrupted in its coding of a cunning request by Beatrice's woolly voice.

"I don't know what you're up to, Dr Bailey. I don't know if I want to know. You came looking for something and you found it."

"Yes," said Maud in a whisper. . . . "It isn't only my secret," Maud hissed. "Or I wouldn't have been disingenuous. I—I don't know *what* I've found, yet. I promise I'll tell you first when I do. I think I know what Blanche Glover told her. Well, one of two or three things it might have been." (233–34)

Maud is here telling the truth, because the existence of the secret has been detected intuitively in spite of her, but all the same she is not telling what the truth is. She admits she is trying to construct a conclusion, but she will not disclose a conclusion to what. A few moments later, when challenged by Dr Fergus Wolff, the most brilliant scholar of the day and her former lover, she denies both his charge and her truth:

"Don't be like that, Maud. I want to talk to you. I'm suffering terribly in equal amounts of curiosity and jealousy. I can't *believe* you've got involved with sweet useless Roland and I can't *understand* what you're doing haunting the Crematorium here, unless you have. . . . Tell me what's going on at least, go on, do. If you tell me I'll be fearfully discreet."

"There's nothing to tell."

"And if you don't tell me, I shall find out, and consider what I find out to be my own property, Maud." (235–36)

It is fascinating to realise how, in the world of research and scholarship, everyone is on the watch for everyone else's movements, and every movement is not only supposed to be a secret but is suspected of being the secret possession of something leading to a conclusion. Degrees and expressions of curiosity vary according to the sense of decency and the gifts of strategy of each individual, but these people are all curious. They are all incessantly trying to conclusions with one another and, over and above everything, trying to conclusions about conclusions.

So act Roland and Maud with all scholars externally, and internally with all texts—all the published works of the two poets; all their unpublished texts; all the published works and unpublished texts of their relations, friends, and acquaintances—dramatically making out their case and more than their case, finding out more than they had bargained for, becoming at once the architects and the sports of their fortune, which is felt to be no longer their own, but the very fortune of conclusion. For poets do not use words for poetry only, and to try to conclusions with their texts, works, and miscellaneous writings is conducive to conclusions that are not exclusively literary.

Poems, however, whose language is essentially a language of clues, are especially rich with dormant conclusions, waiting for someone to perceive them, decode them, and set them free to disclose their secrets. "The Glass Coffin," one of Christabel LaMotte's *Tales for Innocents*, may be read as a metaphoric exemplar of this. It tells the story of "a little tailor" who is given the choice of "three things" (59) and chooses a "little glass key, . . . because he did not have any idea about what it was or might do, and curiosity is a great power in men's lives"; he is then told that it is "the key to an adventure, if [he] will go in search of it" (60), which he does, eventually discovering a Sleeping Beauty imprisoned in "a glass coffin," immediately knowing "that the true adventure was the release of this sleeper, who would then be his grateful bride" (63), delivering her from the spell with the key, and marrying her after having also delivered her brother, her castle, her servants, her gardens, her woods, and her horses. Like the glass coffin, a poem is the repository of enchanted beauty, of encoded truth, ever ready to be read, revived, and restored to its full conclusive power.

This is what happens, literally, when Maud, on seeing "a sudden row of staring tiny white faces, one, two, three, propped against a pillow . . . in a substantial if miniature four-poster bed" in what used to be Christabel's room, exclaims: "Oh, the *dolls*— . . . She wrote a series of poems about the dolls. . . . They were ostensibly for children, like the *Tales for Innocents*. But not really" (81). And she recites:

> Dolly keeps a Secret
> Safer than a Friend
>
> . . . .
> Dolly ever sleepless
> Watches above
> The shreds and relics
> Of our lost Love
>
> (82–83)

—which inspires her to act on the very suggestion of the poem, to search the dolls' bed, and to discover in a "wooden box" under several mattresses a "package" containing the whole correspondence between Ash and Christabel (84).

This is also what happens when Roland thinks of "going through the poems— his and hers—written about then—with the idea that they might reveal something. . . . One might find a cumulative series of such coincidences." And he recites from a poem by Ash:

> We drank deep of the Fountain of Vaucluse
> And where the northern Force incessantly
> Stirs the still pool, were stirred. And shall those founts
> Which freely flowed to meet our thirsts, be sealed?

Maud said, "Say that again."

Roland said it again.

Maud said, "Have you ever really felt your hackles rise? Because I just have. Prickles all down my spine and at the roots of my hair. You listen to this. . . .

> Ah, Melusine, I have betrayed your faith.
> Is there no remedy? Must we two part?
> Shall our hearth's ash grow pale, and shall those founts
> Which freely flowed to meet our thirsts, be sealed?"

Roland said, "Shall our hearth's *ash* grow pale. . . . Which came first? His line or her line? . . . It reads like a classic literary clue. She was a clever and hinting sort of woman. Look at those dolls."

"Literary critics make natural detectives," said Maud. . . .

"I thought you were mad. . . . Now I feel the same. It isn't professional greed. It's something more primitive."

"Narrative curiosity—"

"Partly." (237–38)

There is little need to comment on a text that does its own textual commentary so neatly, except to emphasise that when Roland and Maud make their double discovery—identical lines that have been in print for over a century, for everybody to notice and elaborate upon them—and an *ash* image to introduce them, not in the poem of Ash, whose favourite idiosyncrasy it was to insert such images (of the tree, and of the powdery residue after combustion) in his own poetry as a kind of hallmark, but in the poem of Christabel—they may be said to act according to the full basic meaning of "to discover"—to take the cover off (this is the White Queen's "lovely riddle—all in poetry—all about fishes: Which is easiest to do, / Undish-cover the fish, or dishcover the riddle?"), and of "to invent"—to come in, to find. They do not create sense, they revive it by simply seeing it.

Simply may sound the wrong word and yet be the right notion. To conclude is as simple as that. The prolegomena are involved and perplexing: the conclusion is evident—self-evident. Moreover, Ash and Christabel must have wanted it to be so, otherwise they would not have interwoven their poems with such guidelines, so to speak, such directions for use, such echoing evidence of a common story. For there are other intertextual and extratextual elements to prove that it was not just a literary game for their own amusement.

From that angle, what has been called a trying of conclusions as far as Roland and Maud are concerned may be interpreted as a trial of conclusions as regards Ash and Christabel. In the sense that they have intentionally left scattered about their poems a common body of evidence, awaiting reconstruction and trial. And in the sense that their common story can be read as an attempt to construct and try conclusions together, if not a common conclusion.

Naturally enough, their story begins under the auspices of poetry. They not only admire each other's poems, but they enjoy discussing poetry in general, each other's aims and inspiring principles, each other's projects and work in progress, as they both have the philosophical mind and a profound sense of the moral consequence of an artist's commitment. It cannot be pure chance, but rather what Christabel, in "The Threshold"—a tale about the impossibility "to live free of fate"—defines as "the power of necessity in tales" (155), which means that, when they first meet, Christabel, a poet of short lyrics, is already trying her hand at "an epic, . . . a Saga or Lay or great mythical Poem" (161), the mode of expression that has made Ash famous, while Ash is writing "a long poem, . . . a dramatized monologue" (158) about Swammerdam, the seventeenth-century Dutch naturalist who studied insects, and Christabel's most admired poems are of "Insect life" (158). There is more than one conclusion to be instinctively and reflectively drawn by them from such a happy conjunction of circumstances, a "beginning" that is rendered more "urgent" by mutual attraction, and more dramatic by various material and moral obstacles: Ash is married, Christabel has a passionate guardian friend, Blanche Glover; Ash is an extrovert, very much in the public eye, Christabel is an introvert and a recluse. And they agree that truth must be law between them. "I want from you not illusion but truth," writes Ash in his second letter (158–59). "One must keep truth," agrees Christabel in her answer (159).

Being spiritual moralists, their first common attempt at truth concerns the truth of "the Christian religion"—"so central a truth," as Christabel puts it, declaring Ash's epic poem, *Ragnarök*, to have been "the occasion of quite the worst crisis in the life of my religious faith" (160), while he explains he "meant it rather as a reassertion of the Universal Truth of the living presence of Allfather (under whatever Name) and of the hope of Resurrection from whatever whelming disaster in whatever form. . . . And then there is the whole question of what kind of Truth may be conveyed in a wonder-tale, as you rightly named it" (163–65).

Their metaphysical and literary debate will not be related in detail, since it is not the particular object of the present study, but one must bear in mind nevertheless that the first trial they join in is a search for what seems to them to be the supreme conclusion—about which Ash writes:

I do not know why—or how—but I do know wholeheartedly that it *is so*—so I cannot prevaricate with you, and worse, cannot leave decently undiscussed matters of such import. . . . And if I tell you what views I do hold—what will you think of me? Will you continue to communicate your thoughts to me? I do not know—I only know that I am under some compulsion of truthfulness. (164)

Their second trial considers "the well-attested Phenomena of Second Sight—the gift of pre-Vision, or foretelling or prophecy "(166)—"Spiritual Manifestations" (169)—"Paracelsus, who tells us that there are minor spirits doomed to inhabit the regions of the air . . . and whom we might, from time to time, exceptionally, hear or see" (171)—"the Fairy Mélusine . . . [and] the *Dames Blanches*" (173)—and many other similar subjects, which they take up again, matured, sharpened, and perfected, in their respective poems. This again cannot be related in detail, but it must be noted how their letters, once they have been discovered at the bottom of the dolls' bed and eventually read by Roland and Maud, confirm and amplify all the conjectures their textual criticism of the poems had led them to form about an essential exchange of ideas, and of more than ideas, between the two poets.

On the nature of that exchange, Ash writes:

What can I say? I have never before been tempted to discuss the *intricacies* of my own writing—or his own—with any other poet—I have always gone on in a solitary and self-sufficient way—but with *you* I felt from the first that it must be true things or nothing—there was no middle way. So I speak to you—or not speak, *write* to you, write written speech—a strange mixture of kinds—I speak to you as I might speak to all those who most possess my thoughts—to Shakespeare, to Thomas Browne, to John Donne, to John Keats—and find myself unpardonably lending *you*, who are alive, my voice, as I habitually lend it to those dead men—Which is much as to say—here is an author of Monologues—trying clumsily to construct a Dialogue— and encroaching on both halves of it. Forgive me.

Now if this were a true dialogue—but *that* is entirely as you may wish it to be. (177)

"Have you truly Weighed—what you ask of me?" answers Christabel (178). He has indeed, and he starts calling her "My dear Friend," instead of "Dear Miss LaMotte" and telling her about "obscurely *untouchable* things" (181–82). Their relations have entered a new phase, and she would put a stop to them altogether, because she dreads public conclusions—"the world would not look well upon such letters" (184). But he insists, and, although she explains that "the—*precious*—letters—are too much and too little—and above all and first, I should say, compromising" (186), she agrees, because "the Letters we have written are with me such an Addiction." So they go on writing to each other, but, as Christabel puts it, "the Threat is *there*" (187), the threat of another conclusion.

Trying to conclusions about that particular conclusion is what Ash now does:

You may well ask why I am so tenacious in continuing writing to one who has declared herself unable to maintain a friendship (which she also declared so valuable to herself) and remains resolute in silence, in rejection. A lover might indeed in all honour accept such a *congé*—but a peaceable, a valued friend? . . .

And why am I so tenacious? I hardly know myself. . . . I see that I had insensibly come to perceive you—mock not—as some sort of *Muse*. (188)

From "Friend" to "Muse"—and then from "Muse" to "Love"—this again is "the power of necessity in tales," in Romances, and in life:

I have called you my Muse, and so you are, or might be, a messenger from some urgent place of the spirit where essential poetry sings and sings. I could call you, with even greater truth—my Love—there, it is said—for I most certainly love you and *in all ways possible to man* and most fiercely. . . . We are rational nineteenth-century beings, we might leave the *coup de foudre* to the weavers of Romances. . . .

And now, I write to ask, what are we to do? How shall this be the end, that is in its very nature a *beginning?* (193)

Of the love-story proper let it be sufficient to say that it is short-lived by mutual consent; life-long in its sentimental and moral consequences; destructive in so far as Blanche Glover kills herself, and something dies in Ellen Ash's heart, and Christabel's existence is permanently altered; constructive, because it inspires many poems one way or another; productive, as a child is born; and ultimately destined to immortality.

It is also the occasion for the lovers to come to essential conclusions about each other, their own selves, and the nature of love—during the brief period when they felt love, and made love, and love made them, and they "heard each other's thoughts" (last, unsent letter from Ash to Christabel, several years later; 456), and they "loved each other—*for* each other" (last letter from Christabel to Ash, unread by him, twenty-eight years later; 502)—and during the long period when love had unmade them and they could only hope to give each other "blessing" and "forgiveness" (500), and yet Christabel could still write to Ash on his death-bed: "I would rather have lived alone, *so*, if you would have the truth. But since that might not be—and is granted to almost none—I thank God for you—if there *must* be a Dragon—that He was You—" (503).

But this love-story is also that of the opposition, or apposition, of "possession" with "self-possession" (502), and that of the juncture of false conclusions with real facts, the truth about the child having been falsified, and "Most of what they shared, after all, after all was done, was silence. 'It was all a question of silence'"(449)— Ellen Ash's ultimate summing up of her married life at her husband's death, also suitable to his unmarried life with Christabel, poetry excepted.

En toutes choses il faut considérer la fin. This moral imperative is insufficiently and/or inadequately considered by the nineteenth-century lovers and the twentieth-century scholars, even though passion and possession do not admit of moderation.

The case of the love-child is the most palpable one, and yet, like all the others, it has its own acceptable explanations, in the universe of romance and in the world of facts. That the moral law has nevertheless been transgressed is obvious, not from any condemnatory vituperation, but from the fact that the contravention itself allows only of false conclusion, impasse, and uncompleted ending, which the world of facts will assimilate, but not the universe of romance, over which morality has a much more powerful ascendancy.

Having told neither Ash nor Blanche that she is with child, Christabel seeks refuge with her Kercoz cousins in Brittany and, at the end of her pregnancy, leaves for a convent "where the Bishop has made provision for the care of cast-out and fallen women" (376). She comes back to her cousins without a child and says, "Do not ask, I beg you. . . . Please ask *nothing*" (377–78). And nothing more about it is ever said by her for twenty-eight years. What is there to conclude? Some time later, Ash suspects something and follows her to Brittany, to be told that she has indeed had a child and nothing more about it has ever been known. So he knows. But he does not know what to know. What is there to conclude? Until one day, at a séance that he attends for the sole purpose of meeting her, he calls out "in an uncontrolled and frantic manner, 'Where is the child? Tell me what they have done with the child?'"(397), and she cries, "you have made a murderess of me" (500). What is there to conclude? Will Ash ever know more? On hearing that he is dying, Christabel writes to tell him the truth and never knows for the rest of her life whether or not he died knowing what conclusion there was to know.

This is more or less the position of the twentieth-century scholars, who have collected about the same amount of information when their separate quests are nearing the same uncompleted end and they finally join forces, all of them, or almost all of them, in view of a common conclusion. In the meantime, professional crimes and moral misdemeanours have been committed by many of them, all in the interest of textual passion and possession. Technically, those offences are of two kinds, against the dead and against the living, but inextricably entangled as to the facts.

An outsider—Sir George Bailey, the present owner of Seal Court, where Christabel died and the correspondence was found—and a non-runner, Dr Beatrice Nest, the editress of Ellen Ash's diaries—had given similar warnings as to the moral consequences of conclusion-seeking: "For one thing, I believe in letting dead bones lie still. Why stir up scandals about our silly fairy poetess? Poor old thing, let her sleep decently," says Sir George (86). "This—what you're so excited about—it won't—it won't expose her [Ellen Ash] to ridicule—or—or misapprehension? I've become very concerned that she shouldn't be—exposed is the best word I suppose—*exposed*," says Beatrice (235). And Roland answers Sir George: "We aren't *looking* for scandals. . . . I don't suppose there is any scandal," while Maud answers Beatrice: "It isn't primarily to do with her." "That is not necessarily reassuring," Beatrice concludes, a prophetess *malgré soi* and the one to sound the alarm when she overhears that Mortimer Cropper, the hateful American Ash scholar, and Hildebrand Ash, son and heir to the present Lord Ash, have decided to dig up Ash's tomb in search of an iron box containing the conclusion to all intermediate conclusions.

This, of course, is illegal without a Faculty of the Bishop, but Beatrice is the only one to wish to prevent the outrage. All that the now beleaguered scholars want is to prevent Cropper from running away with the booty. They all find very good reasons for letting the nasty fellow do the dirty work and then for benefiting from it jointly and severally. There is the reason of the controverted legal ownership of the documents in the casket. There is the reason of not allowing them out of England. There is the reason of their huge commercial value. There is the reason of their immense literary value. There is the reason of the editing work to be done. There is the reason of a donation instead of a public sale. There is the reason of Ellen Ash not having destroyed whatever she deposited in the box but saved it from immediate rummaging and poking, preserved it for indefinite discoverers in an indefinite future, and recorded the fact in her diary, like Christabel LaMotte trusting the correspondence to a hiding-place and a mysterious tell-tale poem. There is the reason of consuming curiosity. There is the reason of a real end, a final end, being needed to justify the various means employed to win. There is the reason of the proximity of a conclusion. There is the reason of the actual topsyturvification of lives that can but remain *sens dessus dessous* as long as the hurly-burly's *not* done, for their own sake as much as for that of textual criticism.

These last personal reasons are not voiced so clearly as the first general ones, but they are no less urgent. What Roland and Maud had not considered was that their joint conclusion chase would ultimately round on them, and their lives, like the poems of Ash and Christabel, would become texts they could no longer construe word by word, nor read line by line, outside a dual theme, a parallel purpose, and a common fate, *en toutes choses*: romance is romance is romance . . .

Romance *coronat opus*. But not romance alone. In *Possession*, the art of resolution is glorious in all of its numerous meanings, including the dramatic sense of unravelling complications and reaching a final solution, the musical sense of making discord pass into concord, the psychological sense of boldness and firmness of purpose, and so forth.

Not counting a delightful, prophetic conceit—

"And all's well that ends well," said Euan. "This feels like the ending of a Shakespearean comedy—who's the chappie that comes down on a swing at the end of *As You Like It*?"

"Hymen," said Blackadder, smiling slightly. (482–83)

—I have found six moments of a crowning nature—or contributing to the making of the crowning framework—no doubt there are a few more—before the actual coronation of an epilogue. These are: Ash's death; Roland's solitary return to his Putney flat; the scholars' conference about the buried iron box; the digging up of the box in the churchyard; the reading of the contents of the box; and Roland and Maud's love-making.

I do not mean to scrutinise the chapter of Ash's death in 1889—Chapter 25—but only to note how, in answering certain questions in a pre-concluding way, it puts forth new questions that precipitate the events of the chase and allows the reader of *Possession*, if not to share the narrator's omniscience, at least and at last to know more than the scholar-characters, and so partly to dissociate himself from them for the finale. This is achieved in a symphonic way by using all sorts of sources that the scholars may already know, or will eventually know, or will in fact never know, as the case may be. Ellen Ash's journal, unpublished but accessible. Cropper's biography of Ash, published. A letter of Christabel to Ellen, which she cannot bring herself to answer. An old unfinished letter of Ash to Christabel, which Ellen reads and burns. A very old love letter of Ash to Ellen, which she re-reads and puts into the box. A sealed letter of Christabel to Ash, which she also puts into the box, unread. And Ellen's memories and thoughts, which do not give the same view as her journal, where they are either entirely suppressed or only half silenced. Structurally and thematically, the end of Ash's life thus marks the start of the great all-embracing, all-concluding final movement of the quest, the narrative, and the tale.

In 1987, when Roland, in Chapter 26, comes back to the flat in Putney where he had lived for years with his girl-friend Val—from whom he has become totally estranged during his conclusion quest—he feels that, as far as he is concerned, he is "marginal," and that there are "a great many circles"—those of the legal ownership of Ash and Christabel's letters—"all of which he [is] outside" (437–38). The research he and Maud had kept secret now being public, "their own strange silent games" cannot "survive in the open," and he must "think a few things out" (440–41). He finds the flat empty and letters offering him jobs in Hong Kong, Amsterdam, and Barcelona. "The world opened" (468), but it is a world without Maud, and "He thought of Randolph Henry Ash. The pursuit of the letters had distanced him from Ash as they had come closer to Ash's life. In the days of his innocence Roland had been, not a hunter but a reader. . . . Roland's find had turned out to be a sort of loss. . . . He took down his Ash from the shelf, sat at his desk, and read" (469–70).

The poem he reads is given in the epigraph. It is *The Garden of Proserpina*:

> Since riddles are the order of our day
> Come here, my love, and I will tell thee one.
>
> There is a place to which all Poets come
> Some having sought it long, some unawares,
> Some having battled monsters, some asleep
> Who chance upon the path in thickest dream,
> Some lost in mythy mazes, some direct
> From fear of death, or lust of life or thought
> And some who lost themselves in Arcady . . .
>
>   (463)

Roland's reading is an epiphany. I cannot quote in full nor sum up in a few words the four pages describing his experience "that we the readers, knew it [the text] was always there, and have *always known* it was as it was, though we have now for the first time recognised, become fully cognisant of, our knowledge" (472)— nor the two pages in which he turns from reading Ash's poem to writing poems of his own for the first time in his life: "He had time to feel the strangeness of before and after; an hour ago there had been no poems, and now they came like rain and were real" (475). But everyone will perceive how fine an end, if not a conclusion, this double epiphany might have been. Roland is, after all, the "modern hero" of the contemporary story in *Possession*, the initial thief and dispossessor carried away in a plot where his intellectual, professional, and social betters use him, then defeat him, and finally dismiss or forget him. But he finds himself possessed of two inalienable recompenses. He can read poetry. He can write poetry. This would make a very satisfying end to a "modern" novel.

But *Possession* is not modern in that sense, and, before it comes to its *Romance* conclusion, there is still the "detective story" to be tackled, "the unmasking at the end" rendered all the more necessary by the introduction of a "villain, . . . capable of grave robbery" (483). The conference of the scholars in Chapter 26, which I have already mentioned, turns into a conference of confederate "spies" (485), looking upon themselves as justicers for a profusion of valid reasons. This, of course, starts the quarry again. Who would not wish to be in at the finish?

Chapter 28, however, does not offer direct termination. There is first a Gothic churchyard scene, complete with night and moonlight, crime and conspiracy, a smoking fire, "a huge white owl" and a "creaking" weathercock "in the shape of a flying dragon," and a wind "getting up," which soon becomes "a creature from another dimension, trapped and screaming," while "trees crash all around" (487–95).

There is then a farcical scene of the villains and captors sitting together in a room at an inn after they have escaped from the dangers of the storm, sharing "the sense of communal survival," drinking "coffee and hot milk—and . . . brandy, . . . stupidly good, smiling weakly, damp and chill," dressed in a variety of pyjamas that are not even their own, unable to "find force to be angry or even indignant" (497).

There is the scene of the opening of the box, the reading of the letter and its confessions, confirmations, and conclusions, leading to fresh revelations: "So, in that hotel room, to that strange gathering of disparate seekers and hunters, Christabel LaMotte's letter to Randolph Ash was read aloud, by candlelight, with the wind howling past, and the panes of the windows rattling with the little blows of flying debris as it raced on and on, over the downs" (499).

It is to be remembered that it is a letter that Ash never read, his wife, under whose cover it had been sent, having kept it for one month before he died and then put it unread into the box that was buried with him. It is a very long letter, which confesses to Ash and confirms to the scholars the existence of a child, a girl who never read tales or poetry "for pleasure, . . . Maia (who will have nothing of her 'strange name' and is called plain May, which becomes her)," and who is now "a Squire's wife and comely," and the mother of a boy who "chants verses to the amazement of his stable- and furrow-besotted parents. . . . He is a strong boy, and *will live*" (500–3). The revelation is that the girl was brought up as the daughter of Christabel's sister, Sophie, Lady Bailey, and so was Maud's great-great-great grandmother:

"How strange for you, Maud, to turn out to be descended from both—how strangely appropriate to have been exploring all along the myth—no the truth—of your own origins."
Everyone looked at Maud. (503)

Everyone will perceive again how fine an end, if not a conclusion with a dual epiphany, this might have been. Maud has been, after all, the "modern heroine" of the contemporary story in *Possession* and is ultimately revealed to be the offspring and inheritress of the two poets of the other story, thus making the two stories into one.

But this is a romance, and, just as the two stories have miraculously blended into one, the two possible endings with either Roland or Maud as the central figure must now blend into one conclusion, and a conclusion that is also—"such is the power of necessity in tales"—a *possession*. I should have said long ago that Roland is a craftsman like the little tailor with the glass key, that Maud's hair is blond and long like that of the Sleeping Beauty in the glass coffin, and that for months they have been feeling a mutual attraction that was not wholly textual— so that the conclusion scene must be a love scene.

It begins:

He stroked her wet hair, gently, absently.
    Maud said, "What next?"
    "How do you mean, what next?"
    "What happens next? To us?" (505)

It ends:

Roland finally, to use an outdated phrase, entered and took possession of all her white coolness that grew warm against him, so that there seemed to be no boundaries. . . .
    In the morning, the whole world had a strange new smell. It was the smell of the aftermath, a green smell, a smell of shredded leaves and oozing resin, of crushed wood and splashed sap, a tart smell, which bore some relation to the smell of bitten apples. It was the smell of death and destruction and it smelled fresh and lively and hopeful. (507)

Everyone will perceive how fine an end this is. Love *coronat opus*! Romance *coronat opus*! *Finis coronat opus*! But the coronation is still to come.

In her letter, Christabel had written: "You will think—if the *shock* of what I have had to tell you has left you any power to care or to think about my narrow world—that a *romancer* such as I (or a true dramatist, such as you) would not be able to keep such a secret for nigh on thirty years (think, Randolph, thirty years), without bringing about some *peripeteia*, some *dénouement*, some secret hinting or open scene of revelation" (501). This is exactly what the narrator sets out to do, as a "romancer" and a "true dramatist," in an epilogue whose title is *Post-*

script 1868, and which starts: "There are things which happen and leave no discernable trace, are not spoken or written of, though it would be very wrong to say that subsequent events go on indifferently, all the same, as though such things had never been" (508).

Such a thing is the meeting of Ash with a small girl who tells him her name is May, or Maia: to whom he says that she has "a true look of [her] mother" and "a look of [her] father too": for whom he makes a daisy chain—"a crown": to whom he recites a few lines from a poem: and to whom he says:

"Tell your aunt . . . that you met a poet, who was looking for the Belle Dame Sans Merci, and who met you instead, and who sends her his compliments, and will not disturb her." . . .
    "I'll try to remember," she said, steadying her crown.
    So he kissed her, always matter-of-fact, so as not to frighten her. . . .
    And on the way home, she met her brothers, and there was a rough-and-tumble, and the lovely crown was broken, and she forgot the message, which was never delivered. (510–11)

So Ash knew all along. And nobody knew it. But it is told us, outside the narrative, yet at the very heart of the story. Is this, in 1868, not 1889, not 1987—*the* conclusion, smelling "fresh and lively and hopeful," like the love story, and no less romantic?

In "Sugar," A. S. Byatt says: "I select and confect" (*S* 241). In a *Nouvelle* of Louis XI, quoted by Littré, somebody says: "*Vos semblans et decevantes paroles m'ont conclue et rendue en vostre obeissance.*" Such is the power of necessity in tales. Such is the power of conclusion in *Possession*.

Annegret Maack

Wonder-Tales Hiding a Truth: Retelling Tales in "The Djinn in the Nightingale's Eye"

> All old stories . . . will bear telling
> and telling again in different ways.
> (*POa* 350)

Like her earlier best-seller *Possession: A Romance*, A. S. Byatt's "The Djinn in the Nightingale's Eye" is set within the realm of academia. Once again, its protagonists are literary critics, whose disciplinary concern is the narration and analysis of traditional tales and myths. In the shorter, more recent text, Byatt returns pointedly to a question she had already treated in *Possession*: what is the meaning of storytelling?

Like *Possession*, "The Djinn in the Nightingale's Eye" is profoundly inter-textual, alluding to the Arabian tales from *The Thousand and One Nights*, to Grimm's fairy tales, Coleridge's "Rime of the Ancient Mariner," the *Epic of Gilgamesh*, Euripides's *Bacchae*, Shakespeare's *Winter's Tale*, Balzac's *Peau de Chagrin*, and Wilde's *Picture of Dorian Gray*, to mention only some of the more clearly marked sources. Explicit quotations are made from Chaucer's *Canterbury Tales*, Milton's *Paradise Lost*, and Shakespeare's *Hamlet*. Where the framework of *Possession* is realistic, however, Byatt conceives "The Djinn" as a fairy tale, signalling from the opening formula "once upon a time" that the laws governing our everyday world are suspended. Despite this unreal and alienating perspective, it is nonetheless clear that the events of the story take place in 1991, the year of the Gulf War: "At the time when my story begins the green sea was black, sleek as the skins of killer whales, and the sluggish waves were on fire, with dancing flames and a great curtain of stinking smoke. The empty deserts were seeded with skulls, and with iron canisters, containing death" (*DNE 96*).

Byatt's systemic reference to the fairy tale provides her with a genre that is "intrinsically intertextual," as Lucie Armitt, in *Theorising the Fantastic,* characterises the fairy-tale mode: "perhaps it is this lack of any one originary version of a particular fairy story that makes this sub-genre not only intrinsically intertextual, but also interactive with so many other cultural forms."[1]

The tale here is of a woman who, after the failure of her marriage, concentrates on her professional career as a narratologist, a specialisation she explains as "telling stories about stories" (*DNE* 96). Her family name, Perholt, suggests the name of Charles Perrault, whose *Histoires ou Contes du temps passé* (*Contes de ma Mère l'Oye,* 1697) contains some of the best-known European fairy tales. Gillian Perholt concerns herself professionally with both the scholarly analysis of tales and the act of telling them. Thus, at the two conferences Gillian attends, she not only presents her research about literary texts, but she also recounts stories, for "The best narratologists work by telling and retelling tales" (106). Like Sheherazade, she has "perused the books, annals and legends of preceding Kings, and the stories, examples and instances of by-gone men and things; . . . She had perused the works of the poets and knew them by heart; she had studied philosophy and the sciences, arts and accomplishments; and she was pleasant and polite, wise and witty, well read and well bred."[2]

Gillian is not the only character that bases her stories on previous texts. It is a striking feature of Byatt's tale that several characters tell stories in this same mode: the protagonist's Turkish colleague Orhan Rifat uses the stories from *The Thousand and One Nights,*[3] a museum guide recounts the story of Gilgamesh, and finally the magic djinn tells of his "incarcerations" in the bottle from which Gillian frees him. Byatt's novella contains in these insertions a number of tales concerned "with Fate, with Destiny" (125), around which it, too, takes on the form of a frame-tale—like *The Arabian Nights* or *The Canterbury Tales* to which it so frequently alludes.

In the larger story that provides the frame, Gillian sees herself as "redundant." As a woman over fifty, she must come to terms with her fate, must understand that she is approaching death and overcome her fear of it. In close accord with the laws of the fairy tale, she sees an old woman appearing before her on three different occasions, each an epiphany reminding her of her own mortality. The first occasion is during her lecture in Ankara, when she is suddenly confronted by "a cavernous form, a huge, female form" (118). The second time she experiences a similar "strange stoppage of her own life" in Ephesus (167), where (she is told) the Virgin Mary died. Standing before her, Gillian sees "a real bewildered old woman, a woman with a shrivelled womb and empty eyes, a woman whose son had been cruelly and very slowly slaughtered before her eyes" (166). She interprets this encounter as a meeting with her own destiny: "my fate—my death, that is—waiting for me" (167). The third occasion is in the Haghia Sophia at a pillar where for centuries pilgrims have uttered their wishes, and where she wishes not to be a woman.

Gillian is drawn again and again to thoughts of her own fate, her transitoriness, to the extent that she sees in her bathroom mirror the steam-fogged image of "her death advancing towards her, its hair streaming dark and liquid, its eyeholes dark smudges" (189–90). But in her professional life she is concerned to find a supra-individual pattern in the "stories of women's lives," and at the conference in Ankara—whose title is precisely that—she retells the story of "Patient Griselda" in her lecture. Byatt accentuates the multi-layered intertextuality of the material, making her narratologist into a link in the long chain mediating the legend, from Chaucer's clerk in the *Canterbury Tales* to Petrarch's Latin adaptations of Boccaccio's Italian—although no mention is made here of Perrault's version of "Griselidis" [*sic*].[4] Reading the legend as the "tale of a man seeking the return of spring and youth" (120), Gillian can draw parallels with Shakespeare's *Winter's Tale* and with the Persephone myth, and incorporate "Patient Griselda" into the tradition of "tales of the desire for eternal youth" (267). But at the same time she understands the tale as a story of women's fates, a story of "stopped energies" (121), such as one finds in a more realist context in characters like Fanny Price, Lucy Snowe, and Gwendolin Harleth.[5]

From the two statues of Artemis in Ephesus, Gillian learns the law of metaphorical identity that governs the multiple and proliferating manifestations of underlying structures. Successive cultures have written over the familiar names of gods and goddesses with new names of their own, as in a palimpsest: "the Greek Artemis or the Roman Diana, an Asian earth-goddess, Cybele, Astarte, Ishtar, . . . those dying gods, Tammuz, Attis, Adonis" (157; cf. 144). Gillian Perholt's vision of the mother–god comprehends both the continuity of myth and the finite nature of the individual: "the mother goddess, the Syria Dea . . . was still, and always had been, and in the foreseeable future would be more alive, more energetic, infinitely more powerful than she herself, Gillian Perholt, that she would stand here before her children, and Orhan's children, and their children's children and smile, when they themselves were scattered atomies" (166). Individual histories are the re-enactment of a universal plot to which Gillian ascribes a higher degree of reality: "the goddess of Ephesus is more real than I am" (236).

The adaptation of the matter of literature, the superscription of myth as a process of cultural history, is demonstrated in many examples. At the Museum of Anatolian Civilisations Gillian meets an old man who, as he shows her round the museum, tells her the story of Gilgamesh and his search for the plant that could restore lost youth. Introduced as an "Ancient Mariner," the guide, however, is more than a Coleridgean figure telling his tale as penance for himself and as a lesson for his audience. In the act of telling, he assumes the most varied identities while still retaining his identity: "he was Gilgamesh . . . and became Siduri, the woman of the vine, . . . he became Urshanabi the ferryman of the Ocean" (149).

In *Possession*, Byatt adapted Vico's concept of *corsi* and *ricorsi*, "a 'corso' being a series of three ages or successive stages: the age of gods, . . . the age of heroes, . . . and the age of men,"[6] in order to point to basic recurring structures. According to Vico, human history is more appropriate to the age of men, myth more to that of heroes, but they are merely two ways of dealing with the same subject. Ash's volume of poetry, entitled "Gods, Men, Heroes," uses Vico's stages as the ordering principle for its "dramatic monologues" (*POa* 6). In *Possession*, we are given to understand, the same underlying patterns determine the lives of nineteenth-century poets as they do those of twentieth-century critics: LaMotte and Maud live out the myth of Melusine as Maud and Roland do the romance of Ash and LaMotte. But the process of superscribing myth and romance, of adding layers of new stories, may tend to hide the originally clear pattern and an easily accessible truth. Ash himself was well aware of this when he wrote to LaMotte: "The truth is . . . that we live in an *old* world—a tired world—a world that has gone on piling up speculation and observations until truths that might have been graspable in the bright Dayspring of human morning . . . are now obscured by palimpsest on palimpsest" (164). The process of retelling and of reformulation in language becomes the active process of cognition that tends to make truth comprehensible for the teller and the listener.

In his "Theory of Myths," Northrop Frye observes exactly this type of underlying, structural recurrence. Speaking of structure in myth, romance, and the realist novel, he remarks: "When what is written is *like* what is known, we have an art of extended or implied simile. And as realism is an art of implicit simile, myth is an art of implicit metaphorical identity. . . . In myth we see the structural principles of literature isolated; in realism we see the *same* structural principles (not similar ones) fitting into a context of plausibility."[7]

In *Possession*, myth and legend become "poetic metaphors" conveying knowledge through their essential ambivalence (3).[8] At a different level, both in the stories she tells and those that she is told, Gillian learns to see the potential for multiple metaphorical identities that reflect her own situation in a different and a similar way at the same time. The first story she relates at any length, "Patient Griselda," introduces themes that recur in the later texts: accounts of the workings of fate, of love and renewal, of the power structures that inform the relations of men and women—structures of domination and submission—and finally stories of the fear of death and of the fulfilment of our inmost wishes.

For Gillian, "Patient Griselda" is a "terrible tale" (*DNE* 120). Chaucer's clerk tells of a woman who sacrifices "every other human desire . . . to her vow of obedience,"[9] while her husband Walter torments her in subjection to his remorseless will. Though it is a "moral tale," the moral of Chaucer's clerk is not easy to tell. The clerk refers to Petrarch's allegorical interpretation that we should simply accept the sufferings God sends us, but he also criticises it when, referring to the Epistle of St. James, he observes that God does not deal with us as Griselda's husband did with her: "God cannot be tempted with evil and he himself tempts no one, but each person is tempted . . . by his own desire."[10] As a *teaching story*,

"Patient Griselda" is about a contest in which Griselda's "maistrie" in suffering proves stronger than her husband's in commanding.

Gillian's journeys to Ephesus, Ankara, and Istanbul constitute an introduction to oriental culture and prepare her for the encounter with the magic figure of the djinn, who escapes from a bottle made of an unusual glass called Nightingale's Eye. The djinn is a creature of fire, emphatically male, who possesses eternal life and can change his form at will. That, during a live broadcast, he can conjure tennis star Boris Becker from the television screen to appear in Gillian's hotel room is not a postmodernist play on ontological levels of signification but a straightforward proof of magic powers. By allowing his liberator three wishes as a reward, the djinn, too, shows respect for the rules of the fairy tale. However, although Gillian may be granted "what you most desire," she is also warned of the limitations of wishing: "I cannot delay your Fate" (201). For it is only in dream or myth that "the limit of the conceivable is the world of fulfilled desire emancipated from all anxieties and frustrations."[11] Her first wish, which transforms her into a thirty-five-year-old woman, is the result of her fear of growing old and dying. The second—"I wish you would love me"—can be understood in the same light. Making love to the djinn, Gillian is reminded of the lovers in Marvell's "To His Coy Mistress," who "had not 'world enough and time'" (252)—proof enough that the limits set on her own life determine the pattern of her thought.

When later narrative elements inserted in the tale speak of wishing and ask "what women most desire," they do so in reference to the contest between husband and wife in "Patient Griselda." In giving his own account, Chaucer's clerk had already echoed the Wife of Bath's tale, which asked and answered that very question:

> What thing is it that wommen most desyren?
> . . . .
> Wommen desyren to have sovereyntee
> As wel over hir housbond as hir love,
> And for to been in maistrie him above[12]

This question, which recurs so often in the tale of "The Djinn" (201; 209; 213; 244), again plays on a chain of stories that answer it in similar ways. In John Gower's "Tale of Florent," in the *Confessio Amantis*,[13] and in "The Wedding of Sir Gawain and Dame Ragnell,"[14] the answer is always "sovereignty." The djinn, however, although he has known the Queen of Sheba, does not tell what her most intimate wish was. The Bible gives no details and only reports that the queen's wishes were fulfilled: "And King Solomon gave unto the queen of Sheba all her desire."[15] The djinn's stories are of his various incarcerations in the bottle and liberations from it, and of the women he has loved, the Queen of Sheba and the Princess Zefir. Where "Patient Griselda" describes a relation in which the will of a man has become an instrument of fate for the compliant woman, the djinn and

Zefir speak of a different power over each other, one that is mutual: "my pleasure, in being in her power, and hers, in having power" (230). In the context of the frame-tale, the embedded stories sustain the paradoxical message of "Patient Griselda," that "the power of the will is more evident in submissiveness and restraint than in assertiveness."[16]

At the same time that the "The Djinn in the Nightingale's Eye" is a fairy tale, it is also a metafiction that comments on the rules it follows. The narrator–narratologist compares them with those of tennis. She knows many stories about wishing and illustrates its dangers in a version of the "Tale of the Foolish Wishes" with its string of sausages.[17] In her second lecture in Toronto, on "Wish-fulfilment and Narrative Fate" (257), Gillian reflects on the situation of characters in a fairy tale whose wishes are granted: "We feel the possible leap of freedom . . . and the perverse certainty that this will change nothing; that Fate is fixed" (259).[18] What Gillian tells her audience—which includes Tzvetan Todorov[19]—about the paradox that bonds a character's freedom to the inevitability of a fixed personal fate necessarily plays its part in her own life as well. She recounts in the lecture—evidently against her will—the story of a power relationship: A fisherman pulls a monkey out of the sea, and the monkey must serve him and grant his wishes, but with every wish he makes the monkey shrinks and comes visibly closer to death. As in Balzac's *Peau de Chagrin*, a connection is made between wishing and the approach of death. In Balzac's novel the antiquarian, as he gives the protagonist the magic talisman, warns him: "'*Vouloir* nous brûle, et *pouvoir* nous détruit' ('Desire sets us afire and power destroys us')," and recommends only "*savoir* . . . 'the sublime faculty of making the universe appear in one's head.'"[20] While the only possible way to preserve one's self is in the renunciation of desiring, "telling, as another form of desire" is the only way to portray and explain the self.[21] Balzac's novel already links the motive of the realisation of desire, which is destructive of the self, with the one of salvation from death through storytelling.

In his "superimposition" of Freud's *Beyond the Pleasure Principle* on fictional plot, Peter Brooks understands narrative as "seek[ing] illumination in its own death,"[22] and speaks of the "desire of narrative, driving toward the end which would be both its destruction and its meaning."[23] In her lecture, Gillian quotes Freud, ending her paper with an exposition of Freud's theory of the dual structure of human wishing, the interplay of the pleasure principle and the death instinct: "'*The aim of all life is death,*' said Freud, telling his creation story in which the creation strives to return to the state before life was breathed into it, in which the shrinking of the peau de chagrin, the diminishing of the ape, is not the terrible concomitant of the life-force, but its secret desire" (268).

Byatt seems here to be following Lionel Trilling's interpretation of Freud in "Freud: Within and Beyond Culture," which she mentions approvingly in *Passions of the Mind* (289): "when we take into account the age-old impulse of highly developed spirits to incorporate the idea of death into the experience of life, even to make death the criterion of life, we are drawn to the belief that the assertion of the death instinct is the effort of finely tempered minds to affirm the self in an ultimate confrontation of reality."[24]

On another occasion, in "Van Gogh, Death and Summer," Byatt also refers to Freud's *Beyond the Pleasure Principle*, speaking of the discovery of a "natural desire for death" as "a myth of Freud's which seems to tell us an undisplaced truth about our place on earth" (*PM* 313).[25] Byatt here understands Freud's observations as "a resolutely atheist vision of the same myth of sun, earth, death and lovers" that she sees in Van Gogh's pictures of *The Sower* and *The Reaper* as "the beginning and the end of life" (314; 331). In this context, Freud spoke of recurrence as a psychic mechanism that helps the individual come to terms with an unsolved problem: "to work over in the mind some overpowering experience so as to make oneself master of it."[26]

Freud's concept of repetition and *working over in the mind* is reminiscent of Gillian's strategy of retelling. While rephrasing the story in which the fisherman takes pity on the monkey and allows him to make a wish, Gillian finds out that this tale determines the structure of her own action. Like the fisherman, she too gives her third wish, and it is this wish that sets the djinn free. Like Griselda, Gillian shows mastery in foregoing desire,[27] and the gift of the act of wishing is her attempt "to incorporate the idea of death into the experience of life"[28]—the acceptance, in other words, of her fate. Telling stories helps her to understand that her ultimate desire is unsatisfiable, that she "cannot delay [her] fate" (*DNE* 201)—at the same time, stories become a means to master that fate.

Byatt has stated that her novels grow out of pictures, and at the end of "The Djinn" she visualises the essence of her tale in three images. The story does not end with the traditional fairy-tale formula, which promises a "pseudo-eternity of happy-ever-after" (266), but with Gillian receiving, as a present from the djinn, two glass paperweights. She collects glass paperweights because she sees them as possessed of opposing qualities: glass is "fire and ice, it is liquid and solid, it is there and not there" (271). In these paperweights, Gillian finds a metaphor for art, especially for the stories she tells. Like glass, these are "a medium for seeing and a thing seen at once" (274–75). Byatt understands this duality in terms of Ricœur's use of "Wittgenstein's ambiguous figure—the duck–rabbit—which can be *seen* as a duck or a rabbit, and is itself an ambiguous Gestalt between two terms, partaking of both" (*PM* 15).

The paperweights that Gillian receives from the djinn—one decorated with a snake, the other with a flower—are icons of the cyclic sequence of growth and decay, renewal and ending, which is her fate too. Byatt has used the symbol of the snake throughout her work. The central myth of *Possession*, which LaMotte both writes about and embodies, along with her descendant Maud, is that of Melusine, the serpent–woman. Ash too, writing in his poem "Ragnarök" of the tree Yggdrasil and the snake Niddhögg that digs its way under its roots, antici-pates in these images the threat to his male world represented by LaMotte. Byatt opens "The Djinn" with a quotation from Milton's description of the serpent in *Paradise Lost*, "the snake . . . made of words, and visible to the eye" (100); and the museum guide, although he is called an "Ancient Mariner," speaks not in Coleridgean terms of sea-snakes, but of the flower of eternal youth that Gilgamesh found—only to have it stolen again by the serpent. In Byatt's iconography, glass, flower, and serpent stand for the imagination and for the activity of writing. In *The Game,* she uses as a motto a text from Coleridge that takes the serpent as an emblem for the imagination:[29] "The principle of the imagination resembles the emblem of the serpent, by which the ancients typified wisdom and the universe, with undulating folds, forever varying and forever flowing into itself—circular, and without beginning or end."[30]

Coleridge, who has read and pondered the work of Vico and his concept of poetic wisdom that evolved through metaphors, symbols and myths, conceives of metaphor as "Imagination in action": "This power . . . reveals itself in the balance or reconciliation of opposite or discordant qualities: of sameness, with difference; of the general, with the concrete; the idea, with the image; the individual, with the representative; the sense of novelty and freshness, with old and familiar objects."[31]

In the poem "The Garden of Proserpina," which Byatt inserts into *Possession,* the author draws the central metaphors of the novel together in order to construct upon them "a Vichian interpretation of literature as a way—if not *the* way—of squeezing meaning out of life."[32] She has commented on these central images in the following terms:

it's to do with the image of the tree and the serpent and the woman in the paradise garden . . . Randolph Ash's [poem] about the Garden of Persephone . . . was, in a sense, the central meaning of the novel. It starts with Vico's image of language and mythology as corn. It's exactly the same image as in *The Virgin in the Garden*: language is flowers, the flowers coming from the mouth of the Primavera.[33]

Ricœur describes metaphor "as a word meaning occurring in a new context,"[34] as a transposition into a new context: "Metaphor is . . . a contextual change of meaning."[35] The inserted stories in "The Djinn" suffer a similar "displacement" or "transposition." This is also the term that Kristeva uses to define *inter-textuality*: "The term *inter-textuality* denotes this transposition of one (or several) sign system(s) into another."[36] Like the meaning of *metaphor*, which can only be understood in context, the frame and the chain of stories attribute an interpretation to the embedded intertexts. Like metaphor, the intertexts assume a cognitive function; they share the function to be "both an experience and an act, . . . a deliberate act of understanding" (*PM* 15).

Citing T. S. Eliot's "Tradition and the Individual Talent," Byatt, in *Passions of the Mind,* demands "respect for the tradition" (167). She propounds the thesis that "re-writing" is "Not parody, not pastiche, not plagiarism"; and Gillian, in the same vein, shows the "re-telling of tales" to be a means of understanding one's own life: "We all make meanings by using the myths and fictions of our ancestors as a way of making sense, or excitement, out of our experience on the earth"

(*PM* 312). We understand our life not by attempting to record it realistically but through the mirror of imaginative tales. When Gillian relates the events of her life as they occurred, her account seems to the djinn formless and incomprehensible. The fantastic narrative with its dream-like speech, on the other hand, contains the knowledge that comes from imagination: "it re-arranged, it made clear" (*DNE* 207). Byatt quotes Jonathan Raban on the degree to which literature informs and moulds our lives: "But life itself tends constantly to the second-hand; our responses are so conditioned, our behaviour so stereotyped, that it is immensely hard for us to extricate ourselves from these literary precedents which plot the course of our own feelings and actions" (qtd. in *PM* 168).

Gillian's own reflections on "literary precedents"—notably placing herself as a "being of secondary order" because of the fictions she re-enacts (*DNE* 96)—demonstrate the cognitive function of rewriting and retelling. By recognising "a metaphorical identity," a displacement and a similarity in the often-told fairy tales, she is able to comprehend her situation and to act accordingly. Like Ash, she becomes convinced of the meaning of the past, those "past voices and lives whose resuscitation in our own lives as warnings, as examples, as the life of the past *persisting in us*, is the business of every thinking man and woman" (*POa* 104). Like Sheherazade in *The Arabian Nights*, Gillian is "primarily concerned with epistemological questions, with figuring out how to extend her store of knowledge to stave off her death."[37] The example of Sheherazade reiterates that storytelling is a means to avoid death and to set free both king and storyteller: "In the *Nights,* knowledge of a story and the ability to tell it may assure the survival of an individual."[38]

Gillian does not surrender uncritically, however, to the fictive realities or plots that she re-enacts. Like the protagonist in "The Story of the Eldest Princess," she deliberately chooses her approach: "You had the sense to see you were caught in a story, and the sense to see that you could change it to another one" (*DNE* 66). Byatt illustrates the issues of predestination, fate, and freedom in two narrative-inserts in *Possession*. In "The Glass Coffin" (*POa* 58–67; *DNE* 3–24), the little tailor saves the princess and wins her as his bride. Although he begs her to refuse him, she follows the conventions of the fairy tale of her own free will and marries him. In "The Threshold," a variation of the traditional story of the three caskets, the metafictional commentary glosses the protagonist's choice of the lead casket in the following terms: "And one day we will write it otherwise, that he [the Childe] would not come, that he stayed, or chose the sparkling [caskets], or went out again onto the moors to live free of fate, if such can be. But you must know now, that it turned out as it must turn out, must you not? Such is the power of necessity in tales" (*POa* 155).

Roland and Maud, too, believe themselves caught in a story: "being driven by a plot or fate that seemed, at least possibly, to be not their plot or fate but that of those others" (*POa* 421).[39] Unlike LaMotte and Ash, however, they find a way to create a relationship that respects each other's autonomy. The metaphor of *possession* reveals its ambivalence when Byatt shows how through "the active act of ownership, of taking control over, . . . and in so doing signalling both mastery and authority,"[40] the partners attain freedom.

Myths and fairy tales present models for action, but, at the same time, they present the freedom to change the plot and tell another story. Stories construct a pattern, an ordering system through which we can begin to understand. In an interview with Nicolas Tredell, Byatt makes her position clear: "ideas of the random, of the haphazardness and ungraspability of life, have been grossly exaggerated. When Virginia Woolf says that life hits us as a series of random expressions, it jolly well doesn't. It hits us as a series of narratives, though they may be mutually exclusive narratives. We may be hit by random impressions, but if we're intelligent we immediately put them into order."[41]

Byatt's metafictional fairy tale suggests cultural memory as a matrix within which "tales about things that were unreal" are to be understood (*DNE* 206–7): "A Tale, a Story, that may hide a Truth / As wonder-tales do, even in the Best Book" (*POa* 409).[42] Cultural memory establishes the mental and spiritual continuity in which Gillian participates when she accepts her own contingency and finitude. Ash formulates the same experience of an intertwined permanence and change when he writes: "The individual appears for an instant, joins the community of thought, modifies it and dies; but the species, that dies not, reaps the fruit of his ephemeral existence" (*POa* 4). Through the act of retelling, Gillian participates in the cultural memory of the community. The concept is suggestive of Vico's "recollective fantasia" to which he attributes three different aspects: "memory when it remembers things, imagination when it alters or imitates them, and invention (*ingegno*) when it gives them a new turn or puts them into proper arrangement and relationship."[43] Byatt's narrators appropriate all three qualities, remembering the original tales but altering and reinventing them in the context of their own lives. That the act of retelling tales should accept the task of opening to the listener such fundamental truths shows how far Byatt is departing from postmodernist conceptions of writing and language.

NOTES

1. Lucie Armitt, *Theorising the Fantastic* (London: Arnold, 1996) 21.

2. *The Arabian Nights' Entertainment or The Book of Thousand Nights and a Night*, ed. Bennett A. Cerf (New York: Modern Library, 1932) 13.

3. Both the frame-story of *The Arabian Nights* and the "Tale of Kamar Al-Zaman" are referred to; cf. Joseph Campbell, *The Hero with a Thousand Faces* (Princeton: Princeton UP, 1968) 65–68, 74–77, 226–28.

4. For Perrault's "Griselidis" and its relation to Boccaccio, see Jeanne Morgan, *Perrault's Morals for Moderns* (New York: Lang, 1985) 56–76.

5. Byatt has pointed out the fairy-tale motives and mythical structures of Jane Austen's *Mansfield Park,* Charlotte Brontë's *Villette,* and George Eliot's *Daniel Deronda* (*IC* 114).

6. Ivana Djordjevic, "In the Footsteps of Giambattista Vico: Patterns of Signification in A. S. Byatt's *Possession*," *Anglia* 115.1 (1997): 50.

7. Northrop Frye, *Anatomy of Criticism* (1957; Harmondsworth: Penguin, 1990) 136.

8. For Vico, every metaphor is "a fable in brief." See Donald Phillip Verene, "Vico's Philosophy of Imagination," *Vico and Contemporary Thought*, ed. Giorgio Tagliacozzo and Michael Mooney (London: Macmillan, 1976) 23.

9. Robert Longsworth, "Chaucer's Clerk as Teacher," *The Learned and the Lewed: Studies in Chaucer and Medieval Literature*, ed. Larry D. Benson (Cambridge, MA: Harvard UP, 1974) 64.

10. Longsworth 64.

11. Frye 119.

12. Geoffrey Chaucer, *The Complete Works of Chaucer*, vol. 4: *The Canterbury Tales*, ed. Walter Skeat (Oxford: Clarendon, 1972) l. 904, 1038f; cf. 1254.

13. John Gower, *Confessio Amantis*, ed. Russell A. Peck (New York: Holt, 1968) l. 1607: "That alle wommen lievest wolde / Be soverein of mannes love" (cf. l. 1834).

14. Cf. Donald B. Sands, ed., *Middle English Verse Romances* (New York: Holt, 1966) 323–47; cf. l. 468–69: "Women desire sovereinté, for that is their liking; / And that is ther moste desire."

15. 1 Kings 10.13.

16. Longsworth 65.

17. Perrault's *Contes* contain a version of these "souhaits ridicules"; cf. Charles Perrault, *Contes de Perrault* (Genève: Slatkine, 1980) 3–12.

18. Her example is the story of "The Appointment at Samarra." Cf. Robert Irwin, *The Arabian Nights: A Companion* (London: Penguin, 1994) 195.

19. Cf. Tzvetan Todorov, "Les hommes-récit," *Poétique de la prose* (Paris: Seuil, 1971) 78–79, where he formulates his thoughts on character and fate in the *Arabian Nights*.

20. Qtd. in Peter Brooks, *Reading for the Plot: Design and Intention in Narrative* (Cambridge, MA: Harvard UP, 1984) 52.

21. Brooks 53.

22. Brooks 103.

23. Brooks 58.

24. Lionel Trilling, "Freud: Within and Beyond Culture," *Beyond Culture* (Oxford: Oxford UP, 1980) 85–86.

25. In *The Virgin in the Garden*, Byatt already uses this idea: "He [Freud] said death was bound up with our sexual method of perpetuating ourselves" (309).

26. Sigmund Freud, *Beyond the Pleasure Principle*, trans. James Strachey (New York: Norton, 1961) 10.

27. On the relation between mastery and desire in feminist writing, see Judith Butler, "Desire," *Critical Terms for Literary Study*, ed. Frank Lentricchia and Thomas McLaughlin (Chicago: Chicago UP, 1995) 377.

28. Trilling 86.

29. Cf. Richard Todd, *A. S. Byatt* (Plymouth: Northcote House, 1997) 12.

30. John Beer, to whom *The Game* is dedicated, uses the same quotation as an epigraph for his *Coleridge the Visionary* (London: Chatto, 1970); see also his comments on Coleridge's image of the serpent as representation of "the ideal of creative activity" (71).

31. Samuel Taylor Coleridge, *Biographia Literaria*, ed. George Watson (London: Dent, 1971) 174.

32. Djordjevic 77.

33. Nicolas Tredell, "A. S. Byatt," *Conversations With Critics* (Manchester: Carcanet, 1994) 65.

34. Paul Ricœur, "Metaphor and the Main Problem of Hermeneutics," *New Literary History* 6 (1974–75): 101.

35. Ricœur 99; cf. 96.

36. Julia Kristeva, *Revolution and Poetic Language*, trans. Margaret Walker (New York: Columbia UP, 1984) 59–60.

37. Wendy B. Faris, "Scheherazade's Children: Magical Realism and Postmodern Fiction," *Magical Realism: Theory, History, Community*, ed. Lois Parkinson Zamory and Wendy B. Faris (Durham: Duke UP, 1995) 166.

38. Irwin 236.

39. Cf. *The Virgin in the Garden*: "And she was gripped by that ancient, primal feeling of being in a story one has no desire either to share or to see out" (249).

40. Elisabeth Bronfen, "Romancing Difference, Courting Coherence: A. S. Byatt's *Possession* as Postmodern Moral Fiction," *Why Literature Matters*, ed. Rüdiger Ahrens and Laurenz Volkmann (Heidelberg: Winter, 1996) 126.

41. Tredell 59–60; cf. *PM* 11.

42. Cf. "what kind of Truth may be conveyed in a wonder-tale" (*POa* 165).

43. Verene 31.

Jane Campbell

"Forever possibilities.
And impossibilities, of course":
Women and Narrative
in *The Djinn in the Nightingale's Eye*

The Djinn in the Nightingale's Eye is subtitled "Five Fairy Stories." The tales it contains, however, cleverly subvert the fairy-tale genre, subjecting the form to feminist revision. In *Imagining Characters*, Byatt observes that "the fairy story says life is full of hazards and horrors and terrors and then you will be married and you will live happily ever after." Her fairy stories reject this formula, moving the form closer to the novel, which she describes as saying that "life is full of energy" and as rejecting the happy-ever-after ending (*IC* 190–91). By combining features from the two genres, the *Djinn* volume explores both the "hazards" of women's lives and their creative energies.

Byatt uses the fairy tale to explore the possibilities and limitations of women's lives in the contemporary world. Anne Cranny-Francis states that "Feminist generic fiction . . . critically evaluates the ideological significance of textual conventions and of fiction as a discursive practice."[1] While containing instances of the shape-shifting that is common in the action of fairy tales, Byatt's stories also alter the shape of the conventional fairy tale itself. Understanding the tie between genre and ideology, Byatt performs the task of feminist writers described by Cranny-Francis, of "placing the individual (generic) text within the history of that particular (generic) form,"[2] to reveal the ideological meaning of that history. In doing so, she gives women power in their own lives while exposing the male control that is a stock feature of the genre.

Two of the five stories in *The Djinn in the Nightingale's Eye* were originally published in *Possession*; they shift their shape simply by reappearing in combination with three new stories. Richard Todd shows how these two stories are transformed by their presence in "the narrative matrix of *Possession*,"[3] but the converse is also true. By removing them from their original context and placing them in her new volume, Byatt makes them part of a history of women's stories. "Gode's Story," the one with the earliest historical setting, stresses most heavily the limitations imposed on women by their culture. "The Glass Coffin" gives its female character more freedom, although her liberation is brought about in the traditional way, by a male. The three new stories, imagining richer possibilities for women, go further in deconstructing the fairy tale.

"The Glass Coffin" begins as a familiar story, a version of one of Grimm's concerning the rescue of a lady by a male, a little tailor. The lady, silenced and imprisoned by a magician because she refused to marry him, wishes instead to live with her twin brother and hunt with him in the woods. The tailor finds the sleeping woman and, with a glass key, releases her from her glass coffin. In a parodic moment, she recognises him: "You must be the Prince." But the tailor rejects the name of Prince—"I am . . . a fine craftsman"—and questions the prescribed ending (*DNE* 15). He offers instead a generous, commonsense revision of the old story: "Of course I will have you, . . . for you are my promised marvel. . . . Though why you should have me, simply because I opened the glass case, is less clear to me altogether, and when, and if, you are restored to your rightful place, . . . I trust you will feel free to reconsider the matter, and remain, if you will, alone and unwed" (20–21). By vanquishing the evil magician, the tailor also releases the lady's beloved twin brother from the spell that had transformed him into a dog. The tale ends ambiguously: the tailor, the lady, and the brother live together, the twins occupy themselves with hunting in the "wild woods," and the "one thing . . . missing" from the happiness of the household is not, as one might expect, a child (in fact, the question of marriage is left open). Rather, the work of the tailor, who now orders cloth and threads so that he can make for pleasure what he once made "for harsh necessity" (24), fulfils the genre's expectation for a "happily ever after" ending—but with a difference. Unlike the lady's prototype Snow White, who, as Sandra Gilbert and Susan Gubar point out, is freed from her first coffin only to be trapped by the male voice speaking from "her second glass coffin, the imprisoning mirror,"[4] the princess in this story is liberated from the controlling voice of patriarchy. She is free to pursue her own choices, including that of chastity, which is suggested by her parallel with the huntress Diana. In *Possession*, "The Glass Coffin" is one of Christabel LaMotte's *Tales for Innocents* and is tied to its teller and context. In the *Djinn* volume, it becomes one of a new series that explores the relationship between narrative and female power.

"Gode's Story," the second of the tales from *Possession*, is the most pessimistic of the *Djinn* stories. In *Possession,* it is told by the old servant, Gode, in the presence of the pregnant Christabel, and it points to the entrapment of women in both Victorian society and ancient Brittany, where the story originated. In the new collection, it represents both the imprisonment of women by the code of chastity and the compelling power of language. The miller's daughter, it seems— for the tale is filled with indirection and innuendo—is made pregnant by the sailor, and her child—murdered at birth or still-born?—appears as a "little thing dancing" that leads the mother over the edge of the cliff to her death (33). The sailor, who has married another woman, now also hears the dancing feet. He crosses the boundary between the worlds of the real and the unreal, sees the child, wastes away, and dies. The story reasserts the old tie between sexuality and death while exploring the fairy tale as a form, with its crossing of the threshold between natural and supernatural.

In "The Story of the Eldest Princess," the heroine, doomed to failure in the traditional plot which favours the third sibling, succeeds in her quest—and she does so by redefining the quest itself. Rather than bring back the desired object in a plot laid down for her, she abandons the plot and moves outside it. The quest is for a silver bird whose capture will restore the blue sky that has, for some reason apparently related to the three princesses' growth, turned to variable shades of green. Disobeying the instructions of the patriarchal wizard by leaving the straight road of the traditional plot for the wild wood, the eldest princess recognises in the end that the object of her quest is nothing outside herself; rather, it is narrative freedom. In doing so, she violates both the quest plot and the plot of romance—which, for women, usually form one plot.

The princess, knowledgeable about the story she is in, sees this quest plot as a trap: "I am in a pattern I know, and I suspect I have no power to break it" (48). She meets three creatures, all wounded or imprisoned, and all in need, they say, of the healing powers of an old woman in the forest. Each creature has suffered, like her, from being caught in a story. After rescuing the first, a scorpion, the princess decides to "walk out of this inconvenient story;" she realises that "it would make no difference to the Quest" (52–53). She assumes that the scorpion will sting her, because this is what traditional wisdom tells us; to this, the scorpion retorts that "Most scorpions . . . have better things to do" (51). The toad is bleeding because of the false belief that it has a jewel in its head; it has, however, freed itself from its persecutor by using what is true about it, its poisonous skin. Far from being the loathsome creatures constructed by false narratives, the scorpion and the toad are both handsome, although the toad warns the princess about another false story: she "must not suppose I shall turn into a handsome Prince, or any such nonsense" (55). The third creature, a cockroach, which has been caught in a fowler's trap, is the most skilled of all at refuting false stories. After the princess has been attracted by the fowler's whistle and the hunter's horn and warned by the scorpion and toad to avoid these humans because of their cruelty, she is enticed by a more threatening temptation in the form of the woodcutter's apparently innocent song. This song, a version of "Come live with me and be my love," promises happy pastoral romance, but the cockroach counters it with the *real* story as he knows it from his observation of the fates of the woodcutter's five wives: "And I will beat your back, and drive / My knotty fists against your head" (59). The cockroach, reputedly the most despicable of the three creatures, is a perceptive truth-teller who, by exposing the despicable habits of the woodcutter, becomes a rescuer in his turn.

Now in her own shared story, the princess reaches the house of the old woman and her true goal, an understanding of the therapeutic value of narrative. The old woman, with a house full of creatures, heals the three newcomers by having them "tell the story of their hurts" (64–65). And the princess discovers her vocation: "telling the story, [she] felt pure pleasure in getting it right" (65). The old woman's completion of the stories of the second and third princesses tells how the second princess is also innovative within the traditional plot, claiming for herself the successful quest for the silver bird. In other ways, however, narrative still imprisons her, for she follows the formula to the letter and, obeying the wizard's instructions, burns the bird. Predictably, the ashes produce a phoenix, the sky turns blue, restoring the norms of narrative,[5] and the second princess in due course becomes queen. The third princess, left with no story, meets an old woman—one of those who, says the old woman storyteller, are "always ahead of you on a journey, and . . . behind you too" (71)—and (in this one respect following the convention) chooses the third of three gifts offered to her. She rejects the magic mirror, which would show her her true love and effectively end her story. She also rejects the loom that weaves "thickets of singing birds" (70), choosing instead a fine thread—the narrative of her own free life—which she follows into the forest. By refusing to be caught in the marriage plot, she also rejects the plot of woman's enclosure in a world of simulacra. The women in this story all break the pattern and do so more radically than the figures in the two stories from *Possession*.

Boredom and stagnation in an old plot also contrast the possibility of new stories in the next tale, "Dragon's Breath." Three siblings, Harry, Jack, and Eva, long for escape from the repetitive life of their isolated village. The brothers wish for excitement and variety, while Eva, a weaver working with a limited range of colours to produce traditional designs, dreams of "unknown colours" and an escape from the occupation which she does not perform well but which is prescribed for her gender. She would like to be "a traveller, a sailor, a learned doctor, an opera singer" (78). When the mountains begin to move and the fixed story of their lives is disturbed, the villagers feel "a certain pleasure in novelty" (79). Then the creatures appear—great wormlike dragons that devastate the village, driving the villagers into the forest (where, despite their terror and suffering, they are still bored) and filling the air with the stench of their breath. But after the destruction—and the subsequent loss of Harry, who dashed into the smoke to rescue his beloved pig, Boris—the family's house emerges untouched, and Boris, too, is restored to them. Now everything is transformed; the people have new stories to tell, and, like the eldest princess, they find delight in making beauty out of danger and suffering. Their stories of the dragons, edited to omit the misery of waiting for Harry to return and the "inevitable fate" of the cherished Boris, take their place with the traditional stories, and these tales become "charms against boredom, . . . riddling hints of the true relations between peace and beauty and terror" (92). The people create a new folk tale. And although Eva continues to be a weaver, she now sees the old colours freshly, "as though she had never seen colour before" (90). In her unfinished rug, she reads not only the story of her own imperfect artistry but also, in the traditional design of the tree, fruit, and birds, the communal narrative of the women of her family.

This story highlights the possibility of creativity in repetition, insists on the need (especially for women) to continually re-imagine personal, family, and tribal history, and faces the inescapability of loss, suffering, and limitation. As in "The Glass Coffin," the female figure's closest ties are familial. Although the predictable patterns of community life necessarily involve becoming "lovers, . . . parents and grandparents" (76), there is no hint that this future exists for Jack or Eva, and no suggestion that either will enjoy their dreams of enlarged horizons. Unlike the three princesses, they cannot change the plot they are in, but they can change their relation to it by becoming storytellers themselves. And whereas the male hero of the traditional tales rescues the passive female from the dragon, here the sexes both share in helplessly witnessing the dragons' devastation and in creatively responding to it.

In the novella that is *The Djinn*'s title story, the romance plot is again present but involves a love relationship between Dr. Gillian Perholt, a middle-aged narratologist, and a genie whom she has unwittingly released from his imprisonment in a bottle made from a rare and beautiful Turkish glass called nightingale's eye. From one perspective, "The Djinn in the Nightingale's Eye" is an essay in feminist narratology. In it, Byatt performs magic of her own, blending realism and fairy tale. With the djinn's appearance in Gillian's hotel bathroom, the plot slips, apparently effortlessly, across the generic boundary. But long before this moment, the author has highlighted the marvellous elements of everyday life, including the possibility of independent life for women in Western culture.

Byatt's opening paragraph, through its use of the "once upon a time" formula, identifies the story as belonging simultaneously to realism and fantasy by evoking the wonders of the familiar: "Once upon a time, when men and women hurtled through the air on metal wings. . . ." The airplane is now the magic carpet, and Gillian, a denizen of this world, is introduced through apparent paradox: she was "largely irrelevant, and therefore happy" (95). She enjoys being redundant, "a woman in her fifties, past child-bearing" (101), whose children live far away and whose husband has left her. The reader's creativity is appealed to; we are invited to share Gillian's enjoyment of Milton's description of the serpent "floating redundant" (98), to participate in her reflections on the modern meanings of redundancy, and to construct for ourselves the story of her marriage. We can imagine for ourselves, the narrator says, the fax that arrives by modern magic to tell of Mr. Perholt's decision to leave Gillian for Emmeline Porter, whom we can also imagine for ourselves: "she was twenty-six, that is all you need to know, and more or less what you supposed, probably, anyway" (102). Realistic and fairy-tale elements are smoothly blended in the opening of this story.[6]

As in the other stories in the volume, the marriage plot is marginalised. Gillian has outlived that plot, and, instead of the grief she "imagined herself" feeling, she experiences (in language that anticipates the escape of the djinn from his bottle) "lightness . . . like a bird confined in a box, like a gas confined in a bottle, that found an opening, and rushed out" (103–4). Gillian is an "unprecedented being" (105), thanks both to modern science, which has extended her life span far beyond that of her ancestors, and to the Western world's acceptance of women scholars. Far from being caught in a story like the helpless females in fairy tales, she is a powerful interpreter of narrative and, indeed, ready to create a plot that will enhance her freedom.

Two stories told by Gillian at academic conferences frame the main story. The first, narrated at a conference in Ankara on "Stories of Women's Lives" (105), is Chaucer's tale of Patient Griselda and her testing by her husband Walter. Gillian's analysis, a severe critique of patriarchal control of women's stories, shows, once again, Byatt's concern with the ethics of narrative. After completing her presentation, which is interrupted by a terrifying vision of her own aged and dying self, Gillian becomes a listener to other stories about women, including her friend Orhan Rifat's paper on *The Arabian Nights* (whose principle of embedded stories "The Djinn" follows)[7] and the tales that are told by a mysterious, eloquent guide at the Museum of Anatolian Civilisations. These stories prepare for Gillian's sharing of stories with the djinn and for the second conference, where Gillian creates a story which summarises the understanding of narrative and of mortality that she has now reached.

Gillian retells Chaucer's "Clerk's Tale" about Griselda's meek endurance of her husband Walter's grotesque tests of her obedience as a story of the stopping off of women's energies; this, she tells her audience, is the common subject of women's lives in fiction. A resisting reader, Gillian rejects the moral offered by the Clerk that, like Job, we must patiently endure suffering. Noting that the Clerk himself has already rejected the obvious, gender-specific moral that all wives should follow Griselda's example—thus showing the interpretation of narrative as an ongoing, communal task—she moves to her own assessment of the story. "The story is terrible because Walter has assumed too many positions in the narration; he is hero, villain, destiny, God and narrator—there is no *play* in this tale" (120). Since Griselda's voice is so effectively silenced, she can, in the end, speak authentically only through her body, clasping her restored children so tightly that she becomes unconscious. "Chaucer does not say . . . that she was strangling them, but there is fear in his words, and in the power of her grip" (119). Griselda's attempt to rewrite Walter's ending by performing the story of her oppression fails, of course, and Chaucer gives the "happily ever after" ending that Gillian finds so outrageous. Her reshaping of the tale aligns it not with Job but with *The Winter's Tale*, a story with a "plotted dénouement" for a life most of which "has been taken by plotting" (114).

The story of Patient Griselda prepares the way for Orhan's paper on "Powers and powerlessness: djinns and women in *The Arabian Nights*" (106), which itself both builds on Gillian's paper and prepares for the rest of the novella. By focusing on Scheherazade as powerful storyteller and powerless possession of King Shahriyar, Orhan again links the two subjects of narrative and women's lives. He tells how Scheherazade, by her narrative skill, saves her own life and the lives of the other virgins intended to replace her. This is possible, he says, because her "plotting" is powerful enough to overcome Shahriyar's obsessive sexual egotism and vengefulness (125). Orhan then analyses one of Scheherazade's stories, one that again brings together freedom, control, and sexuality.

From this point on, Gillian encounters a series of narratives of women's lives. Her self-appointed guide to the museum tells her of the history of the construction of woman and of Gilgamesh, whose friendship with Enkidu was destroyed by another powerful female, Ishtar, who killed Enkidu because Gilgamesh had rejected her. The tale of Gilgamesh's successful quest—for the flower of immortality, his loss of it to a snake who stole it, and his own death—returns to the topic of mortality, which had interrupted Gillian's conference paper. Then, in Ephesus, Gillian reflects on the figures of Artemis and the Virgin Mary, on the power and powerlessness of woman, and on factual versus imaginative truth. She decides that "real–unreal [is] not the point" (166); the point is the imaginative energy generated by well-told stories.

After Gillian buys the bottle that, she is told, may or may not be made of nightingale's-eye glass, the lines between real and unreal simply disappear; wonder becomes naturalised, and language moves easily and often comically between the two realms. After the djinn, fascinated by the television in Gillian's hotel room, which to him is true magic, moves into the reality of the tennis game to pluck the figure of Boris Becker and set it on the chest of drawers, the commentator announces that Becker has had a seizure. This "delighted the djinn, who had indeed seized him" (199). Later, when Gillian tells him she is ready to make her third and last wish, he replies: "I am all ears" and expands his "to the size of elephants' ears" (269), erasing the line between word and act. The most telling instance of linguistic boundary-crossing is Gillian's name, which the djinn pronounces "Djil-yan Peri-han" (206). Thus Gillian, a collector and scholar of tales (Perholt/Perrault) becomes also a magical figure, a peri (a Persian elf) *in* a tale, and her affinity with the djinn is reflected in both parts of her new name. Floating redundant in a new dimension, she understands that "she might move suddenly"—or the djinn might—"into some world where they no longer shared a mutual existence" (207). In her dreamlike state she does not question his presence, his assurance that the bottle is truly nightingale's eye, or the story he tells of his history; real–unreal is not the point when we meet images from the world of our imagination.

Unlike Sleeping Beauty, who dreams as she sleeps in her glass casket, Gillian, in her dream state, is fully active as her narratologist self; her professional life is enriched, not suspended, by her relationship with the djinn. Again she becomes a listener to and learner from stories, as the djinn, telling the history of his previous incarcerations, explores with her the question of women's freedom. He tells of his relative, the Queen of Sheba, the only female he has known who has matched Gillian's description of herself as an independent woman, who willingly gave herself to Suleiman, and, at the other end of the spectrum, of women who, prisoners of patriarchy, had no power of their own at all. One of these, Zefir, was a secret artist, embroidering stories in silk and feeling herself to be "eaten up with unused power" while she was kept by her husband "like a toy dog . . . in a cage" (223–24). She and the djinn loved each other, but he sacrifices the possibility of her freedom to his enjoyment of her company. Their story ends in imprisonment for both; as a result of her carelessly wishing that she could forget him, he is enclosed in a bottle again.

Taking her turn as historian of her life, Gillian reciprocates with stories that place herself in relation to women's narratives. She tells about herself as a girl, confused and terrified by the power of her newly emerged perfect body, wishing she were not female. She also tells about her early, abortive attempt to write fiction when, feeling imprisoned at boarding school, she invented a male alter ego called Julian, who disguised himself as a girl, Julien. This story was abandoned because Gillian was unable to separate realism, reality, and truth; "my imagination failed" and, because of this failure, she thinks, "I am a narratologist and not a maker of fictions" (233). Her third story is about an old Ethiopian woman, starving along with all her people, and unable to act: "if only I were not a woman I could go out and do something" she told an interviewer from within the cage-like structure of her body (248). Through this story, Gillian relates herself to the issue in a personal way and exposes the gaps—already indicated by the presence of traditionally garbed Moslem women at the conference in Ankara—between the worlds in which twentieth-century women live.

Up to this point, Gillian has made three wishes. Two are in the ordinary, pre-djinn world, where, at the temple of Artemis, she wishes for an invitation to a conference in Toronto; then, forced against her will to wish on a pillar in the Haghia Sophia, she repeats her girlhood wish to not be a woman. With the djinn, she makes a third wish (the first of three that he is obligated to grant her): to have her body once again as it was at thirty-five, "when I last really *liked* it" (201). Now, her fourth wish is that the djinn will love her—a wish, he says, which might not have been necessary, "since we are together, and sharing our life stories, as lovers do" (250). After their strange and beautiful love-making, she and the djinn go to England where a letter awaits, granting her first wish to attend the conference in Toronto, where she will tell her last story and make her last wish.

This story sums up what Gillian has learned about wishing and about narrative and shows her understanding of their connection. It also shows that she is now not only a narratologist, "a being of secondary order" (96), but also a maker of fictions. She knows the importance of wishing wisely, and she understands that, when narrative control is too rigid, it produces unsatisfactory fictions. Her story of the fisherman and the apes, which introduces her paper, exemplifies these principles. The djinn, in disguise, silently collaborates with her to bring about the ending that both participants desire. Instead of wishing extravagantly for great wealth, Gillian's fisherman asks from the ape he has rescued only a shop, a house with a garden, and a loving wife. There is, however, a snag. With each wish the ape is diminished; he is wasting away. Gillian now understands what her own last wish must be; she tells how the fisherman gives his last wish to the ape to "wish for your heart's desire" (265). The ape vanishes, and the fisherman lives contentedly to the end of his natural life. As cooperative narrators, Gillian and the djinn have crossed another boundary, obliterating the distinction between the one who wishes and the one who grants the wish. With the djinn's help Gillian has fulfilled her own requirement that there should be play and freedom in narrative, even to the point of risking loss of control of one's own story. She later accuses the djinn of making her paper "incoherent" by introducing "the freedom of wishing-apes" into a story she had intended to be "about fate and death and desire" (269). She concludes her paper with reflections—related to the fisherman's eventual death—on Freud's discovery that death, not pleasure, is humans' deepest wish. This story mirrors the structure of the enclosing main story; it blends the fairy tale, where, as Gillian points out, characters are "subject to Fate and enact their fates," and the novel, where characters have "choice and motivation" (258).

There is no need for women characters as actors in this new story, for, with the illogical logic of dreams, fisherman and ape stand in for Gillian and the djinn. The djinn has indeed "introduced freedom": he has contrived his own release from Gillian's control—for he must stay with her until he has granted three wishes—and at the same time has helped her to fulfil her own wish to give him something. With the help of the story, Gillian is able to accept the loss of the djinn and the inevitability of her death. Like the fisherman, she acts generously, giving her last wish to her friend, who, before taking his freedom, chooses to remain with her long enough to give her a gift in return. His gift, a glass paper weight, lends an image for their relationship and the form of their stories by suggesting, in its combination of multicoloured fluid shapes, what he calls "forever possibilities. And impossibilities, of course" (227). The djinn then disappears, and Gillian resumes her life in "normal" reality where, "two years ago" (270) in the narrator's time, he returns in another disguise to present her with two weights that image the flower and snake in the tale of Gilgamesh. Holding the snake, which waits to steal the flower, Gillian, though still in her thirty-five-year-old body, notices an age mark on her hand and is able to see this portent as "pretty," a "soft dried-leaf colour" (276). Her body, despite its temporary reprieve, is still travelling towards death, but she no longer finds the sign of mortality terrifying. At the beginning of "The Djinn," Gillian had rejected the image of the wise old crone as applicable to herself. Now she is ready to become the crone when her time comes. Meanwhile, she is "happy," because she has, for a time, recaptured her childhood ability to recognise "things in the earth . . . that live a life different from ours, . . . that cross our lives in stories, in dreams, at certain times when we are floating redundant" (277). Earlier, Gillian's story of the imprisoned Griselda was interrupted by a ghoulish apparition of her own aged self, and she heard her own voice echoing "inside a glass box" (117). Now, she is the possessor and namer of glass, which is "a medium for seeing and a thing seen at once. It is what art is" (274–75). With its paradoxical quality of being "fire and ice, . . . liquid and solid, . . . there and not there" (271), glass is a "solid metaphor" (274). Gillian can now see possibilities in glass other than the story of woman's captivity told in "The Glass Coffin" and its antecedents: glass has become a multiple signifier.

The djinn, who has moved from being the prisoner of glass to the buyer and bestower of glass, has also matured as a storyteller. In his previous incarcerations, he has failed to encourage his temporary owners to use their wishes wisely; he was either too slow to act to change the story and help the woman escape death or, in the case of Zefir, too reluctant to break the tie between them, which depended on her remaining in the cage of her marriage. He wanted, Gillian thought, "to be both liberator and imprisoner in one" (227). Now he and Gillian together achieve as much freedom as is possible for each. In the story of their relationship, furthermore, the ending balances the satisfaction of closure and the promise of open-endedness. As they part, the djinn says that he will "probably" come back to visit her again; Gillian adds "If you remember to return in my lifetime," and he responds: "If I do" (277).

In these stories, Byatt re-visions the traditional female story and questions its ideology. Beginning with the old image of the woman unconscious, enclosed in glass, the collection ends with the woman free, active, and an interpreter of glass. Rescue is a reciprocal act in this story. Even in "The Glass Coffin," in which a male is the rescuer, he is able to free the woman without imposing a new slavery, and the woman lives out her own choices. "Gode's Story," the story most tied to convention, both shows a woman imprisoned by her culture and, at the same time, demonstrates the power of women's imagination, for it is the miller's daughter who, by the force of her language, compels the sailor to see and hear the dancing child. "Dragon's Breath" tells of a woman's discovery of her own and her foremothers' creativity. "The Eldest Princess" and "The Djinn in the Nightingale's Eye" feature women who confront the old stories in a conscious informed critique and construct new stories demonstrating openness and community.

In all five of the stories, too, a space is opened for the reader. In traditional fairy stories, Rosemary Jackson observes, the closed structure and authoritative narration keep both protagonist and reader passive;[8] in Byatt's stories, however, readers as well as characters are active. Familiar with the structure and motifs of fairy tales, we are alert to notice deviations: the absence of evil stepmothers, the transformation of the act of leaving the prescribed path from a dangerous punishable offence to a first step to freedom; most striking of all, the deletion of the marriage ending. The "system of rewards" in the classic tale—summarised by Marcia K. Lieberman as "being beautiful, being chosen, and getting rich"—is displaced.[9] Byatt's heroines are not praised for their youth and beauty, and their riches derive from their own resourcefulness and creativity. These stories all critique the inherited stories described by Karen Rowe, "which glorify passivity, dependency, and self-sacrifice as a heroine's cardinal virtues."[10] Whereas the ending of the classic tale answers all our questions, Byatt's tales leave us still wondering. If the guide at the museum was the djinn in one of his disguises, how did he escape from the bottle of nightingale's eye before Gillian bought it and took it to her hotel? We are in a realm where ordinary logic is suspended, where loose ends are irrelevant, and where mysterious forces and beings exist "somehow out there on an unexpected wavelength" (118).[11] Or, to put it in other terms, we are in contact with the "romance of language" which Gillian sees as the meaning of the "golden boy," Julian, "more real than reality" (236), whom she invented to be her childhood companion and who is now present in the form of the djinn, whose name resembles Julian's.

Byatt's book, described by a reviewer as "an elegant reflection on the nature of narrative,"[12] is another step in framing a feminist narratology. The stories do not contain a precise answer to Freud's question "what do women want?" about which Gillian speculates, but they point to one clear answer: women want to be free in their own story in a multiplicity of flexible, self-directed plots. Furthermore, they want to participate in shared stories, arising from and constructed around community and reciprocity. These stories are full of "forever possibilities."

Like the adult fairy tales examined by Jack Zipes, these stories show "liberation and transformation" for women. At the same time, however, they take what Zipes identifies as a "guarded position . . . with regard to the possibilities for gender rearrangement."[13] Byatt reveals the potential of the female imagination and envisions the possibility of a male–female relationship that is not based on power and dominance, but only one story, "The Djinn in the Nightingale's Eye," depicts a satisfying sexual relationship, and, in it, the male figure is not human. In "The Glass Coffin" and "Dragon's Breath," heterosexual love is marginalised and the sister–brother relationship is privileged; in "The Eldest Princess," storytelling replaces romantic love; and, in "Gode's Story," the result of sexual union is death for both partners. Furthermore, except for "The Glass Coffin," where the language of the "happy ever after" is still present, the stories assume that their characters will die. In this sense, the stories also praise the acceptance of limits, the "impossibilities" spoken of by the djinn. In her comment accompanying her contribution of "new" poems by Christabel to the editor of *Victorian Poetry*, Byatt describes *The Djinn in the Nightingale's Eye* as "a self-referring fiction about the life and death of the (female) body."[14] Certainly both the energy and the vulnerability of women's bodies are highlighted in these stories. But it is important to remember that Byatt is writing as Maud Michell-Bailey, and her statement reflects Maud's scholarly interests and language. Byatt's own paramount interest remains the telling itself,[15] the production of narratives about women that interrogate and revise old stories and create new ones.

NOTES

1. Anne Cranny-Francis, *Feminist Fiction: Feminist Uses of Generic Fiction* (New York: St. Martin's, 1990) 9–10.
2. Cranny-Francis 18.

3. Richard Todd, *A. S. Byatt* (Plymouth: Northcote House, 1997) 43.

4. Sandra M. Gilbert and Susan Gubar, *The Madwoman in the Attic: The Woman Writer and the Nineteenth-Century Literary Imagination* (New Haven: Yale UP, 1979) 42.

5. I owe this valuable suggestion to my former graduate student Sally Braun-Jackson.

6. Byatt says that she enjoys "writing the narrative expectations of a fairy story into a realist short story"; Jean-Louis Chevalier, "Entretien avec A. S. Byatt," *Journal of the Short Story in English* 22 (1994): 21. She also acknowledges the difficulty of making the transition from the "fairytale atmosphere" to "concrete reality" (*IC* 165).

7. Robert Irwin draws attention to Todorov's analysis of embedded narrative in the *Arabian Nights*. See Robert Irwin, *The Arabian Nights: A Companion* (London: Lane, 1994) 226. Byatt acknowledges her indebtedness to Irwin's book (*DNE* 279) and also comments on the effect that the device has on the reading experience. It "turns the writer into a reader and it turns the reader into a reader of a reading; and it somehow lines the reader up with the writer as a reader of this text within a text" (Chevalier 20).

8. Rosemary Jackson, *Fantasy: The Literature of Subversion* (London: Methuen, 1981) 154.

9. Marcia K. Lieberman, "'Some Day My Prince Will Come': Female Acculturation Through the Fairy Tale," *Don't Bet on the Prince*, ed. Jack Zipes (New York: Methuen, 1986) 190.

10. Karen E. Rowe, "Feminism and Fairy Stories," Zipes 210.

11. Richard Todd points out the "veiled puzzlement" that Byatt creates in "The Glass Coffin" by the unexplained vanishing from the story of the "little grey man" who initiated the tailor's quest (44). The mystery surrounding the djinn/museum guide is another instance of this effect.

12. Alev Adil, "Obeying the Genie," rev. of *The Djinn in the Nightingale's Eye*, *Times Literary Supplement* (6 Jan. 1995): 20.

13. Zipes 19.

14. Maud Michell-Bailey [A. S. Byatt], "Letter to the Editor," *Victorian Poetry* 33 (1995): 2.

15. Acknowledging that "The Glass Coffin" contains "obvious Freudian imagery" that would interest the feminist critic Leonora Stern in *Possession*, Byatt says that her own interest, by contrast, is in "the kinds of things that exercise Christabel," ways of breaking the "narrative structure" of fairy tales. See Richard Todd, "The Retrieval of Unheard Voices in British Postmodernist Fiction: A. S. Byatt and Marina Warner," *Liminal Postmodernisms*, ed. Theo D'haen and Hans Bertens (Amsterdam: Rodopi, 1994) 108.

Sally Shuttleworth

Writing Natural History: "Morpho Eugenia"

And is love then more
Than the *kick* galvanic
Or the thundering roar
Of *Ash* volcanic
Belched from some crater
Of earth-fire within?
Are we automata
Or Angel-kin?

(*POa* 273)

This ventriloquised poem of the fictive Randolph Ash could well stand as the epigraph of A. S. Byatt's *Angels and Insects*, which takes further many of the issues and questions first addressed in *Possession*. The discourses of natural history and spiritualism that were so complexly intertwined in *Possession*'s explorations of the nature of history and of forms of afterlife become the respective defining narrative modes of the two novellas—"Morpho Eugenia" and "The Conjugial Angel"—that comprise *Angels and Insects*. Ash's poem, which prefaces Byatt's account of the "honeymoon"/natural history tour taken by Ash and Christabel LaMotte, sets human love in the context of recent discoveries in the physical sciences, questioning the hierarchy of Being constructed by the Christian religion. If "natural history" were truly written, would we be set down with the insects or float free with the spirits?

Like *Possession*, "Morpho Eugenia" takes its starting point from this distinctly Victorian set of questions. Even more than its predecessor, it also attempts not merely to represent but to work within, to actively inhabit, Victorian forms of discourse. Such fascination with the forms and thought of the Victorian age is not, of course, unique to Byatt's fiction. The critical success of *Possession* in 1990 marked the beginning of a veritable deluge of Victorian-centred novels published in the British Isles, which currently shows no signs of abating. Such novels generally display an informed postmodern self-consciousness in their interrogation of the relationship between fiction and history. They reveal, none-theless, an absolute, non-ironic fascination with the details of the period and with our relations to it.

"Morpho Eugenia" is one of a number of contemporary texts dramatising the Darwinian moment in Victorian history, placing the focus on the sense of crisis evoked in 1859 when Darwin's *On the Origin of Species* was published and the profoundly ahistorical forms of natural history espoused by the natural theolo-gians gradually gave way to the new science of evolutionary biology. Although they adopt very different forms, there are remarkable similarities in some of the plot elements of "Morpho Eugenia" and Graham Swift's *Ever After* (also pub-lished in 1992). Both feature a male protagonist who is a naturalist and follower of Darwin and who finds himself fundamentally at odds with his clergyman father-in-law. Science and religion are set against each other as the representative of the new science attempts to communicate his new beliefs to a father-in-law still deeply wedded to the picture of the world drawn by natural theology. The story in both cases is one of intellectual, generational, and marital conflict and has been told many times before, not least in the Victorian age itself. Why should two writers choose to retell it in 1992? What are the attractions of this particular story for writers and readers in our post-modern age? And what does this particu-lar historical convergence tell us about our own era?

The answers to these questions must embrace, on the one hand, the extraordi-nary popularity in England at the current time of the historical novel (in all its new postmodern guises), and on the other, the explosive growth of the Darwin industry in recent years. There seems to be an insatiable appetite for high-brow historical novels, Darwinian biographies, and television spectaculars.[1] Interest in Darwin was revitalised by the publication in 1991 of the Desmond and Moore biography,[2] but this does not in itself explain why such extensive media attention was accorded to it. Similarly, the popularity of Byatt's *Possession* does not explain the resurgence of fictional interest in the Victorian period since this work was in itself part of a wave of retro-Victorian fiction, with many texts already underway before the publication of Byatt's novel.

Such a blossoming of interest in the Victorian period is even more curious when placed in the context of Frederic Jameson's diagnosis of the "historical deafness" of our postmodern age, our inability to perceive how our present has evolved linearly out of the socio-economic and psychological conditions of the past.[3] Jameson does not wish to suggest, however, that historical images are entirely absent from our culture and our thoughts. The very reverse is the case:

at the very moment in which we complain, as here, of the eclipse of historicity, we also universally diagnose contemporary culture as irredeemably historicist, in the bad sense of an omnipresent and indiscriminate appetite for dead styles and fashions; indeed, for all the styles and fashions of a dead past.[4]

What he is here defining is the appetite for "retro" so evident in the fashion and advertising industry at present, where styles of the past swiftly replace one another, without any sense of the cultural and social baggage they had previously carried. Diachrony becomes synchrony, temporality is transformed into spatiality, history into image.[5] Our current addiction to the photographic image, Jameson suggests, "is itself a tangible symptom of an omnipresent, om-nivorous, and well-nigh libidinal historicism."[6]

Is our current addiction to the historical novel similarly an outcome of a "libidinal historicism" that actually destroys the historicity of its objects? It is significant that Jameson's diagnosis of the American situation is clearly not applicable in England. He suggests that the historical novel

has fallen into disrepute and infrequency, not merely because, in the post-modern age, we no longer tell ourselves our history in that fashion, but also because we no longer experience it that way, and, indeed, perhaps no longer experience it at all.[7]

In England, however, the historical novel is alive and thriving. Admittedly, it generally carries with it a self-reflexive consciousness about the problems of writing history in our postmodern age. But it also usually displays a deep com-mitment to recreating the detailed texture of an age, to tracing the economic and social determinants that might structure these imaginary lives.

The evolution of the current historical novel can itself be defined historically. One evident progenitor of the retro-Victorian novel is John Fowles's *The French Lieutenant's Woman* (1969), which intertwines sexuality and natural history through the life of its male protagonist, an amateur naturalist and follower of Darwin. Past and present are brought together in the narrative voice, which carries all the arch knowingness of the twentieth-century observer.

A second progenitive model for the contemporary historical novel is to be found in Jean Rhys's *Wide Sargasso Sea* (1966), which is one of the first in a long line of texts that have sought to open up the silent spaces of history or classic literary texts. The impetus for these growing number of novels comes now both from feminist and post-colonial theory, as writers seek to give voices to women or the racially oppressed, who have been denied a voice in history.[8] Rather than adopt a knowing or agonised twentieth-century narrator, texts in this model have gone for total immersion, frequently employing first-person narrative, in an attempt to create an authenticity of voice. The second text in *Angels and Insects*, "The Conjugial Angel" is partially in this tradition (although not first-person narrative). It attempts to reclaim Hallam from Alfred Tennyson, and to tell the story of Hallam's true "widow," not Alfred, but Emily Tennyson.

The third model for contemporary historical texts is illustrated by A. S. Byatt's *Possession*, where nineteenth- and twentieth-century stories intertwine and the recovery and interrogation of the past forms the basis of the central protagonists' own attempts to construct their identity. Swift's *Ever After* also follows this latter pattern, oscillating between the first-person framing narrative of a contemporary narrator and his attempts to come to terms with his own relation to history, and extracts from the notebooks of one of his ancestors, which record his loss of religious faith. As in *Possession* or Swift's *Waterland* (1983), the problems of writing history in the late twentieth century form an explicit preoccupation in the book.

In Byatt's *Angels and Insects*, the contemporary frame has gone. The two stories continue the exploration of the Victorian preoccupation with natural history and the spirit world started in *Possession*, but there is no point of reference outside the nineteenth-century frame. Perspective here is spatial rather than temporal; William Adamson's experiences in the closed aristocratic world of Bredely Hall are set in counterpoint to his memories of the tribal rituals of the Amazon rainforest. "Morpho Eugenia" is characterised by a narrative movement that hones in ever more closely on the intricate, often tortured, discourses of the nineteenth century. This, it seems, is storytelling armed with the collector's box and magnifying glass, intent on revealing, both literally and metaphorically, what G. H. Lewes called "that great drama which is incessantly enacted in every drop of water, every inch of earth."[9]

Impersonal narrative in "Morpho Eugenia" gives way to a whole sequence of further *texts*: Harald Alabaster's interminable, circular text, where he attempts to defeat Darwin through natural theology; the text of Matty Compton and Adamson's book on ants, *The Swarming City*; Adamson's personal, agonised jottings on instinct and intelligence; and Matty's fable of insect life, "Things Are Not What They Seem." The effect is extraordinarily dense, a form of double layering of natural history. We are given not only the details of a Victorian natural history text in the study of the ants, but a natural history of the lives and beliefs of the protagonists who are alike subjected to the scrutiny of the magnifying lens. The textual form of "Morpho Eugenia" itself mirrors that of Victorian natural history as it moves increasingly inward with a dizzying sense of detail. Natural history functions as both trope and narrative model for Byatt in this novella.

The hallmark of Victorian natural history was indeed its celebration of the world of the minute, as evidenced by the variety of teeming life to be found in one small water drop. Philip Henry Gosse, in his highly popular *The Romance of Natural History* (1860), for example, devoted thirteen action-packed pages to depicting the drama of life to be found within a single water drop.[10] Byatt draws on this Victorian sense of excitement at the discovery of a world beyond the bounds of normal sight in her creation of the poem "Swammerdam" in *Possession*:

> I saw a new world in this world of ours—
> A world of miracle, a world of truth
> Monstrous and swarming with unguessed-at life.
>
> (207)

The problem for the Victorians, however, as Byatt's text suggests, is that it was precisely this form of close scrutiny of the minute forms of nature, encouraged by natural theology, that produced, in Darwin's work, an image of the autonomous, destructive, and evolving world of nature that completely overthrew the entire framework of natural history and theology. Celebrations of static order and evidence of Divine Design were supplanted by a world of change and chance, random mutations and futile waste. The study of the order of nature transmuted into a lament for its disorder. "Morpho Eugenia" is situated at precisely this transition. Adamson has made the switch but is haunted by the implications of his new beliefs; Harald Alabaster accepts Darwin's findings but is insistent that they must be reconciled somehow with his old beliefs.

If natural history, like its companionate discourse and predecessor, natural theology, draws its rhetorical strength from the invocation of a realm of extra-human order, its fascination for the twentieth-century novelist, both as narrative trope and as mode, lies, however, in its tendency to unravel and implode. Neither term in the equation remains stable. Like the Victorians, we have—although in very different ways—lost our sense of what is "natural" while our sense of what it is to write history is similarly under threat.

In *Possession,* natural history and spiritualism, as figured in the interests of Ash and LaMotte, exist initially in peaceful tension, before being violently dissevered at that fateful séance where Ash reaches for the medium's arm in an attempt to offer scientific proof of forgery. Such violent questing after scientific truth, however, brings only increased disorder and mystification, sealing irrevocably Ash's separation from LaMotte. His "scientific" evidence also carries little weight in a text preoccupied with the verbal hauntings of the past, where both Victorian and modern protagonists express their fears that their recreations of the past are themselves forms of forgery. Ash wonders whether, in his pursuit of "scientific history," he is merely lending "verisimilitude to a colossal Lie with my feverish imagination" (168). The modern critic Blackadder views his work as a form of natural history, the painstaking dissection of an owl's pellet "in order to reconstitute the dead shrew or slow-worm which had run, died, and made its way through owl-gut." He considers making a poem about this rather macabre image, only to discover that Ash had been there before him; he is left uncertain whether "his mind was primed with Ash's image, or whether it had worked independently" (29). Both critical and creative powers, it seems, form part of the ongoing cycles of natural history.

The processes of natural history and myth-making do indeed constantly intersect as Byatt replicates in her structure the Victorian preoccupation with origins, which embraces both the evolution of life and the construction of history, whether religious, mythic, or critical. Unbeknownst to themselves, Blackadder and the other characters inhabit and re-enact the myths of the past which Victorian scholars had already firmly located as primitive accounts of the cycles of birth and death within nature. In *Middlemarch*, Casaubon, absorbed in writing his "Key to all Mythologies" while woefully behind the scholarship of his day, had, "in bitter manuscript remarks on other men's notions about the solar deities, . . . become indifferent to the sunlight."[11] Despite himself, and his belief that all mythic systems were mere "corruptions of a tradition originally revealed,"[12] Casaubon comes to play Dis, the god of the underworld, against Will Ladislaw's sun god, in the myth of Persephone that animates the novel. *Possession* is similarly framed by that myth of natural renewal, Persephone. It is in researching origins and sources for Ash's *Garden of Proserpina* that Roland comes across the Ash and LaMotte correspondence that is to lead, eventually, to Roland and Maud's own rebirth into the green, sunny world of love. Ash's *Proserpina* had been read as a poem of religious doubt, "a meditation on the myths of Resurrection" (3), but in Ash's manuscript comments in the Vico, it is linked also to the natural world of species survival: "The individual appears for an instant, joins the community of thought, modifies it and dies; but the species, that dies not, reaps the fruits of his ephemeral existence" (4).[13] Through the myth of Persephone, or Proserpina, natural history, religion, and mythic storytelling intersect in *Possession* as Byatt interweaves past and present texts in order to explore that peculiarly fraught question for the Victorians: the significance of individual human life.

In a sense, the narrative structure of *Possession* carries its own forms of redemption, as mythic re-enactment offers one mode of resolution to the all-important questions of human survival and significance. "Morpho Eugenia," however, forgoes the emancipatory potential of a twentieth-century frame, setting natural history, science, and loss of religious faith at the very heart of the text. In place of *Possession*'s historical sweep, "Morpho Eugenia" turns inward and dramatises the contortions and agonies of intellect that accompany such crises of belief.

Both novellas in *Angels and Insects* offer complex explorations of loss: the material loss of loved ones ("The Conjugial Angel") and the emotional loss of faith, both in the spiritual domain and in the Victorian domestic idyll of family life. Each story explores Victorian preoccupations with life behind the veil: the veil that hid the world of spirits and what G. H. Lewes termed the "obscuring screen of familiarity" that veiled all the minute actions of the natural world from our view.[14] The pursuit of natural history and of spirit rappings were both motivated by a desire to extend the boundaries of knowledge, to broaden apprehension beyond the confines of daily life.

Fittingly, "Morpho Eugenia" explores the intricacies of a two-fold perspective at all levels of the text. William Adamson possesses what he terms a "double consciousness" (*AI* 24). English social rituals and sexual mores are placed in the context of Amazonian rites and Adamson's memories of uninhibited sexual

abandon with naked dark-skinned women. Despite himself, he acts simultaneously as anthropological observer and critic of Victorian sexual hypocrisy. Natural history is then mapped on to anthropology. Throughout the text, life at
the aptly named Bredely Hall is paralleled to that of an insect colony, both
implicitly and explicitly. Morpho Eugenia is both a shapely, exotic butterfly and
Adamson's future wife. The punning is continued in her name: *eugenesis* means
both "the quality of breeding well or freely" and "the production of young by the
union of individuals of different species or stocks."[15] Eugenia certainly enacts the
first of these meanings but defiantly flouts the latter. All her young remain
curiously true to the Alabaster stock.

The parallels between insect and human life start on the physical level of
resemblance and quickly extend to social organisation and the social and sexual
division of labour. Like the ant colony and the beehive, the Hall is serviced by an
army of non-individuated workers. The recognition, attributed in *Possession* to
Swammerdam, that we have not lords of the anthill and beehive but queens, is
enacted in the text with the powerful but idle figure of Lady Alabaster and the
equally somnolent and fertile Eugenia. The structure is matriarchal, but unlike
the recent figuration of this structure in James Cameron's film *Aliens*, where the
queen ant is seen as a terrifying figure who impregnates all creatures she can
grasp, these queens seem, as Adamson observes, "Prisoners of Love" (102).[16]
Adamson's babies are "passed from hand to hand" while Eugenia "dozed and
sewed and her attendants fed and groomed her" (74). The scandal in the text,
however, is not that of matriarchy but rather the central anagram whereby IN-
SECT is transformed into INCEST. Eugenia has not been producing young
through union with different stock but has rather been mating with her brother.[17]
Harald Alabaster's sermon on love, which begins "with the natural ties between
the members of the family group, . . . the closeness of brothers and sisters" (23),
becomes, in the light of subsequent revelations, an exposure of the incestuous
dynamics that lay at the heart of Victorian ideologies of the family.

As in the ant colony, the female is the object of desire of all the males. The
scene in the conservatory where Eugenia is literally covered in moths gives
expression to this desperate level of sexual need: "They advanced, a disorderly,
driven army, beating about Eugenia's head, burring against her skin, thirty, forty,
fifty, a cloud, the male Emperors propelling themselves out of the night towards
the torpid female" (54). Within the framing perspective of insect life, Eugenia's
brother Edgar becomes not an immoral, evil figure, but rather a desperate, driven
creature, and Eugenia an amoral, complacent being eager to resume her "self-
nurture" and "self-communion" (159). Indeed, in view of the mass slaughter of
the unwanted males in the ant colony, the sexual politics in the human sphere
appear quite tame. Adamson imagines the worker ants "feeling a certain compla-
cency at their immunity from the terrible desire, both murderous and suicidal as
well as amorous, which drives the winged sexual creatures" (101).

Both the social and sexual division of labour are viewed in this text from the
perspective of the insect world. Like Darwin, Adamson draws human analogies

with the slave-making ants, and, as in Swift's *Ever After*, the issue of American slavery is linked to the conditions of workers in the Lancashire cotton mills (where much of the Alabaster money comes from).[18] However, the level of entrancement with the minute world revealed in the ant colonies is so strong in the novel that this sense of social perspective tends to be squashed. Such is the devotion to the recreation of the textual density of Victorian natural history and of the voices of social and religious doubt that our attention tends to be drawn ever inward, so that we as readers start to inhabit that world of wonder and doubt, rather than standing outside it.

For the contemporary imagination, it seems as if the Victorian age is best encapsulated not in the sweeping industrial developments made possible by science, but in the individualised crisis of faith and the discourses that served to articulate it. Is there an analogue for this crisis of faith in the 1990s? Or is that precisely the point, that there is no such parallel, just an empty space?

If we look at the ways in which science is currently entering into the popular imagination, we find that prevalent fears no longer focus on the relationship between man and the animal kingdom but on the relationship between man and machine, the human brain and the microchip. AI—not *Angels and Insects*, but Artificial Intelligence—is devoted precisely to this issue, while in science-fiction movies such as *Bladerunner,* our nightmares are given direct embodiment with androids, or replicants, who fail to realise that they are not human. Developments in genetic engineering further reinforce our culture's terrified reassessment of the boundaries of the human. Faced with what appear to be frightening technological capabilities with regard to the control of human and animal reproduction, the Darwinian order, with its endless vistas of minute change and its base within a self-governing natural order, takes on a reassuring, almost sentimental appeal. Is the current upsurge of interest in the Darwinian revolution, then, a displacement of contemporary fears concerning the indivisibility of man and machine onto the no longer threatening relationship between human and animal life? Significantly, the ever-proliferating television series on the natural world now tend to focus more directly on the predatory, wasteful, Darwinian aspects of natural life. Nature is no longer cleaned up for us. Photography and commentary that high-light the speed, beauty, and efficiency of an animal moving in on the kill disarm our anthropomorphic moral responses. Anthropomorphism still works, however, but at a deeper level. Lulled into wonder at the beauties of the operations of natural selection and a sense of pride at our kinship with such animal systems, are we subconsciously led into a process of assent to the principles of *social* Darwinism? Is a double displacement at work, so that fears about the interface of man and machine in this age of information culture are displaced onto a reassuring animal kingdom, only then to be subtly recuperated into an emotional defence of the excesses of capitalism—itself the very embodiment of our ahistorical, tech-nological, computer age—under the idea of a natural order?

The recent popularity of the Darwinian story can also possibly be traced to the fact that the Darwinian revolution appears a very manageable one in human terms. For an age wanting heroes, Darwin seems an ideal candidate. The Darwin industry, in its populist form, has created a heroic image of an individual who almost single-handedly changed the fundamental framework of Western thought, redefining psychological, social, and religious understanding. He stands as an image of a man who has defeated history by conferring his own lasting order. Such deification then stands in direct contrast to our own age, where no such human agency seems at work and individuals appear as slaves to their own technological productions. Nor is there any decisive break, no November 1859, when we can symbolically pinpoint the precise day when history changed.[19] Nor, more worryingly, is there a sense that there is a framework of belief waiting to be ruptured. Perhaps this is the ultimate key to understanding the current nostalgia for the Darwinian era. For the Victorians there was a decisive crisis of faith, a sense that the world was shaking under them, an ecstatic agony of indecision. For the postmodern era no such form of crisis seems possible, for there are no fixed boundaries of belief. It is an age of "ontological doubt" without any fixed points of faith against which it may define itself.[20]

Many retro-Victorian texts are informed by a sense of loss, but it is a *second-order* loss. It is not the loss of a specific belief system, but rather the loss of that sense of immediacy and urgency that comes with true existential crisis. We look back nostalgically not to an age of safe belief, for that holds few attractions for us now, but rather to a point of crisis. It is the intensity of emotion and *authenticity* of experience at that moment that we long to recapture.

In "Morpho Eugenia," Matty Crompton poses the question of whether future generations would shrug at the vista of meaninglessness that so appals her contemporaries: will people "be *happy* to believe that they are finite beings with no afterlife?" (117). Maybe not happy exactly, but we seem to find some consolation at least in our appropriations and reworkings of the old discourses of doubt and despair. Byatt's devotion to the replication of Victorian discourse, both in tone and texture, itself raises a whole series of questions around the issue of authenticity. Harald Alabaster's rambling text and Matty's insect fables are so perfectly within the models of their era. Why has Byatt chosen to devote such care to the seemingly impossible task of writing as a Victorian in the 1990s? According to Jameson, current writers do not produce parody, which has a healthy sense of irony, but rather pastiche:

Pastiche is, like parody, the imitation of a peculiar or unique, idiosyncratic style, the wearing of a linguistic mask, speech in a dead language. But it is a neutral practice of such mimicry, without any of parody's ulterior motives, amputated of the satiric impulse, devoid of laughter and of any conviction that alongside the abnormal tongue you have momentarily borrowed, some healthy linguistic normality still exists. Pastiche is thus blank parody, a statue with blind eyeballs.[21]

With the collapse of the high modernist ideology of style, Jameson suggests, the producers of culture have nowhere to turn but to the past: the imitation of dead styles.

Is Jameson, in this rather damning analysis, merely showing his own addiction to the originality thesis which is itself part of a progressivist (and hence anti-postmodern) theory of history? Imitation was, of course, for the Renaissance writer, the highest form of art. In *Possession* we have a perfect embodiment of what Jameson has termed pastiche in the creation of Ash and LaMotte's poetical writings. Although I would not wish to claim that these poems have the force of the original models, they could only have been created by the precise attention to history that Jameson claims is lacking in our postmodern age. They spring from a perfect internalisation of the poetic themes and forms of the period. We also have parody in *Possession*, in the descriptions of Leonora Stern's critical writings on LaMotte. Once again, Byatt has caught the idiom of her chosen model. A certain form of feminist criticism is here transfixed: her readings are not unintelligent—indeed, they are perfectly plausible. Their very predictability, however, and the ease with which they can be so condensed renders them empty in our eyes. We turn then to the pastiche itself, to the simulacra of Victorian texts, for our sense of authenticity. This displacement is reinforced by the two love stories where the twentieth-century tale seems pale and uninteresting in comparison with the story of Ash and LaMotte, which engrosses our emotional energies. The whole experience is a peculiar turning on its head of our instinctive responses and reading patterns. The language and experiences of our own era become mere pastiche, and the evident artefact, the postmodern recreation of Victorianism, becomes our measure of authenticity.

Authenticity is, however, a difficult illusion to sustain. In depicting Ash and LaMotte's walking and natural history tour, Byatt draws details from George Eliot's journals and letters written when she was on a similar trip with G. H. Lewes.[22] Ash's subsequent researches into the sexual propagation of sea creatures and whether they feel pain follow the concerns of G. H. Lewes in *Sea-Side Studies* which was based on these trips. Authenticity here helps to illuminate Victorian emotional preoccupations and the reasons for their fascination with the realm of natural history. Why, however, does Byatt include the detail that Ash was to have been accompanied on his trip by Frances Tugwell, author of a work on sea anemones? Fact is here teasingly interwoven with fiction. Eliot scholars will recognise Frances Tugwell as the figure described by Eliot in one of her Ilfracombe letters as "the little zoological curate, Mr Tugwell, who is really one of the best specimens of the clergyman species I have seen."[23] While such recognition might bolster scholarly vanity, it also then turns the text into a tissue of historical quotations to be spotted and identified, thus, paradoxically, disrupting our experience of it as history and the illusion of authenticity. In her playful reconstructions, Byatt never allows us to inhabit fully one domain; the inclusion of such fictive "facts" underscores the fictionality of the whole.

Both *Angels and Insects* and Graham Swift's *Ever After* can be seen as exercises in nostalgia, produced in part by a second-order sense of loss, a yearning for the authenticity of emotional experience and engagement which can only be produced when a solid framework of belief is lost. Byatt, for example, reveals an utter fascination with the depth of Adamson's worries about instinct as a form of predestination and his fears that intelligence belongs not to the individual but to the group. There is, however, a very different feel to the two books. *Ever After* ends with a foreboding of suicide, and Matthew Pearce, our hero in the Victorian Age, is drowned as soon as he sets out for the New World. "Morpho Eugenia," by contrast, is, like *Possession*, essentially a romance. *Possession* had confirmed the conservative romance of family life. Maud discovers that all her historical research leads back in the end to her own family line. As Blackadder comments: "How strange for you, Maud, to turn out to be descended from both—how strangely appropriate to have been exploring all along the myth—no the truth—of your own origins" (*POa* 503).

Myths, truth, and origins all coalesce in the text as Byatt explores the diverse ways in which we can be possessed by the past. Her wonderfully evocative title captures the demonic possession of love, or the acquisitiveness that drives Cropper, whose sense of his own identity rests so precariously on his ability to possess Ash's material belongings. It also conjures with ideas of imaginative possession: the ways in which the mind can be haunted by the tales and language of the past, having "an inner ear full of verbal ghosts" (145). Readers and characters alike participate in this spiritual legacy, which is replicated in biological terms when Maud's physical descent from both Randolph Ash and Christabel LaMotte is, literally, unearthed.

Just as the rhythms of the linguistic past haunt the brain, so do its narrative structures. Roland is aware that he, like "almost everyone in the Western world," is being controlled by the "expectations of Romance." He assumes, however, that "Romance must give way to social realism" (425). In this he is mistaken. The genre in which he has been cast and in which he feels most comfortable is firmly maintained by Byatt. That archetypal Romantic form, the quest narrative, is given a traditional conclusion with Maud's discovery of her ancestry and her simultaneous possession by Roland and by Ash. The importance of patrilineal descent is reaffirmed in the postscript, which returns us back to the Victorian era, revealing that Christabel's earlier attempts to deny Ash his paternity have failed. Unbeknownst to Christabel, Ash has long ago discovered his daughter.

"Morpho Eugenia" ends with Matty and Adamson setting off for the New World; Adamson's "sexual sorting" is correct this time. Unlike Matthew Pearce, they are not drowned. The text ends with the spirit of wonder of natural history as outlined by Captain Papagay (the embodiment of sexual vitality who miraculously returns from the dead at the end of "The Conjugial Angel"): "As long as you are alive, everything is surprising, rightly seen" (*AI* 160). Where *Possession* returns us to the law of the father, "Morpho Eugenia" embraces a more defiant, Darwinian interpretation of natural history. Adamson turns his back on those "white faced babes" whose paternity he now wishes to deny, focusing his energies on the "dusky"-skinned Matty, member of a hardier stock than those effete, interbred specimens produced by the leisured aristocratic life at Bredely Hall. Survival, not destruction, is the message of this tale.

Byatt's novellas no doubt are nostalgic texts, but defiantly so, offering a celebration of nineteenth-century sensibility. As such, *Angels and Insects* probably is a symptom, as Jameson would claim, of the poverty of our own culture. Its sheer narrative verve, however, like that of *Possession*, acts as an antidote to that poverty. Through its density of texture, its depth of engagement with Victorian texts, it operates as an implicit corrective to our fifteen-second culture of photomontages where history, as in *Bladerunner*, is displaced into spatiality. In many ways it could be seen as the perfect hermeneutic text, in which perceptions of the 1990s are interwoven within the discourses of the Victorian age. There remains the problem, however, of why the Victorian era in particular should prove so attractive to our postmodern souls. *Angels and Insects* emphatically distances itself from the political rhetoric of the 1990s by offering firm criticism of Victorian family values, which are here seen to be founded on the destructive inward turning of incestuous sexual energies. While Conservative politicians in Britain turned to the Victorian era for an image of order and stability, Byatt unveils the forms of conflict and crisis that lay at its heart. Nonetheless, it is significant that the endings of *Possession* and "Morpho Eugenia" actually reinforce the two primary strands of Victorian social ideology: familial continuity and the energy of individualism. No return to history can be innocent.

NOTES

1. Under the heading "historical novel," I wish to include what Linda Hutcheon has termed "historiographic metafiction" (*A Poetics of Post Modernism: History, Theory, Fiction*, London: Routledge, 1988) as well as contemporary texts set in the Victorian period, such as Matthew Kneale's *Sweet Thames* (London: Sinclair-Stevenson, 1992), which do not include any overt historiographic reflections.

2. Adrian Desmond and James Moore, *Darwin* (London: Michael Joseph, 1991).

3. Frederic Jameson, *Postmodernism or: The Cultural Logic of Late Capitalism* (London: Verso, 1991), 284.

4. Jameson 286.

5. Jameson's lament for the eclipse of historicity could itself be seen as an exercise in nostalgia. Edward Soja, for example, in *Postmodern Geographies: The Reassertion of Space in Critical Social Theory* (London: Verso, 1989), celebrates the demise of historicism, which he defines as "an overdeveloped historical contextualisation of social life and social theory that actively submerges and peripheralizes the geographical or spatial imagination" (15). Whatever their perspective on the postmodern, however, contemporary theorists are in general agreement as to the primacy they accord to spatiality with respect to postmodern culture. David Harvey, unusually, does not separate time and space but reforges them in the concept of "time–space compression" (*The Condition of Postmodernity: An Enquiry into the Origins of Cultural Change*, Oxford: Blackwell, 1989).

6. Jameson 18.

7. Jameson 283–84.

8. Recent examples of these two forms of work would be Jane Rogers's *Mr Wroe's Virgins* (London: Faber, 1991) and Caryl Phillips's *Cambridge* (London: Bloomsbury, 1991).

9. George Henry Lewes, *Sea-Side Studies*, 2nd ed. (Edinburgh and London: 1860) 58. George Eliot also drew on this image in *Middlemarch*, but, significantly, it is used not to celebrate the wonders of nature, but rather to unveil a world of rapacious destruction. See George Eliot, *Middlemarch*, vol. 1 (Edinburgh: 1878–80) 86.

10. Cf. Philip Henry Gosse, *The Romance of Natural History* (London: 1860) 158–71.

11. Eliot, *Middlemarch*, vol. 1, 303.

12. Eliot, *Middlemarch*, vol. 1, 33.

13. Ash's notes, significantly, are written on the back of a bill for candles: the springtime renewal of sunlight is set against a wavering, ephemeral form of light, which has to be purchased. They are written in response to Vico's meditation on the golden corn (or apples) of the myth as the origin of "commerce and community." Roland, in his response to Ash's jottings, notes that Proserpina as species is a very nineteenth-century idea; he wonders whether Ash made his observations before or after the publication of *Origin of the Species* and observes that ideas of development were current throughout the century.

14. Lewes is discussing the new sense conferred by the microscope: "We all begin, where most of us end, with seeing things removed from us—kept distant by ignorance and the still more obscuring screen of familiarity" (*Sea-Side Studies* 57).

15. "Eugenesis," *Oxford English Dictionary*, 2nd ed. (1989).

16. *Aliens*, dir. James Cameron (1986). The figuration of the queen ant in this film is literally of a phallic mother who both penetrates her victims and implants her eggs within them.

17. The anagram would appear to be an intertextual reference to Nabokov's *Ada or Ardor: A Family Chronicle* (London: Weidenfeld, 1969). Van looks lovingly on as Ada and Grace create anagrams of insect. "Scient" is transformed into "nicest" and then into "incest" (85). The sequence from "scient," or "knowing" (with a pun, presumably, on the biblical sense) through to "nicest incest" is revelatory of Ada's future responses to her brother Van. As in "Morpho Eugenia," the world of incestuous sexuality is interwoven with that of entomology in this text (reflecting Nabokov's own professional interests as Curator of Entomology at the Harvard Natural History Museum). I am indebted to John Christie for this Nabokov reference. Incest has, in recent years, become a feature of retro-Victorian fiction. *Waterland*, of course, revolves around an incestuous procreation, and Matthew Kneale's *Sweet Thames* also features father–daughter incest.

18. *Ever After* has a stronger sense of science as a technological and material threat than does "Morpho Eugenia." It not only invokes questions of slavery and conditions in factories, but it also makes the nineteenth-century hero a surveyor for the railways. In the twentieth century such developments are paralleled by the rise of plastics, medical technology, and, most importantly, the atomic bomb.

19. This construction of Darwin's pre-eminent role and the narrow historical location of the crisis of faith around the watershed of 1859 has of course been heavily criticised in recent historiography. Adrian Desmond, in *The Politics of Evolution: Morphology, Medicine, and Reform in Radical London* (Chicago: U of Chicago P, 1989), and Desmond and Moore, in their biography of Darwin, have traced highly politicised evolutionary and materialist trends and anxieties back to the 1810s and 1820s.

20. See Roy Boyne, "The Art of the Body in the Discourse of Postmodernity," *Theory, Culture and Society* 5 (June 1988): 527–42 (here 527).

21. Jameson 17.

22. George Eliot and G. H. Lewes had extended naturalising expeditions to Ilfracombe, Tenby, the Scilly Isles, and Jersey in 1856–57 in order to enable Lewes to write a series of

articles for *Blackwoods Edinburgh Magazine,* which were then published in 1858 as *Sea-Side Studies.* Extracts from Eliot's letters and journals at this time are published in John W. Cross, *George Eliot's Life as Related in Her Letters and Journals,* 3 vols. (Edinburgh: 1878–80), and also in Gordon S. Haight, *George Eliot: A Biography* (New York/Oxford: Oxford UP, 1968).

23. George Eliot, "To Sara Sophia Hennell," 29 June 1856, *The George Eliot Letters,* ed. Gordon S. Haight, vol. 2 (London: Oxford UP/New Haven: Yale UP, 1954) 257.

Michael Levenson

Angels and Insects:
Theory, Analogy, Metamorphosis

IN THE SHADOW OF THEORY

Byatt has spoken back riskily against the encroachments of literary theory—
riskily because her academic background has shown her the force of the theoretical advance. Theory, she knows, is a question not only of new ideas but of new
institutional power, as even those of us sympathetic to the movement must
acknowledge. The reputation of "serious writers" depends increasingly on the
attentions of academic lectures, conferences, and essay collections, and in the
face of the sheer determined energy of theoretical writing, it is mere sentimental-
ity to pretend that novelists do not notice the concepts arranged to display them.

Feminist theory has of course been the most pointed case for Byatt. Long
committed to the social aims of feminism, she has bristled against the demands of
a "theory" or a "program" that would limit the freedom of writing or the play of
reading. In her most brazen mood, Byatt has suggested that a glowing tradition of
contemporary women's fiction has now waned under the chill shadow of feminist theory. Even when praise gets sent to her for the accuracy of her portrayals of
women, she can bite her lip in refusal: "I think in metaphors, not in propaganda."[1]

In its twentieth-century plot, *Possession* plays out the comic polemic stirred by
this anger and by the insight that "critics are tiny people compared to writers:
which is not a fashionable thing to say." "The modern characters," Byatt goes on,
"are very secondary to the interest in the nineteenth century."[2] Part of the event of
Angels and Insects is to live up to that recognition and to invent plots unmediated
by our contemporary quandaries. To write her way past *Possession* was to leave

the confines of a present university setting, escaping not only its smallness but its limited modal resources, the resources of either farce or romantic comedy.

Yet, the problem of theory does not disappear in the leap to the nineteenth century. Two initial examples will help to set the case. The first, the easiest, comes in the middle of "The Conjugial Angel," the second of the two novellas in *Angels and Insects*, where Mr. Hawke, the ponderous, prurient Swedenborgian, robs a séance of its mystery by launching into garrulous hypotheses. "Mr Hawke, Mrs Papagay thought, would theorise if a huge red Cherub with a fiery sword were advancing on him to burn him to the bone; he would explain the circumstances, whilst the stars fell out of the sky into the sea like ripe figs from a shaken fig-tree" (*AI* 203).

The second example is more challenging. It involves Arthur Hallam, described at one point as more mourned and missed than any other departed being. "The Conjugial Angel" evokes his fiancée, Tennyson's sister, who married and became Emily Jesse, and it asks how grief appears, not within the great literary lament of *In Memoriam*, but within a lengthening everyday life, stretching through the years, unresolved, unrhymed. Emily recalls loving Hallam during the four scattered weeks of their acquaintance and also recalls the demand that she love her dead fiancé eternally. But part of the work of the novella is to show how hard it is to mourn the dead.[3] When they return to us, they do not always gleam with virtues; they also shake their unlovely wings. Emily Jesse remembers conversations in which her splendid Arthur divided the sexes in sharply separated compartments: "The Nous is male and the Hyle female, as Ouranos the sky is male, and Ge, the earth, is female, as Christ, the Logos, the Word is male, and the soul he animates is female." To which Emily responds, "Why?" and when he asks, "Why what?" she puts the bracing question, "Why is inert Matter female and the animating Nous male, please?" What follows is a cramped and awkward exchange, where we learn that "Arthur was not good at teasing. He spoke too decisively, as though beginning a lecture." The uneasiness only ends with his peremptory declaration: "Women shouldn't busy their pretty heads with all this theorising" (227–28).

"Theorising," in both these examples, is the work of those who claim spiritual authority. But to note Byatt's choice of the word is not to suggest that she is subtly referring to contemporary academic discourse. The case seems rather the reverse. As Byatt has reflected painfully on the conditions of late-twentieth-century writing—the barriers to freedom, the strength of literary orthodoxy, the temptations of a critical system—she has seen how they recapitulate the religious struggles of the nineteenth century. The attempt to preserve Christian faith often took the form of mastering experience through conceptual agility. If Lyell's geology and Darwin's biology threatened the integrity of faith, there remained the hope, continually enacted in *Angels and Insects*, that the new unsettling facts could be accommodated through nimble argument. In this sense, our own literary theory is a late, parodic form of a once momentous conflict. We too rely on the ingenuity of concepts and lend authority to those who wield them well. But the force of Byatt's historical recovery is to present the mid-Victorian struggle of faith and doubt as *unsurpassable*, as the originating moment of our modernity, which we must be willing to encounter again.

BOGGLE HOLE, UGGLEBARNBY

In the first of the paired novellas, the insect tale "Morpho Eugenia," the Reverend Harald Alabaster flails against his doubt. As an amateur naturalist, he sees the point and force of Darwin; he understands the challenge of the fossil record and the animal exempla; but he cannot accept the loss of faith. In a psychically tortured passage, Alabaster describes the span of his representative life. He is "old enough to have believed *without question* in the Divine Birth on a cold night with the sky full of singing angels" and has lived to be "presented with a world in which we are what we are because of the mutations of soft jelly and calceous bone matter through unimaginable millennia—a world in which angels and devils do not battle in the Heavens for virtue and vice, but in which we eat and are eaten and absorbed into other flesh and blood" (59). The rehearsal of his religious agony prepares for the desperate response. Despite the challenges of science, Alabaster cannot relinquish "arguments from the analogy between the Divine Mind and the human mind which he accepted, which supported him, which he did not discard" (58).

"Analogy" is the name for an activity that disturbs and fascinates Byatt. It disturbs her because it can so quickly become the cheap resource of all theoretical minds, the religious minds who defend against the challenge of science, and also the literary theoretical minds who lord it over the mere practitioners of fiction. In the hands of a master, analogy can absorb unruly experience within the safety of concepts; it gives the illusion of understanding, a substitute for faith. So Mr. Hawke the Swedenborgian converts the disorganized stir of human beings into a stately dance of angels. And Harald Alabaster contains Darwin by finding resemblances to Christian design.

The gifted naturalist William Adamson, rescued from shipwreck as he returned from the Amazon, is now a guest in the Alabaster family home. The good Reverend himself has been an ardent collector of natural specimens, sent to him from around the world: monkey skins, preserved lizards, dead beetles, and the like. He invites Adamson to organize the collection—"Set it all in order, don't you know? Make sense of it, lay it all out in some order or other"—as if the act of classification will ratify the Divine order. Adamson undertakes the work conscientiously. He makes labels and rearranges the beetles and frogs. But he finds that he cannot "devise an organising principle," a system that might rationalize the diversity (25). He is left simply attaching labels to specimens, ticketing each particular item, without any concepts to govern the whole.

We can take this as one exemplary tableau of the agon between religion and science. The dogged man of faith insists on a supervening order, but the naturalist, the observer, can only make individual labels that fail to compose a system and that make a mockery of theory. The brute activity of label-making, of finding names for things, is central not only to "Morpho Eugenia" but to Byatt's entire literary vocation. In much of her criticism, she worries over the recession of Names. When high theory grew confident and proud in the mid-1970s, it was all too easy to replace one piece of folk wisdom (words name things) with a new academic cliché (words only refer to other words). Against the wash of the cliché, Byatt did not attempt anything as bald as a philosophic refutation; rather, she responded with images of another temperament and tone (her own), which found energy in contemplating, not the purity of reference, but the *nearness* of words and things. In her 1990 conversation with Nicolas Tredell she offered this characteristic account:

The reason I love North Yorkshire so is that for me language and the earth are really intertwined there. There are these wonderful words like the Boggle Hole, Jugger Howe, Ugglebarnby. It's a sort of image of a paradisal state as in our idea, Foucault's idea, of a sixteenth century in which words denote things. And of course, that's why I get so distressed by literary theories which say language is a self-supporting system that bears no relation to things. Because I don't experience it in that way. I don't have any naive vision of words and things being one-to-one equivalents, but they're woven, like a sort of great net of flowers on the top of the surface of things.[4]

The passage is striking. Byatt makes no attempt to hold fast to obsolescent views of correspondence: the reference in language is not simple, direct, or univocal. And yet in refusing what sometimes counts for theoretical wisdom—language as an infolded garment—she looks to the past. Here the recourse is to the sixteenth century, but as she demonstrated in *Possession* and elaborates in *Angels and Insects*, it is the nineteenth century that comes to offer a richer scene of instruction. What animates the historical turn in *Angels and Insects* is not a longing for a past epoch, but a conviction that history is now. We have indulged fantasies of sophistication; we have patronized the past and preened in our modernity. But the force of these historical fictions is to insist that although our time is not their time, their problems remain ours.

FABLES OF REALITY

The overlooked, underdressed, dependent Matty Crompton writes a radiant fable embedded inside "Morpho Eugenia," which she calls "Things Are Not What They Seem." It turns on the wanderings and sufferings of Seth, the third son of a farmer, who leaves to seek his fortune but is then shipwrecked and cast with his crew upon an unknown island. A sinister fairy enchantress, Cottitoe Pan Demos, tempts the sailors with luscious food. As soon as they eat, she transforms them into hogs and pigs with a touch of her wand. Seth himself has swallowed only three pomegranate seeds and so is only partially changed and able to devise an escape. Yet we read that at the moment of crisis "Seth was interested in the variety of the pig-forms, despite his own great danger" (123). This is a telling remark. The vocation of the protagonist is precisely to register transforming nature in all its variety, even under conditions of emergency. Within the ostensibly anodyne terms of the animal fable, Seth depends on a benevolent ant, attentive caterpillars, and a wide-flying moth. But what gives edge to the tale is the imperative demand for visual heed and, even more, linguistic attention. Through the help of the insects, Seth meets young Mistress Mouffet, vulgarly associated with "Little Miss Muffet." The genuine Mistress Mouffet has no fear of spiders; she is the Recorder of the garden, specifically the recorder of the "names and natures" of the creatures within it. "Namegiving" is indeed her occupation (131). Seth's trial will lie in his encounter with animals and their names. The tale thus becomes a fable of realism. But what are we to make of that peculiar conjunction: a *fable*? of *realism*?

As William Adamson begins to languish among the Alabasters and as his mysterious marriage to Eugenia fails to flourish, Matty Crompton rises from her colorless insignificance to suggest that Adamson return to his vocation. How? he asks. How can he resume the Amazon researches here in the green and tended English countryside, especially when he has no "settled opinions"? Matty's brisk answer is "I did not mean *opinions*. . . . I meant a book of facts. A book of scientific facts, such as you are uniquely qualified to write" (92). The Amazon may be distant, "But nearer to hand—nearer to hand, lie things you could observe and write about" (93). In place of the exotic butterflies of South America, the crawling ants of England can be the subject of natural history.

Here is the call for a reinvigorated realism, a demand to pay close attention, *wherever one finds oneself*—in the words of *Middlemarch*, to study "this particular web" rather than the "tempting range of relevancies called the universe."[5] The scene recalls Byatt's favorite sentence from Murdoch's "Against Dryness," the defense of the "hard idea of truth" against the "facile idea of sincerity."[6] In coming to England and in curling within the marriage to soft, beautiful Eugenia, Adamson has drifted into the zone of fantasy, the close, dangerous cousin to mere sincerity: "He had yearned for Eugenia, and he *had* Eugenia, and he was bodily in thrall to Eugenia" (105). Within the Murdochian/Byattian ethic, our urgent task is to escape the temptations of easy subjectivity (opinion, sincerity, fantasy) and to encounter the hard world beyond the self.

What complicates and enriches this ethics/aesthetics is the recognition of a second motive alongside, or even within, the realism of hard truth. Slowly emerging out of her brown servile indistinctness, Matty Crompton becomes the chief protagonist of "Morpho Eugenia." Partly, her importance lies in rousing Adamson to recover the realist vocation; more substantially, it lies in finding a vocation of her own. Her tale of Seth and his wanderings allows for extravagant romance and fantasy: men are changed to pigs; Seth becomes the size of a small insect; he flies on the back of a moth. As Adamson recognizes, the force of the story depends on the "flight of imagination": Matty "had always seemed dry, and this tale, however playful, was throbbing with some sort of emotion" (140).

Beginning from an antithetical genre, she releases a form of seeing only available within the rhythms of romance.

It looks as if they are contraries: the man of science, the woman of imagination. Yet nothing is more determined in *Angels and Insects* than the will to develop the insight already struggling within *Possession*: a sense of the intimacy, even the deep identity, of these modes. After Matty Crompton has shown him the way, Adamson describes the goal of his natural history: "To appeal to a wide audience, by telling truths—*scientific truths—with a note of the fabulous*." Then Matty describes her own intention to write "some *real fables* of my own": "to emulate La Fontaine—the tale of the grasshopper and the ant, you know—only more *accurately*" (104; first emphasis added). These careful phrases record a complex adjustment of genres. From the side of science, William moves toward the "fabulous," while Matty begins in the tradition of fable and advances toward "accuracy."

In both of the novellas in *Angels and Insects* this ardent choreography is performed. On the one hand, Byatt writes as the rigorous fictive historian, one who will study sources and read up-to-the-minute scholarship in order to ensure the "hard truth" of the represented world. The country-house world of the mid-nineteenth century, including its architecture and domestic sociology; the state of science and literary taste; the circumstances of religious controversy; the deliquescence of the upper classes; the rise of spiritualism and séances—all these features of the age are carefully recovered in the spirit of an austere devotion to fact. At the same time, both novellas insist on scenes of imaginative transformation that change the mode and tone. Matty's fable enacts the modal change in "Morpho Eugenia," while in "The Conjugial Angel" it occurs even more challengingly in Sophie Sheekhy's vision of the dead. Does Arthur Hallam really appear to her? Are her visions real or imagined? The labor of the story is to sap that distinction of its force. Through the most strenuous labor of sympathy, Sophie Sheekhy tries to see what others long to glimpse. In her terror and exhaustion, the sublime images appear; she describes them for the others, who glow under the radiance of her vision. Were they, then, reflections of something that exists? Who can say? And then what finally matters is not that they were *images of the real*, but that they were *real images*.

THE SMELL OF LIFE

During the 1980s and into the 1990s, Byatt's critical thinking and fictive imagining returned repeatedly, even obsessively, to our fall into modernity, the "demythologizing" of the Christian world, the loss of the sacred canopy. The historical narrative is austere and unsparing: once there was the splendor of faith, the sun as "a choir of the heavenly host" (*PM* 313), but now the myths of glory have become mere fictions for us. It seems that our task is nothing more, but nothing less, than "to look clearly" at the mere, sheer, sensuous universe, to represent what Byatt calls the "bareness" of a post-Christian world (*PM* 313; 323).

Under the sign of "bareness," Byatt's first impulse has often been to defy concepts with the senses. The sheer quickening of the animal world, the heat of the sun, the exploding pigments, green and yellow and red—if we only give ourselves fully to them, we might overcome the weak temptations of analogic thinking. We could love a world unredeemed by concepts. Stirred by the touch of the earth, we might become strong enough not to need a sacred canopy. William Adamson, who has returned from the surging life of the Amazon, now lives within the comfort (and within the theory) of the Alabaster home. Intoxicated by the beauty, most of all the beauty of his wife-to-be Eugenia, he begins to ignore the call of the sensuous world. Only when prodded into taking nature rambles does he feel "his old self again, scanning everything with a minute attention that in the forests had been the attention of a primitive hunter as well as a modern naturalist, of a small animal afraid amongst threatening sounds and movements, as well as a scientific explorer" (*AI* 29). The vividness of the world, its colors, its smells, will heal him.

Matty Crompton smells. It is a "peculiar smell, a slightly acid armpit smell" (96) that contrasts with the fresh sheets in Eugenia's bedroom. The good stain of sensual life emanates through Matty's smell, and as it draws William toward her and away from his white and sterile marriage, it reaffirms the call of the body, whose upsurge defeats theory. So, too, at the end of "The Conjugial Angel," when Arturo Papagay (alive after all) returns to his wife, he pulls her toward him and she meets "his live smell, salt, tobacco, his own hair and skin, unlike any other hair and skin in the whole world, a smell she had kept alive when it had seemed wiser to let it die in the memory of her nostrils." (289) Even the "rich, decaying smell" (286) of Mrs. Jesse's dog Pug is an undeniable, inassimilable fact of life before theory.

In her comments on the writing of *Still Life*, Byatt describes her attempt to compose a novel "eschewing myths and cultural resonances—a novel, I even thought, which would try to forgo metaphor" (*PM* 9). Ford Madox Ford and William Carlos Williams were presiding figures in this ambition, inspiring her to a belief "that accuracy of description is possible and valuable." The novel would be "very bare" (*PM* 11), a still life indeed, which looked to "contiguity rather than analogy"—things alongside other things (*PM* 13). Yet, as she openly confesses, the project fails. The novel could not be written according to the canons of bareness. Metaphors kept erupting, like the return of the repressed. A telling moment, says Byatt, came during an encounter with Van Gogh's yellow chair. At first it seemed a triumph of worldly description, "a mimetic rendering of the thing itself," but as she gave herself to the image, "it turned out to be a complex metaphor, psychological, cultural, religious, aesthetic"(*PM* 14). Things and metaphors inevitably commingle—this was the decisive thought, and it participates in the still larger reflection on the place of spirit in an age of science.

If Byatt is drawn so consistently back to the nineteenth century, back especially to Van Gogh, it is because he occupies a difficult but opportune place between spirituality and bareness. Indeed, the very word "between" is a frequent resource in her essays—as in "Van Gogh stands, for me, between Browning and Wallace Stevens, sharing some of the preoccupations of each" (*PM* 6). Or again: Van Gogh "stands between the old myth of sacrifice, death and resurrection and the new world, in which all we can do seems to be to look clearly" (*PM* 313). The *place between* marks a condition of suffering, repeatedly enacted in *Possession* and *Angels and Insects*, but it always stirs the imaginative life. Memory and desire mix: the memory of a fading conviction, and the desire to keep the world luminous.

"*We* are not Nature," says one of the Alabaster children, to which Matty Crompton tartly responds, "What else are we?" (*AI* 32). This is Byatt's own rigorous question, enacted through the recovery of the Victorian crisis of faith and doubt. How can we accept the corrosions of science and still retain ideals of hope, visions of beauty? How can we picture ourselves as nothing but nature and at the same time richly and distinctively human? The risk is that such questions will seem hoary clichés, and a large part of Byatt's historical motive is to return us to the moment when the questions were alive and demanded urgent answers.

At the vital center of "The Conjugial Angel," Lilias Papagay, mourning for her apparently dead husband, has drifted into the community of spiritualists. She has gradually become a practitioner of automatic writing and has befriended Sophie Sheekhy, who can see farther than she. Even amid her passion to find her dead husband, Mrs. Papagay wonders at the hunger for the visitations of spirit. Why now, in the middle of the nineteenth century, is there such a yearning to see the dead? It can't always have been this way. Once the dead didn't haunt the living, returning "with raps, taps, messages, emanations, materialisations, spirit-flowers and travelling bookshelves" (*AI* 170). But now, an age of doubt has released a craving to witness signs of survival beyond the grave. Or, as Byatt has put it in her essay on Browning, "Spiritualism was the religion of a materialist age" (*PM* 62).

"The Conjugial Angel" thinks beyond the historical explanation, and, through the reflections of Mrs. Papagay, it looks to other motives for spirit-seeking. It was not really for the reassurance of immortality

that she travelled to séances, that she wrote and rapped and bellowed, it was for *now*, it was for more life *now*, it was not for the Hereafter, which would be as it was, as it always had been. . . . she wanted *life*. And this traffic with the dead was the best way to know, to observe, to love the living, not as they were politely over teacups, but in their secret selves, their deepest desires and fears. (*AI* 171)

The vision is of a worldly existence that depends on straining toward a Beyond. We can only love this world by seeking its limits. We can only break the grip of the everyday by traveling to the very end of the comprehensible and the known, indeed by reaching the point where comprehension shatters and a more fully human state is glimpsed in those "secret selves" and "deepest desires and fears." The Beyond is not only high above; it is deep within.

The friendship and partnership of Lilias Papagay and Sophie Sheekhy is an alliance of Life and Limit. The one is quivering, responsive, sensuous, and desirous; the other is inward and abstracted, at once matter-of-fact and visionary. By placing them together, in mutual care and fondness, Byatt unveils their need for one another. Like the intimacy between realism and fabulism, the close dance between Life and Limit is seen as the arduous condition of a post-Christian epoch. We can survive without Christianity, but we cannot survive—at least not well, not with grandeur or integrity—if we cease to strain past the existence that confines us. Only through the will to transcend do we preserve the glory of the immanent. The séance may collect fakery and fanaticism, but in its creaky way it preserves the dignity of hope and the sublimity of mystery.

Within Matty Crompton's fable, the sinister Dame Cottitoe Pan Demos culti-vates the abundance of her walled garden: a profusion of fruits and flowers and trees. But when Seth escapes, he learns that her garden is only "part of the realm of a much more powerful Fairy than Dame Cottitoe" and that there are many creatures not subject to her rule, those who come from "beyond-the-wall" (*AI* 130–31). If we recall the rendering of her name as "for all the people," we can recognize in Dame Cottitoe the figure of a dominating human will, a desire to constrain, enclose, and control. Here we have another image of those theorists, literary and religious, who tame the unruly and domesticate the visionary. Else-where in "Morpho Eugenia," when Adamson meets Sir Harald Alabaster, he is reminded of the Portuguese missionaries in the Amazon "who failed to compre-hend the incomprehension of the placidly evasive Indians" (24). To speak of an incomprehension beyond our comprehending is one way to put it; another is to posit a realm "beyond-the-wall" of our human will.

METAPHORIC MADNESS

I have spoken of Byatt's resistance to theory, literary and religious, her brazen assertion of our animality that precedes and exceeds our concepts. Speaking of women's role in child-rearing, she has erupted, "damn it, one's instincts are there, you can't theorize them away."[7] Yet for all this telling polemic, Byatt engages in what we can only call a theoretical activity of her own.

We have seen how *Angels and Insects* exposes the hollowness of the analogiz-ing mind, the cozy notion of similitude that defends against vivid experience. Within "Morpho Eugenia," the sentimental governess Miss Mead joins her em-ployer, Sir Harald, in willfully extracting solace from William's close observa-tion of the ants. Miss Mead "made little speeches to the little girls about the *kindness* of the ants" (41), and in his late desperate writings in defense of faith, Sir Harald clings to an image of "the sisterhood of ant-workers, who greet each other with great shows of affection and gentle caresses, always offering sips from their chalices of gathered nectar, which they are hurrying to carry to the helpless and dependent inhabitants of their nurseries" (86). But William has seen the insects bite off one another's heads, and his response to his patron's "Proof by the Ants" is to say: "You may argue anything at all by analogy, Sir, and so consequently nothing. . . . You might as well say, we are like ants, as that ants may develop to be like us." He invokes Feuerbach's claim that "We have made our God by a specious analogy" (89) and later remarks to Matty that "Analogy is a slippery tool. . . . Men are not ants" (100).

And yet immediately afterwards we read that William is hard put "not to see his own life in terms of a diminishing analogy with the tiny creatures" (100). Indeed, from his first appearance in country-house society, he has been struck, even disoriented, by the power of analogy. Even before he feels his life mirrored among the ants, he has noted similarities between the rituals of genteel privilege and the ceremonies performed by the Amazon tribes. William Adamson is as inveterate a user of analogy as all those defensive theorists who seek to disarm the world's contingency. Yet, the difference, which is all the difference, is that his analogical imagination makes no attempt to stabilize the world. The ants no more give the final truth about humanity than do parallels to the South American peoples. Similarities proliferate; comparisons multiply. Here is the more challenging provocation to the theoretical mind: not simply the acrid smell of the sensuous world, the irreducible blaze of yellow, but the endless intimations, the infinite allegories, stirred by the senses. The sharpest challenge to cozy analogy (those kind ants who show the benevolence of the Creator) is not the sharp shock of fact, but the lush production of *many* analogies. As William puts it, "We find parables wherever we look in Nature, and we make them more or less wisely" (116).

The natural world for Byatt is only intermittently a design; chronically, it is an abundance, a plenitude. What she draws from the agitations of nineteenth-century sciences—from geology, anthropology, biology—is a tableau of continual seething, a churning transformation that mocks the apostles of benevolence, the allegorists of order. As William squirrels away at Sir Harald's collection of specimens, he loses any sense of a consoling natural design, seeing instead

a huge, inexorable random constructive force, not patient, because it was mindless and careless, not loving, because it was remorseless in its discarding of the ineffectual or the damaged, not artistic, because it needed no wonder to fuel its subtle and brutal energies, but intricate, but beautiful, but terrible. And the more he delighted in his own observations of its gradual workings the more vain and pathetic he felt Harald's attempts to throw a net of theology over it, to look into its working and churning for a mirror of his own mind, to demand of it kindness, or justice. (73)

This is Nature as a sublimity that trounces our mere human conceptions, as a "mystery," which William proposes not only as "another name for God," but also as "another name for matter" (60). It can be a name for both, because in Byatt's strenuous re-vision, the religious sense must now live on within a radiant materialism. The surging, remorseless natural world—what Lilias Papagay simply calls "life"—is not forlorn or spiritually abandoned; it is the very home of our sense of spirit, its luminous dwelling. "It is not possible to avoid the myth of incarnation for long"—so writes Byatt in her indispensable essay on Van Gogh (*PM* 308). This is why he epitomizes for her, as do Browning and George Eliot, a moment of both terror and beauty, a nineteenth-century moment, when old beliefs were tottering but had not yet fallen, when the very emergency in religious faith excited a desire to make the world sacramental, to find the infinite within the finite, to incarnate God within Nature, Mystery within Matter.

Within this context, Matty Crompton's fable in "Morpho Eugenia" must be read as a tale of incarnation and metamorphosis. Its meticulous account of the "transfiguration" of insects, especially the breaking of the chrysalis and the birth of the moth, displays a view of Nature as a scene of mystery and a stage of change. Just when we think we can fix the world in place, its aspect turns: what "looks like the decay of putrefaction . . . is the stuff of life and rebirth itself" (133). From the perspective of this metamorphic naturalism, we can abandon the net of Christian theology and still retain the sublimity of transfiguration. In the last stages of "Morpho Eugenia," we watch as human beings perform transfiguring acts as momentous as the caterpillars. When William realizes the long deception of his marriage—Eugenia locked in incestuous pairing with her brutal brother—he finally understands that his real mate is the overlooked Matty Crompton. Yet he hesitates, and only her eruptive strength breaks through the chrysalis of old habits. Announcing that she will sail with him to the Amazon, he still falters:

"It is *no place* for a woman—"
"Yet there are women there."
"Yes, but not of your kind."
"I do not think you know what kind of woman I am." (156)

Indeed he does not, because he has not understood that a metamorphosis is underway. Matty, too, is not what she seems, and at the transfiguring moment she is nearly unrecognizable as she takes on a new form of being. She demands that he *see* her; only when he does can he accept the transformation of his own life: the break with his wife, the departure from England, the abandonment of a decaying social order.

RECALLING THE DEAD

Historical memory may look back to the radiance of transfiguration, but has it disappeared from our lives, lives that are many steps further along the road to demythologization? Is the summoning of the nineteenth-century moment finally an act of nostalgia? A postmodernist yearning for the pre-modern? "I don't want to go back," Byatt has said. "I never have wanted to go back."[8] Yet she insists on the endurance of an older world, a nineteenth-century world, that we like to pretend to have surpassed. When B. S. Johnson refused nineteenth-century literary forms as "anachronistic, invalid, irrelevant and perverse" (qtd. in *PM* 165–66), he was promulgating a false contemporaneity, repeated now within an imperial theory telling us what we can no longer believe. Byatt, always looking to the inspiration of Murdoch, denies the rupture of Modernism and insists on recovering continuity with the Victorians.

The difficulty lies in finding figures for this continuity. How can we picture ourselves still living at a time when the stakes are limitlessly high? How can we conceive ourselves as actors within a momentous drama that has not yet been played out? Partly, the answer is that historical fiction, like history itself, can reanimate the dead and make their extremity live for us. Both novellas in *Angels and Insects* work to revive the old shudder of Darwinism. Why shouldn't we still shudder?—this is what the stories implicitly demand. What have we become that we have forgotten the shock of our origins? The insight that seems to have been clarified for Byatt through the writing of *Possession* is that a novel might not only be *about* the act of faith in an age of doubt; it can itself *be* the act.

In her essay on Browning she pondered the case of Michelet, the French historian, who, in choosing a name for his history, rejected "Narrative" and "Analysis" in favor of "Resurrection." To write history is to resurrect the dead; it is to raise Lazarus; this is the decisive thought. Byatt, too, might well choose "Resurrection" as the name for her literary calling. At the end of "The Conjugial Angel," when Mrs. Papagay's husband thrillingly returns to her, Sophie Sheekhy watches "as they clutched and touched and babbled. And she thought of all the people in the world whose arms are aching and empty to hold the dead, and of how in stories, and very occasionally in sober fact, the cold and the sea give back what they have taken" (290). The miracle happens only occasionally in life, but stories can perform it often. A narrative can bring a drowned sailor back to life. And then beyond the workings of plot, the very act of writing historical fiction is a raising of the dead; it brings to life a buried past and so counts as a contemporary spiritual gesture.

There is another answer to the question. We writers exist in continuity with our nineteenth-century ancestors because we still use their language, and because the activity of speech and writing is itself bound up with belief, spirit, transfiguration. When Matty Crompton shows Adamson that she is a different "kind" of woman from the one he imagined, she takes on a new name: now she is "the new hungry Matilda"(158). To bestow a name, we see again, is to enter the shifting web of language; it is to change the aspect of the world. "It is amazing," says Matty, "how much—how much of mystery, of fairy *glamour*—is added to the creatures by the names bestowed upon them." And William agrees: "There is something wonderful about *naming* a species. To bring a thing that is wild, and rare, and hitherto unobserved under the net of human observation and human language" (118). The two characters share a passion for Linnaeus, recognizing his great taxonomy not as a wooden system but as a witty, vital verbal construction, rich with a sense of "character" and "myth." Matty's fable takes its inspiration from Linnaeus, one of "the great Namegivers" (131), and the labor of her protagonist Seth is to understand the vast burgeoning of Nature by grasping the protean powers of language. In a resonant statement consolidating so many of Byatt's imaginative investments, Mistress Mouffet instructs Seth that "Names, you know, are a way of weaving the world together, by relating the creatures to other creatures and a kind of *metamorphosis*, you might say, out of a *metaphor* which is a figure of speech for carrying one idea into another" (131–32).

Within language are the resources that bind us to the unsurpassable struggles of the nineteenth century. We have seen that Byatt refuses the strain in post-structuralism which regards language as a "self-supporting system that bears no relation to things," but she also resists a naive theory of correspondence in which one word simply names one thing. Language does not create a world; it weaves the world beyond itself, inventing connections, illuminating obscurities. Because the making of metaphors is the central act, language can never be a stable instrument; it is an active, mobile instability, and as it evokes the world, it changes worldly experience. This is the sense in which metaphor is metamorphosis and language incarnation.

A defensive Christian apologetics and literary theory are, for Byatt, both inimical to this imaginative venture. Their analogies are stiff and predictable: they assimilate sensuous experience into their stable constructions. The grander work of analogy, its distinctive glory, lies in exploiting the abundance of metaphor, a perpetual variety that settles nowhere. There is no one true metaphor. There are only new attempts to describe the world, resurrecting dead cliché into living speech, and straining to point at a world beyond the words, as human beings still strain to see beyond the reach of their eyes.

NOTES

1. Nicolas Tredell, "A. S. Byatt," *Conversations with Critics* (Manchester: Carcanet, 1994) 61. Even before the painful contest with feminist theory, Byatt had joined with Iris Murdoch in resisting the "single vision" of the crystalline modern novel. And then beyond the question of Modernism and its narrowness, she has held out against all demands for a programmatic mission: "my temperament is agnostic, and I am a non-believer and a non-belonger to schools of thought" (*PM* 2).

2. Tredell 58.

3. See Christien Franken's discussion of mourning in "The Conjugial Angel," where the story is read against the background of Freud's distinction between mourning and melancholia, in "The Gender of Mourning," *The Author as Character: Representing Historical Writers in Western Literature*, ed. Paul Franssen and Ton Hoenselaars (London: Associated UP, 1999) 244–47.

4. Tredell 65–66.

5. George Eliot, *Middlemarch* (Harmondsworth: Penguin, 1965) 170.

6. Iris Murdoch, "Against Dryness" [1961], *The Novel Today*, ed. Malcolm Bradbury (London: Fontana, 1990) 19. See the discussion of "Against Dryness" in Byatt's "'Sugar' / 'Le Sucre,'" *PM* 24.

7. Tredell 62.

8. Tredell 69.

A. S. Byatt

True Stories
and the Facts in Fiction

Better and better, man. Would now St Paul would come along that way, and to my breezelessness bring his breeze! O Nature, and O soul of man! how far beyond all utterance are your linked analogies! not the smallest atom stirs or lives on matter, but has its cunning duplicate in mind.

(Melville, *Moby Dick*, Chapter LXIX "The Sphinx")

He fastens each natural object to a theologic notion; a horse signifies carnal understanding; a tree, perception; the moon, faith; a cat means this; an ostrich that; an artichoke this other; and poorly tethers every symbol to a several ecclesiastic sense. The slippery Proteus is not so easily caught. In nature, each individual symbol plays innumerable parts, as each particle of matter circulates in turn through every system. The central identity enables any one symbol to express successively all the qualities and shades of real being. In the transmission of the heavenly waters, every hose fits every hydrant. Nature avenges herself speedily on the hard pedantry that would chain her waves.

(R. W. Emerson, "Swedenborg, or the Mystic,"
Representative Men)

"I must buy that. It would give me new metaphors."

(A poet, my friend, on the telephone, after my enthusiastic
recommendation of E. O. Wilson's *Insect Societies*)

I

This essay is about the relations of precise scholarship and fiction—largely historical fiction. The example I have used is the writing of my two linked historical novellas, "Morpho Eugenia" and "The Conjugial Angel," published together as *Angels and Insects*. The first version of the essay was written shortly after I finished writing the stories and reflects the moment-to-moment preoccupations with problems of accuracy and invention of the writing.

Both stories arise directly from my teaching in the English Department of University College London. It is customary for writer–academics to claim a kind of schizoid personality and state that their research, or philosophical thinking, has nothing to do with their work as makers of fiction. I don't know whether this is from fear of being thought to be amateurs in one or the other of their professions, or from fear, particularly in Britain, that the rigorous forms of the life of the intellect might be felt to inhibit their "creativity." I have myself always felt that reading and writing and teaching were all part of some whole that it was dangerous to disintegrate. "The Conjugial Angel" sprang directly from a lecture I used to give on the presence of Arthur Henry Hallam in Tennyson's *In Memoriam*. "Morpho Eugenia" is related to the reading of Darwin in connection with George Eliot's novels and essays, and also to modern Darwinian ideas and fictions. The same ideas could have turned into academic papers on "Swedenborg, Spiritualism, the energetic principle of love for the beautiful, The Human Form Divine and other uses of the human body in *In Memoriam*." Or "Arthur Hallam, Alfred Tennyson, Emily Tennyson and Emily Tennyson: Male Friendship and Victorian Women." Or "The Life after Death in the Victorian Imagination" or "Sexual Selection and Insect Societies in Victorian Thought." Or "The Earthly Paradise: Adam, Linnaeus, Wallace, Bates, the English Hedgerow and the Amazon Jungle." Why did these particular ideas form themselves into fictions?

This brings up the question of why the past is the subject of so much modern fiction? When I began writing novels, we were being lectured by C. P. Snow and Kingsley Amis about how good fiction *ought to* describe the serious social concerns of contemporary society. It seemed perfectly adequate to dismiss historical fiction as "escapism," and defences were unconvincing, apart from Lukács's powerful account of the European Walter Scott. We were later exhorted by Malcolm Bradbury and *The Guardian* to find new forms, now-this-minute, to describe the collapse of communism and Thatcher's Britain. The fall of the Berlin Wall, Bradbury rightly said, has changed our world. There should be new fictive forms, he also said, experimental forms, based perhaps on new means of information, television, satellite surveillance, to take on these rapid changes.

And yet there is a large body of serious and ambitious fiction set in the past, not for the pleasures of escapism or bodice-ripping, but for complex aesthetic and intellectual reasons. Some of it is sober and some of it is fantastic, some of it is knowing and post-modernist, some of it is feminist or post-colonial rewritings of official history, some of it is past prehistory, some of it is very recent. The writers include Golding, Burgess, Barnes, Carter, Swift, Coetzee, Calvino, Ransmayr,

Winterson, Unsworth, Michèle Roberts, Marina Warner, Jane Rogers, Caryl Phillips, Timothy Mo, Peter Ackroyd, Peter Carey, Elaine Feinstein, Penelope Fitzgerald and Toni Morrison—and many more.

There are all sorts of possible reasons for this. One, I think, which certainly affects me, is the vanishing of the past from the curriculum of much modern education in schools and increasingly in colleges and universities. A-Level[1] courses are increasingly preoccupied with contemporary texts to which students can hypothetically "relate." And yet my sense of my own identity is bound up with the past, with what I read and with the way my ancestors, genetic and literary, read, in the worlds in which they lived. A preoccupation with ancestors has always been part of human make-up and still, I think, comes naturally. Freud wrote in 1933:

Science is very young—a human activity which developed late. Let us bear in mind, to select only a few dates, that only some three hundred years have passed since Kepler discovered the laws of planetary movement, that the life of Newton, who analysed light into the colours of the spectrum and laid down the theory of gravitation, ended in 1727—that is to say, little more than two hundred years ago—and that Lavoisier discovered oxygen shortly before the French revolution. The life of an individual is very short in comparison with the duration of human evolution; I may be a very old man today, but nevertheless I was already alive when Darwin published his book on the origin of species. . . . And if you go further back, to the beginnings of exact science among the Greeks, to Archimedes, to Aristarchus of Samos (about 250 B.C.) who was the fore-runner of Copernicus, or even to the first beginnings of astronomy among the Babylonians, you will only have covered a small fraction of the length of time which anthropologists require for the evolution of man from an ape-like ancestral form, and which certainly comprises more than a hundred thousand years.[2]

The older I get, the more I habitually think of my own life as a relatively short episode in a long story of which it is a part. Darwin and Freud—and Tennyson, and even Swedenborg—do seem to me more central and urgent in this story than much of what is on television (in which I am also interested) or even the day-to-day movements in Kuwait or Sarajevo. It is always said of Browning's various resurrected pasts in his dramatic monologues that they are about Browning and the nineteenth century, and of course this is true—but it is not always added that they are also truly about the time when the New Testament was written, or about Renaissance Christianity and Art, though they are, and are illuminating about those matters. It is not either–or. At its best it is both–and. I do believe that if I read *enough*, and carefully enough, I shall have some sense of what words meant in the past, and how they related to other words in the past, and be able to use them in a modern text so that they do not lose their relations to other words in the interconnected web of their own vocabulary. At a time when certain kinds of criticism and ideological activity are happy to dispense with close attention to the history of words and their uses, it seems somehow important to be able to make coherent texts using words as they were used, together. Writing serious historical fiction today seems to me to have something in common with the difficult modern enterprise of Borges's Pierre Menard, rewriting the Quixote, in the "same" words, *now*.

This brings me to language. The journalist Chris Peachment interviewed various novelists about ten years ago about why they were writing historical novels, expecting some answer about paradigms of contemporary reality, and got the same answer from all of them. They wanted to write in a more elaborate, more complex way, in longer sentences, and with more figurative language. (I think the novelists interviewed were Golding, Ackroyd, Fowles, and Swift, but am not sure about this.) This surprised Chris Peachment but interested me. I associated this answer with a story of John Cheever, "Mene, Mene, Tekel, Upharsin," in which a man finds that the graffiti in an imposing marble-partitioned gentlemen's lavatory are long literary–aesthetic paragraphs, and with Anthony Burgess's *1985*, where the skinheads are secretly learning Latin in garages, because it is forbidden. Cheever's narrator is baffled by forms resembling (or perhaps they are) Poe, Pater, and Wilde and compares the archaic texts to the paperback books of "graphic descriptions of sexual commerce" in the "noble waiting room." "What had happened, I supposed, was that, as pornography moved into the public domain, those marble walls, those immemorial repositories of such sport, had been forced, in self-defence, to take up the more refined task of literature." His final discovery in an airport men's room, written on tile, is "'Bright Star! . . . would I were stedfast as thou art—Not in lone splendour hung aloft the night . . .'."[3] Rhetoric has become shady and a secretive pleasure.

I do have a strong sense of what a good *modern* sentence is. I found myself making this sense precise when I read V. S. Naipaul's novel, *The Enigma of Arrival* (1987). A good modern sentence proceeds evenly, loosely joined by commas, and its feel is hypothetical, approximate, unstructured, and always aiming at an impossible exactness which it knows it will not achieve. Naipaul's book is about a very well-read West Indian making sense of a local Wiltshire landscape and society by constant revision of his preconceptions and constant formation and reformation of new hypotheses. Consider, for example, the following paragraphs from the first section, "Jack's Garden," which begin with precise enumerating description and end with uncertainty about what Jack saw in the same facts.

The elaborate garden, with all its time-eating chores, was flattened. What was left didn't need much attention. No bedding-out plants now; no forking over of the ground below the hawthorn tree; no delphiniums in the summer. The garden was flattened, all but two or three rose bushes and two or three apple trees which Jack had pruned in such a way that they bunched out at the top from a thick straight trunk. The hedge, once tight at the top, mud-spattered and ragged at the bottom, a half or quarter barrier between garden and rutted farm-road, the hedge began to grow out into trees.

Now more than ever the cottages appeared to have neither front nor back, and to stand in a kind of waste ground. It matched the people and their attitude to the place. It matched the new way of farming, logic taken to extremes, the earth stripped finally of its sanctity—the way the pink thatched cottage on the public road, once pretty with its rose hedge, had been stripped of its atmosphere of home by the people who looked to it only for shelter.

But that might have been only my way of looking. I had known—for a short time—the straight stretch of the droveway open and unfenced. It had been fenced down the middle in my first year, and had remained fenced; but I carried that earlier picture. I had arrived at my feeling for the seasons by looking at Jack's garden, adding events on the river and the manor river bank to what I saw in his garden. But there were other ways of looking. Jack himself, giving the attention he gave to a meaningless hedge—a hedge that ran down the length of his garden and then abruptly stopped—saw something else, certainly.[4]

It is in a sense a paradigm of *scholarly* habits of mind, the search for impossible precision, and this, I think, can be said about other texts which strike me as quintessentially modern (always thinking on the Freudian timescale when the 1960s is a very short time ago). I think oddly of Doris Lessing's *The Golden Notebook* and more obviously of Michel Butor's *L'Emploi du Temps*, which is also about a foreigner making sense of an alien reality, in his case Manchester. Lessing's novel is about the breakdown of language and of fictive forms adequate to describe the sexual and political reality of the immediate present. All three texts are haunted by literary ancestors. Naipaul knows his Dickens and corrects his Dickensian London against 1950s reality. Butor, in his baffled text, alternates desperately precise passages of attempts to find geographical bearings with parodies of Proust's elaborate architectural cathedral metaphors. Lessing's novelist–heroine expresses exasperation that a text is no longer possible that can draw the whole world together as Tolstoi could.[5] Lessing demonstrates the fragmentary nature of the world her heroine lives in with a series of texts within texts, parodic and semi-parodic, a novel within a novel, parodies of women's magazine stories, sentimental film "treatments" of novels, Stalinist narratives and theories, fragments of headlines, all made of different kinds of restricted vocabularies. The moments in the *prose* of *The Golden Notebook* that most excited me when I first read it were little self-correcting sequences of sentences about how to say things, how to get things right. I was haunted for years, without quite understanding why it was so important, by the following paragraph:

I've thought about that often since. I mean, about the word nice. Perhaps I mean good. Of course they mean nothing, when you start to think about them. A good man, one says; a good woman; a nice man, a nice woman. Only in talk of course, these are not words you'd use in a novel. I'd be careful not to use them.

Yet, of that group, I will say simply, without further analysis, that George was a good person, and that Willi was not. That Maryrose and Jimmy and Ted and Johnnie the pianist were good people, and that Paul and Stanley Lett were not. And furthermore, I'd bet that ten people picked at random off the street to meet them, or invited to sit in that party under the eucalyptus trees that night would instantly agree with that classification—would, if I used the word *good*, simply like that, know what I meant.[6]

The passage is about moral authority in the world, and it is not insignificant that it is about a group of communists in Africa. But the phrase that haunted me as a writer was "these are not words you'd use in a novel. I'd be careful not to use them." Doris Lessing has made it possible for herself to use them by declaring her—or her heroine's—suspicion of them, her *care* as a writer to avoid them. Partly what moved me in the 1960s was the way it made me think about the vocabulary of a whole text as a *field*, a coherent field in which certain words worked and others didn't. But partly it was the excitement and freedom of the self-reflexive narrative transgression. "I'd be careful not to," she writes, and then does what she "cannot" do. I think this is related at some distance to the way in which Menard's Quixote and Cervantes's Quixote are different fields, in which the words have different values. In a "modern" text one may examine them in the questing way of Doris Lessing/Anna Wulf. Using words like "good" in a modern text written with the loaded vocabulary, say, of the Victorian fairy tale makes a different field again.

And the passages that troubled me, as well as exciting me, were the ones in which the novelist resisted her psychoanalyst's pleasure in her dreaming of ancient myths and paradigms and fairy tales. For these powerful metaphors and analogies, she felt, obscured and impeded her quest for the impossible accurate record of *now*. They were a form of aesthetic closure, agreeable, but not exactly useful. Anna tells the psychoanalyst she recognises her pleasure when she describes a dream of wolves, or ruined temples and blue seas.

"I know what the look means because I feel it myself—recognition. The pleasure of recognition, of a bit of rescue-work, so to speak, rescuing the formless into form. Another bit of chaos rescued and 'named'. Do you know how you smile when I 'name' something? It's as if you'd just saved someone from drowning. . . . no sooner do you accomplish that than you say quickly—put it away, put the pain away where it can't hurt, turn it into a story or a history. . . . I'm tired of the wolves and the castle and the forests and the priests. I can cope with them in any form they choose to present themselves. But I've told you, I want to walk off by myself, Anna Freeman."[7]

I connect this sense I have of fiction's preoccupation with impossible truthfulness with modern scholarship's increasing use of the techniques and attitudes of art. And indeed, artfulness. It is as though the two have changed places in a dance. Recent years have seen much discussion of the idea that history is fiction, and the understanding (not as new as it is sometimes said to be) that all narratives are partial and intrinsically biassed. It has been pointed out that critics are writers, which of course they are and always have been—but emphasis on this fact is problematic in an academic establishment of literary studies where there still exists, in some sense, a body of primary texts that are the object of critical study. Barthes and others have put forward the idea that texts are constructed, in some sense "written," by readers, which was an idea the writer in me used to find exciting before it became a commonplace. Writing a text does feel both the same as and different from reading one, and vice versa. But Barthes and others use it as a way of denying the authorship and authority of writers.

As writers of fiction become preoccupied with truthfulness and accuracy, writers of literary history and literary criticism seem to have taken on many of the rhetorical postures and attitudes of imaginative licence that once went with the artfulness of art. An example that springs to mind, because I reviewed it with a mixture of admiration[8] and irritation with its postures and style, is Mary Jacobus's *Romanticism, Writing and Sexual Difference*. Jacobus as writer claims her text with a series of erudite and not-so-erudite jokes and puns, often designed to diminish the writer she is studying, Wordsworth, who is character-ised as "the nutter of Nutting" and "the spoiled brat of *The Prelude*." She even manages to suggest that the paradigmatic narrative she is discussing requires the death of Wordsworth's mother, whether or not it happened in fact. What are we, as readers, to make of the tone of the following? What status as opinions or narrative or joke have these sentences? "Wordsworth's mother really did die early. But Rousseau's *Émile* suggests that if she were not already dead, she would need to be killed off; that autobiography comes into being on the basis of a missing mother."[9] The proposition itself is dubious, but it is the fictive "killing off" that I find rhetorically interesting. By whom? When? In what real or in-vented world? I am also interested in the narrative posture of the writer who can say, discussing the narrative genre of *The Prelude*: "Genre might be called the Frenchification of gender, and it was in France that (having left his French letters at home, as they say in England) Wordsworth discovered the literal implications of engendering."[10]

What relation do these anachronisms—nutter, French letter, engendering of texts—bear to the inventive anachronisms of Pierre Menard, scholar and writer? What *use* are they to, what relationship do they set up with, the reader of scholarly historical studies of Wordsworth?

Mary Jacobus's project is to reread, and in a riddling sense to rewrite *The Prelude* in the light of her own political preoccupations. Thus she is able to tell her readers that

the passions that blind the feminist reader to the text are one form of error that she might want to endorse. To paraphrase Rousseau on women readers, since "The world is the book of women," the feminist reader would be one who "will read in men's [texts] better than they do"—while deliberately misreading in the blinding light of her own desire. Of course, such a reading of *The Prelude* is itself didactic. Even error is deliberate, even blindness a form of knowledge.[11]

She is also able to construe Wordsworth's lines about "Newton with his prism and silent face / . . . Voyaging through strange seas of Thought, alone"[12] as a significant omission of the fact that Newtonian science had been used in the development of navigation which had led to the slave trade, which had been the occupation of the castaway, John Newton, who had spent his solitude learning Euclid.[13] Her argument rests on the coincidence of the names (it is true that Wordsworth had read John Newton and quotes him—on geometry)—and a certainty of her own right to judge Wordsworth's subject-matter. Slavery, right. Geometry, wrong. These are the worthy political preoccupations of the 1980s. This is Jacobus's text.

This is a kind of rewriting, or writing between the lines which fiction does with more tact, less whimsy, and infinitely more power. Caryl Churchill's *Cambridge,* a modern nineteenth-century text, written by a black man in the persona of a white woman visiting a slave plantation, rereads both the feminine novel of sensibility and the slave narratives. And Toni Morrison's great novel *Beloved* gives a voice, a new life, a life *now* to the silenced slaves of the slave narratives and rewrites, or at least radically changes the reading of the great nineteenth-century American novels. Hawthorne, Melville, Poe, Twain, and Stowe oppose black and white, embody the fears and anxieties of white men, connect these with the colours of Heaven and Hell, however subtly, however variously. Morrison makes black skin into a rainbow of subtle colours and life and makes white into the appalling *absence* that it is in Melville's chapter on "The Whiteness of the Whale." Poe's *Narrative of Arthur Gordon Pym* makes the abyss milky white— Morrison's imagery both endorses and shows up the human limitations of the uneasy understandings of Melville and Poe. Morrison's escaped slaves are fierce and real men and women. They transform the imagined world, permanently. Mary Jacobus complains that Wordsworth's poem leaves no openings for a female consciousness. Morrison simply *makes* new openings—black, female, both then and now.

Jacobus's rhetoric requires her to take a central and controlling and very visible position in her own text. It is a kind of deliberate vanity which it is instructive to compare with the extreme vanity of Norman Mailer in *Armies of the Night,* an account of the 1968 march on the Pentagon, divided into two parts, "History as a Novel" and "The Novel as History." Mailer uses his own central consciousness as narrator, participant, and commentator to *exasperate* the reader with his egoism and partiality. He describes his own self-indulgent drunk rhetoric, the fact that he is attended on the protest march by a documentary film-crew concerned with his own self-advertisement, his overweening competitiveness with other writers present. He then asks the same reader to make sense of the later part of the story which the narrator did not see, the imprisonment of the Quaker pacifists, for which contradictory and obviously inadequate newspaper accounts have to be used. Even such a partial ordering consciousness—especially one so transparently partial—he is arguing, is more use than mere reporting. The result is technically interesting in terms of narrative, of figurative language, of the relations between objective and subjective recording or telling. Both Mailer and Jacobus exhibit their own partiality. But it is the fiction writer who believes that the idea of truth may, through all the obfuscation and rhetoric—his is supremely a text about rhetoric—have meaning.

It is perhaps no accident that my exemplary "modern" texts are all written in the first person—a first person preoccupied with the desirability and impossibility of objectivity and truthfulness—and this is true even of Mailer's deliberate egocentric narration. I began as a writer with a deep mistrust of the first person—as a fictional narrative method, or as a voice for critical commentary. I think it is changes in the rhetoric of criticism that leads me to write commentary more and more overtly in an exploratory and "authorial" first person. I have only written one "fictive" text in the first person,[14] which was the only one that consciously used these "modern sentences"— "Sugar," a family history cast as an autobiography. My instinct as a writer of fiction has been to explore and defend the unfashionable Victorian third-person narrator—who is not, as John Fowles claimed, playing at being God, but merely the writer, telling what can be told about the world of the fiction.

II IMAGINARY PASTS

What follows is a brief, partial and exploratory account of the construction of my two historical fantasies, discussing the origins of the stories, the original ideas behind them, the "research" both conventional and fictional, and the discoveries—for me—the writing led to. Informing both the stories and this account of the stories is the concern I have already tried to describe with the field of available language, with truthfulness or accuracy, and with appropriate rhetoric.

"The Conjugial Angel," like "Precipice-Encurled," a story I wrote about Browning in the 1880s, began with what might be called a marginalising footnote. In the case of "Precipice-Encurled" it was in a book about Browning's hypothetical last love for Mrs Bronson in Venice. The author of the book recorded that Browning did not go to Ischia because a young house-guest of his prospective host had died after a fall from a cliff while sketching.[15] Absence of information starts the imagination working—I wondered about the dead young person whose life and death were contained in a footnote. (This is a professional extension of a normal reading process, in history or fiction, making a fuller, more vivid, more hypothetical narrative precisely around what we are *not* told.) In this case I decided to *invent* the faller—I did not even know whether it was a man or a woman—and to describe the fall, the sudden death, in a fully imagined third-person narrative, involving the reader as fiction does. Around this fictive window I arranged other pieces of narrative, in other styles—the "hypothetical" style of the researcher, the borrowed quotations from Browning himself, about mountains, about accidents, about writing, narrative thefts from Henry James's story "The Private Life," itself a hypothetical and playful structure about the relations between the private and the public selves of Robert Browning.

"The Conjugial Angel" also started with a footnote—in this case a footnote to the *Collected Letters* of Arthur Henry Hallam, in which Fryn Tennyson Jesse, Emily Tennyson Jesse's granddaughter, tells the story of Emily's life after Arthur Hallam, to whom she was engaged when he died in 1833. The engagement had been forbidden until he was twenty-one, and they must have spent only a few weeks in each other's company. Emily mourned him until 1842, when she married Lieutenant Jesse, amid a cloud of contemptuous criticism—for instance from Elizabeth Barrett, who wrote:

Miss Tennyson is a very radically prosaic sister for the great poet,—does her best to take away the cadence & rhymes of the sentiment of life. What a disgrace to womanhood! The whole is a climax of *badness*—! to marry at all—bad!—to keep the annuity, having married—worse! to conglomerate & perpetuate the infidelity & indelicacy, by giving the sacred name to the offspring of the "lubberly lieutenant"— worst of all!! That last was a desperate grasp at "a sentiment"—& missed.[16]

Fryn Tennyson Jesse tells the story of Emily Jesse's spiritualist experiences in the 1870s in Margate.

One spirit, I have always heard, told my grandmother that in the future life she would be re-united to Arthur Hallam, whereupon she turned to my grandfather and said indignantly: "Richard, we may not always have got on together and our marriage may not have been a success, but I consider that an extremely unfair arrangement and shall have nothing to do with it. We have been through bad times together in this world and I consider it only decent to share our good times, presuming we have them, in the next."[17]

Emily Jesse, like Tennyson's brother Frederick and another sister, Mary, did become members of Swedenborg's New Jerusalem Church. Swedenborg believed that angels were composed of a man and a woman conjoined, and that these androgynous angels were known as conjugial angels. My own interest in Swedenborg and in spiritualism came from working on Henry James, and the curious world of "isms"—feminism, spiritualism, Swedenborgianism, Fourierism—which informs *The Bostonians* and led me back to Henry James the elder, who, according to Emerson, wrote the *Secret of Swedenborg* and kept it. Elizabeth Barrett Browning, like many of her contemporaries, took these things with passionate seriousness, and Balzac, so often thought of as the arch materialist and realist, cannot be understood without understanding his Swedenborgian interests—his short novel *Séraphita* is an account of the marriage of a conjugial angel to itself. Alex Owen's excellent book *The Darkened Room*[18] is a gripping feminist account of nineteenth-century mediumship as one of the few professions open to women and one that relied heavily on what were traditionally thought of as "feminine" qualities of passivity, receptiveness, lack of "reason."

The original impulse for "The Conjugial Angel" was in this sense revisionist and feminist. It would tell the untold story of Emily, as compared to the often-told story of Arthur and Alfred in which Emily is a minor actress. I would write the séance in which the angel appeared and was rejected.

One of my *données* was Emily Tennyson's *exclusion.* She was excluded from Hallam Tennyson's *Life* of his father after Hallam's death, though he recorded the scene where she first came downstairs after a year of secluded mourning, "with one white rose in her black hair as her Arthur loved to see her."[19] She was almost excluded from *In Memoriam,* apart from Tennyson's reference to Hallam's possible marriage and his own possible nephews and nieces:

> I see thee sitting crowned with good,
>   A central warmth diffusing bliss
>   In glance and smile, and clasp and kiss,
> On all the branches of thy blood;
>
> Thy blood, my friend, and partly mine;
>   For now the day was drawing on,
>   When thou shouldst link thy life with one
> Of mine own house and boys of thine
>
> Had babbled "Uncle" on my knee;
>   But that remorseless iron hour
>   Made cypress of her orange flower,
> Despair of Hope, and earth of thee.[20]

Although *In Memoriam* ends with the celebration of a marriage, the marriage is that of another sister, Cecilia, to another Apostle, Edmund Lushington. Tennyson talks steadily of himself as the widow in the poem. I thought about this and tried to imagine what Emily Tennyson may have thought and felt.

It was in this context that I came up against the problem I initially thought this essay was "about"—how far can one change "truth" in fiction. I found myself troubled about Emily Tennyson herself—she had a dry wit, in what letters of hers I had read, and a rhapsodic note I was less happy with. If I had been writing biography or literary history, I should have ransacked the papers at the Tennyson centre in Lincoln—whereas as a writer of fiction, I felt a strong inclination to *stop* with the information I had, from Hallam's letters, Fryn Tennyson Jesse, and various writings of Sir Charles Tennyson. I had the facts my imagination wanted to fantasise about, and I wanted space for the kind of female consciousness I needed, to which perhaps Emily Tennyson did not quite fit. Partly to get round this, I decided to invent two mediums—Lilias Papagay and Sophy Sheekhy—named for the female angels often described as having been in Paradise before Adam, Lilith and Sophia or the Shekhinah, who according to some theologies created matter. Mrs Papagay represents one reason for involvement in spiritualism—narrative curiosity. She is interested in people, their stories and secrets, she *will* imagine, she is a version of Sludge-as-Browning, the medium as artist or historian. Sophy actually *sees* things, images, finally both Hallam and the halfangel. She likes poems and is impatient of novels. I also invented a Swedenborgian *flamen* called Mr Hawke and a grieving mother of five dead infant daughters, Mrs Hearnshaw. Mrs Papagay and Sophy, like Joshua, the cliff-faller in "Precipice-Encurled," were my "window" for pure fictive activity, and made it less necessary to *make up* Emily Jesse, so to speak. (In the sense in which Virginia Woolf speaks lovingly in her notebooks of mornings spent "making up" the characters of *The Waves* or *The Years*).

But I was also interested in both Tennyson and Hallam. (Indeed I only came to be interested in Emily because *In Memoriam* is a very great poem, and I did not want to forget that.) My interest in Hallam started with an observation of Marshall McLuhan's in a brilliant essay of 1951, "Tennyson and Picturesque Poetry," in which he discussed Hallam's review in 1831 of Tennyson's poems. Hallam praised Tennyson for being, in Keats's terms, a "Poet of Sensation rather than Thought." McLuhan connects Hallam's praise of sensuous images to modernist imagism and sees Tennyson's landscape poems as precursors of symbolist landscape (*The Waste Land*).

Whereas in external landscape diverse things lie side by side, so in psychological landscape the juxtaposition of various things and experiences becomes a precise musical means of orchestrating that which could never be rendered by systematic discourse. Landscape is the means of presenting, without the copula of logical enunciation, experiences which are united in existence but not in conceptual thought. Syntax becomes music, as in Tennyson's "Mariana."[21]

McLuhan thought that Hallam and Tennyson did not take the final step into cubist "landscape of the mind" which puts "the spectator always in the centre of the picture, whereas in picturesque art the spectator is always outside."[22] But when I read this essay I was already influenced by the morals of the fictions of Iris Murdoch and Doris Lessing, who are both afraid of the mind losing external reality in an arrangement of images and analogies. Both Lessing and Murdoch are concerned in their fiction, and in their other writings, to detect the dangerous distorting power of "fantasy." I liked Hallam and Tennyson because their sensuousness was a guarantee of something resistant "out there" as opposed to *paysage intérieur*.

So I read all Hallam's essays, and his translations of Dante, and much later, his letters, and found that he had a cosmic myth of a Creator so much in need of Love that he created His Son in order to experience "direct, immediate, absorbing affection for one object, on the ground of similarity perceived, and with a view to more complete union," and that he created His Son as the object of his love, and the Universe as it is, "full of sin and sorrow," as the necessary solution of the difficulty of making an object of Love finite, less perfect, not identical to the Lover, though still divine.[23] Both Hallam's aesthetic and his theology are erotic, and material.

Thomas Mann once said that the *directed* reading for a piece of fiction was one of the great pleasures of his work (he was talking about *Dr Faustus*). Once I had a framework and characters I simply immersed myself—over a period of years—in a disparate set of texts. Biographical texts about Hallams, Tennysons, and Swedenborg. Swedenborg's writings. Angels in dictionaries of angels, and the Book of Revelation. Victorian theories of the afterlife. *In Memoriam,* again and again. It is a process like trawling, or knitting, and recurring themes and patterns began to make themselves. Birds, for instance. Emily Tennyson kept a pet raven. Swedenborg said that the thoughts of angels were perceived in the world of spirits in material form as birds. He also said that ravens and owls were symbols of evils and falses [*sic*] because they were birds of night. (Emerson was right to detect something pedestrian in his symbolism.) *In Memoriam* is haunted by birds—larks, linnets, doves, nightingales, rooks,

> birds the charming serpent draws,
> To drop head-foremost in the jaws
> Of vacant darkness and to cease.[24]

Tennyson's poem "Recollections of the Arabian Nights" uses the nightingale as a symbol of deathlessness, like Keats's Ode. This bird sings something which is

> Not he: but something which possessed
> The darkness of the world, delight,
> Life, anguish, death, immortal love,
> Ceasing not, mingled, unrepressed,
>   Apart from place, withholding time.[25]

and is surely related to the later bird of *In Memoriam*:

> Wild bird, whose warble, liquid sweet,
>   Rings Eden through the budded quicks,
>   O tell me where the senses mix,
> O tell me where the passions meet,
>
> Whence radiate: fierce extremes employ
>   Thy spirits in the darkening leaf,
>   And in the midmost heart of grief
> Thy passion clasps a secret joy.[26]

Emily Tennyson, on the other hand, wrote a most prosaic, *outsider's* account of a real nightingale in Lincolnshire to Hallam's sister, after his death.[27] Michael Wheeler has pointed out that Rossetti, in his illustrations, connected Poe's raven in "The Raven" with the vision of the conjoined Lovers in the heaven of the Blessed Damosel, since both were illustrated by him with one left-behind-mourner on earth and conjugial angels in heaven.[28] There is a pleasure to be found in making up real fictive birds and connecting them with images already active in the field of the language the fiction draws on.

I found, as I went on reading, that I was feeling out, or understanding, the Victorian fear that we *are* our bodies, and that, after death, all that occurs is natural mouldering. *In Memoriam* is permeated by Tennyson's desire to *touch* Hallam, Hallam's hands, particularly, and speculation about the decay of the body, tossed with tangle and with shells, netted by the roots of the yew in earth, eaten by worms.

> I wage not any feud with Death
>> For changes wrought on form and face;
>> No lower life that earth's embrace
> May breed with him, can fright my faith.[29]

Spiritualism offers precisely the reassurance of the bodily identity of the departed—they can indeed *touch* and make themselves apparent to the senses. Intelligent thinkers like James John Garth Wilkinson defended Swedenborg's religious beliefs, and Swedenborg's account of his own journeys in the worlds of angels, devils, and spirits, as a proper faith for a *materialist* age, and were comforted by the conjunction of metallurgist and visionary in Swedenborg himself. Tennyson was able, "thro' repeating my own name two or three times to myself silently" to put himself into a state of trance, where

out of the intensity of the consciousness of individuality, the individuality itself seemed to dissolve and fade away into boundless being, and this not a confused state, but the clearest of the clearest, the surest of the surest, the weirdest of the weirdest, utterly beyond words, where death was an almost laughable impossibility, the loss of personality (if so it were) seeming no extinction but the only true life.[30]

"This might," he said, "be the state which St Paul describes, 'Whether in the body I cannot tell, or whether out of the body I cannot tell'."

St Paul's story of the man who was caught up into the third heaven "whether in the body, I cannot tell; whether out of the body, I cannot tell,"[31] which I only knew in terms of Tennyson's trances turned out to be a recurring image. Swedenborg used it to preface his own visits to Heaven and Hell, Hallam read Dante who uses the same passage to prefigure his own bodily journey to Heaven at the beginning of the *Paradiso*. Tennyson's assertion "I loved thee Spirit, and love, nor can / The soul of Shakespeare love thee more"[32] read differently in terms of this preoccupation with the afterlife of the body. Discoveries keep on happening. It was only on checking Keats's letter in which he wrote "Oh for a life of Sensations rather than Thoughts!" that I found that he spoke in the next sentence of enjoying the same bodily pleasures in the afterlife as here on earth.[33]

"The Conjugial Angel" is a ghost story and a love story. As a ghost story it is concerned with live and dead bodies; as a love story it is concerned, among other things, with male and female bodies. One of my early germs of story was a letter of Hallam to Emily in which he talks about the *Theodicaea Novissima*. He says:

I was halfinclined to be sorry that you looked into that Theodicaea of mine. It must have perplexed rather than cleared your sight of those high matters. I do not think women ought to trouble themselves much with theology: we, who are more liable to the subtle objections of the Understanding, have more need to handle the weapons that lay them prostrate. But where there is greater innocence, there are larger materials for a singlehearted faith. It is by the heart, not by the head, that we must all be convinced of the two great fundamental truths, the reality of Love, & the reality of Evil. Do not, my beloved Emily, let any cloudy mistrusts & perplexities bewilder your perception of these, & of the great corresponding Fact, I mean the Redemption, which makes them objects of delight instead of horror. Be not deceived: we are not called to effect a reconciliation between the purity of God & our own evil: that is done freely for us. . . . All our unhappiness comes from want of trust & reliance on the insatiable love of God.[34]

What interests me in this, apart from the usual patronising tone towards women, is the vocabulary of heart and head, feeling and thought. We have seen that Hallam set feeling before thought in poetry, and here he makes the completely usual conventional distinction between men and women as creatures of thought and feeling, respectively. Tennyson too, in *In Memoriam,* uses the same convention. Lyrics 31 to 33 deal with the Lazarus story: 31 asks whether the resurrected man had desired to hear his sister weeping, and where he had been, which "remaineth unrevealed"; 32 is about the deep love of Mary Magdalene for both "the living brother's face" and for Christ, "the Life indeed"; 33 admonishes an undefined "thou"

> Whose faith has centre everywhere
> Nor cares to fix itself to form,
>
> Leave thou thy sister when she prays,
>   Her early Heaven, her happy views;
>   Nor thou with shadowed hint confuse
> A life that leads melodious days.
>
> Her faith through form is pure as thine,
>   Her hands are quicker unto good:
>   Oh, sacred be the flesh and blood
> To which she links a truth divine![35]

This is an application of "O for a Life of Sensations rather than Thoughts" to theology. The woman is happier because her response to the Christian faith is through form, to flesh and blood—and I could spend a whole paper teasing out the complexities of placing these sentiments just here in this poem, next to Lazarus, the riddling exemplar of bodily survival of death. *Whose* flesh and blood? *Whose* sister? Here the Incarnation and the death of the body appear differently to male and female. But I want at this point only to emphasise the connection of woman with flesh and matter and of man with mind. This is an

example of thinking by false analogies—impregnation of females by male se-
men, impregnation of inert Matter by the divine Nous, which I think all feminists
ought to deconstruct. Instead of which many of them have aligned themselves
with earth religions of the Mother, as though both men and women were not both
body and spirit or mind, related in complicated ways. This is an analogy that has
always troubled me since I first met it in seventeenth-century neoplatonism, and
which tends to turn up in my writings when I am not looking, as though it was
what I was really looking for all along. Once I saw that it was at work—*really
and naturally* at work—in "The Conjugial Angel," all sorts of other discoveries
began to connect to it, like filings attracted to a magnet. For instance, that the
literary society formed by the Tennyson sisters and some women friends to
discuss the sensuous poems of Keats, Shelley, and Tennyson was called The
Husks (how sad) and that their highest term of praise was "deadly." Or for
instance that Swedenborg's female angels corresponded to "good, will and affection" in Heaven, while the males were "Truth, understanding and thought," but
that after marriage the qualities were all part of the male, to whom the female was
subordinate, as the Church was to Christ. And I found a wonderful piece of
theology in Swedenborg for my final séance.

Swedenborg believed that the whole Universe was one Divine Human, containing both male and female conjoined, and that heaven and hell were situated
within this Divine Human, attached to the appropriate corresponding organs. He
also claimed to have revealed, himself, to angels and to inhabitants of other
planets, that the Divine Human had been incarnate in a finite human body, at one
point in space and time, on earth, in Christ. Swedenborg taught that the incarnate
Lord had *both* a mortal human form from his mother and an eternal human form
from the fact of his Divine Self, his Father. On earth he successively *"put off"* the
Human assumed from the Mother, and "put on" the Human from the Divine in
himself. He had two states on earth, one called the "state of humiliation, or
exinanition, . . . the other a state of glorification or union with the Divine, which
is called the Father. He was in the state of humiliation" or exinanition so far as,
and when, "he was in the human from the mother; and . . . in the state of
glorification" so far as, and when, "he was in the Human from the Father."[36] His
Crucifixion was a necessary shedding of the corrupt humanity He had from the
mother, in order to experience glorification and union with the Father.

Here the same analogies between women and matter (dead or deathly matter in
this case) and men as mind are at work as are at work, *mutatis mutandis,* in
Hallam's mixture of Keatsian sensuality and neoplatonic theology. I don't have
time to go into the relations between mind and matter in *In Memoriam,* though
the story does. Nor do I have time to tell the story. But I will say briefly how the
discoveries of the metaphors at work changed the writing.

Firstly it meant that the whole story became very *fleshly*, both about the living,
real and imaginary, and about the dead. When Sophy Sheekhy does see the dead
Hallam, the important thing about him—though he speaks—is that he is a *dead
body*, a dead weight, and clay-like—I took some images from the terrible dead

man in Keats's sensuous and ghostly masterpiece, "Isabella." The Hallam Sophy encounters knows that poems are the sensuous afterlife of men.

In the second place, it led towards the way to write the fact (according to Fryn Tennyson Jesse) that the Jesses' séances were given up because of obscene messages. I wrote a series of obscene theological stanzas in the metre of *In Memoriam* incorporating something I found in Jung's *Alchemical Studies* about Sophia and the calling of chaos into matter,[37] and a reference to the stinking corpse of Fair Rosamond actually made by Hallam in his review of Tennyson— more specifically of the "Dreams of the Arabian Nights"—where he quotes the "monkish tag"—*non redolet sed olet, quae redolere solet.* "Bees may be redolent *of* honey; spring may be 'redolent *of* youth and love;' but the absolute use of the word has, we fear, neither in Latin nor English any better authority than the monastic epitaph on Fair Rosamond: '*Hic jacet in tombâ Rosa Mundi, non Rosa Munda, non redolet, sed olet, quae redolere solet.*'"[38]

I wrote

> The Holy Ghost trawls in the Void
> With fleshly Sophy on His Hook
> The Sons of God crowd round to look
> At plumpy limbs to be enjoyed
>
> The Greater Man casts out the line
> With dangling Sophy as the lure
> Who howls around the Heavens' colure
> To clasp the Human Form Divine
>
> .   .   .   .
>
> And is my Love become the Beast
> That was, and is not, and yet is,
> Who stretches scarlet holes to kiss
> And clasps with claws the fleshly feast
>
> Sweet Rosamund, adult'rous Rose
> May lie inside her urn and stink
> While Alfred's tears turn into ink
> And drop into her quelque-chose

(*AI* 285–86)

And the third is a moment of fictive narrative I wrote in which Emily, the outsider, stands on the Somersby lawn, where Alfred and Arthur are trailing their hands, with their fingers not quite touching, and talking about divine love. Emily asks Arthur why Hyle is female and Nous is male, and he fobs her off in the tone of the "Theodicaea" letter. Later Alfred remembers the same scene—the hand he misses, an analogy with Michelangelo's God the Father and Adam (Hallam had "the bar of Michael Angelo" on his brow), "The man I held as half-divine."[39] Emily has in her basket two texts Hallam sent her—*in fact*—*Emma* and *Undine*. He sent her *Undine* because he felt she resembled Undine in her wildness and naturalness. Undine was, I realised while writing this paper, a water-spirit without an immortal soul.

I do not think I would have made many of the connections I made between Hallam's aesthetic, his theology, Emily's Swedenborgianism, the sociology of spiritualism, body and soul, by thinking in an orthodox scholarly way—or, for that matter in a deliberately *unorthodox* scholarly way, in feminist–deconstructionist critical puns. The direction of my research was wayward and precise simultaneously. And the combination of the pursuit of the excluded Emily and the attempt to understand the ideas and images of the two young men did, I think, change my ideas about love and death in Victorian life and literature.

III

What I found—not, I think, imposed—in the writing of "The Conjugial Angel" was an anthropomorphic metaphor for the construction of the Universe, in its nineteenth-century form, though informed by many other versions. "Morpho Eugenia" is an entirely fictitious tale—intended as a kind of robust Gothic allegory, which initially I saw as a film, because one of its sources was the new visions of life afforded by cameras inside antheaps and termite hills. It had two germs. One was the observation that in *Middlemarch* Mr Farebrother the clergyman and collector of pinned dead insects was the old-world order, and Lydgate, who wanted to examine living connective tissues, was the new. The other was Mæterlinck's anthropomorphic imagining of the Ant Queen after her nuptial flight. I read a great deal about insect life, for mixed reasons. I see insects as the Not-human, in some sense the Other, and I believe we ought to think about the not-human in order to be fully human. Insects are the object of much anthropomorphising attention—we name their societies after our own, Queen, Soldier, Slave, Worker. I think we should be careful before we turn other creatures into images of ourselves, which explains why I was worried by my poet–friend's wish to find metaphors in E. O. Wilson's *Insect Societies*. Wilson's own extensions of his thought into human sociology have led to anxieties about political incorrectness, but he does have the ability to make us imagine the *antness* of his ants—at least as construed by this particular scientist. Mæterlinck's flight of fancy is particularly bizarre:

Each female has five or six mates, whom she often carries off with her in her flight, and who wait their turn; after which, falling to the ground, they perish in a few hours' time. The fertilized female alights, seeks shelter in the grass, discards her four wings, which fall at her feet like a wedding-gown at the close of the feast, brushes her corselet, and proceeds to excavate the soil in order to cloister herself in an underground chamber, and there attempt to found a new colony.

The foundation of this colony, which frequently ends in disaster, is one of the most pathetic and heroic episodes of insect life.

The ant who will perhaps be the mother of an innumerable population buries herself in the ground and there makes for herself a narrow prison. She has no other food than that which she carries in her body, that is, in the social crop—a little store of honey-dew—her tissues, and her muscles, and above all the powerful muscles of her sacrificed wings, which will be entirely reabsorbed. Nothing enters her tomb save a little moisture, pluvial in origin, and, it may be, certain mysterious effluvia of which we do not as yet know the nature. Patiently she awaits the accomplishment of her secret task. At last a few eggs are spread about her. Presently a larva emerges from one of these eggs; it spins its cocoon; other eggs are added to the first; two or three larvæ emerge. Who feeds them? It can only be the mother, since the cell is impervious to everything but a little moisture. Now she has been buried for five or six months; she can do no more, for she is nothing but a skeleton. Then the horrible tragedy begins. On the point of death—a death which would at one blow destroy the future which she has been preparing—she resolves to eat one or two of her eggs, which will give her strength to lay three or four more; or she resigns herself to devouring one of the larvæ, which will enable her, thanks to the imponderable aliments whose nature is unknown to us, to rear and nourish two more; and so, from infanticide to parturition, from parturition to infanticide, taking three steps forward and falling two back, yet steadily gaining on death, the funereal drama unfolds itself for close upon a year, until two or three little workers emerge, weakly because ill-nourished, from the egg, who pierce the walls of the *In Pace*, or rather the *In Dolore*, and seek, in the outer world, their first victuals, which they carry to their mother. From this moment she has no more cares, no more troubles, but night and day, until her death, does nothing but lay her eggs. The heroic days are gone; abundance and prosperity replace the long famine; the prison expands and becomes a city, which spreads underground year after year; and Nature, having here played out one of her cruellest and most inexplicable games, goes farther afield, and repeats the same experiments, whose morality and utility are as yet beyond our understanding.[40]

My idea for the story was fairly simple. A young scientist marries the daughter of an old clergyman–collector and becomes trapped in a country house which turns out to resemble an ant-heap, in that it is uncertain whether the source of authority is the incessantly childbearing females or the brisk sexless workers. For a long time I had only these three characters in my head—the Lydgate-like young man, the Farebrother-like old man, and the fecund daughter, who was always associated in my mind with Austen's Lady Bertram. My idea for the film was that the screen would be able to interweave the images of the two communities—ants and people—so as at once to reinforce the analogy and to do the opposite—to show the insects as Other, resisting our metaphorical impositions. I decided quite early to make my hero an Amazon explorer from the lower middle classes like Wallace and Bates and Spruce. I called him William and the old collector Harald out of a blatant reference to Scott's historical vision of old and new rulers, Saxon and Norman. I called the eldest daughter Eugenia, because she was well-born and because the story was something to do with Sexual Selection as well as Natural Selection. Much later in my thinking I saw that I needed another woman, not confined to her biological identity, and invented Matilda—who masquerades through the early part of the story as Matty Crompton, a kind of governessy poor relation, making herself useful in the schoolroom.

Then, as with the other story, I read. Ants, bees, Amazon travels, Darwin, books about Victorian servant life, butterflies and moths—resisting, rather than searching out useful metaphors, but nevertheless finding certain recurring patterns. For instance the Amazonian explorers' use of the imagery of Paradise, which to Wallace in South America was an English field and hedgerow, but in England became the openness of the native people and the fecundity of the virgin forest. Knowledge of both places unsettled the images of both, in terms of the Other. I had called William "Adamson," as a kind of ironic reference to the first man in the first Garden. I discovered quite late in my work the full beauties of the Linnaean system of naming the lepidoptera.

Linnaeus found a treasure-house of names in the Greek and Roman literature which formed the basis of contemporary education. For the swallowtails he turned to Homer and especially the *Iliad*. He applied the names of Trojan heroes to those that had the thorax marked with red, starting with Priamus, king of Troy. The names of Greek heroes (Achivi) were given to those that lacked this red, headed appropriately enough by Helena, "the face that launched a thousand ships," and her rightful husband Menelaus. . . .

After the Equites or Knights came the Heliconi which took their names from the Muses and Graces that dwelt on Mt Helicon. . . . The third section are the Danai. Danaus . . . conveniently had fifty daughters, a splendid source for names. . . . The Nymphales follow . . . After the Nymphales, we have the Plebeji or Commoners (the smaller butterflies).[41]

I thought this was a strange and innocent form of colonialism—the Englishmen wandering through the Virgin Forest in pursuit of creatures called Menelaus and Helen, Apollo and the Heliconiae, and all the Danaides. I was particularly pleased when I discovered in Bates—long after the name of my character was settled—a passage about the Morphos—the large blue butterflies—and discovered that there was one called Morpho Eugenia (a congener of Morpho Menelaus and Morpho Rhetenor, according to Bates).[42] I was even more pleased when I discovered elsewhere that Morpho is one of the ways of naming Aphrodite Pandemos, the earthly Venus. I was pleased in the way one is when one *discovers* a myth still alive and working, despite the fact that part of my intention was to undo anthropomorphic imaginings and closures—for reasons akin to those Doris Lessing gives to Anna Wulf, criticising her psychoanalyst for closing off thought with mythic "wholeness."

A characteristic of working out a story through the metaphors, and the metaphors through the story, is that you have repeated moments when you discover *precisely* and intellectually something that you always knew instinctively. (Though the story calls in question any definition of instinct.) In this case I realised I was working towards a conversation between Harald who was writing a book on Design in a universe that he accepts is accurately described by Darwin, and William, who is a Darwinian agnostic. Harald uses the arguments of Asa Gray, the Harvard biologist[43]—including Gray's quotation of the places where

Darwin still talks of the Works of the Creator, in his description of the development of the eye,[44] and the places where Darwin is led to personify Natural Selection as a kind of Dame Nature.[45] Harald is concerned with the origin of ethical values, and tries to deduce God, the Father of a Family, from human love. (He also uses the arguments used by Kingsley, about God the embryologist, revealed in Psalm 139.) William retorts that argument by analogy is only what Feuerbach said it was, projection of the human being to fill the Universe. *Homo Homini Deus est*. Harald answers that it is just as much of an error to suppose that we are no more than automata, on the analogy of the way some naturalists look at insects. This too is dangerous analogy.

William is gloomy, since he is coming to see himself in terms of the male inhabitants of the hive or the anthill. (He would; I made him so; this is a fable.) I felt as though I had found out for the first time that this story, Darwinian, Linnaean, Amazonian, is just as much about analogy, the body, and its sexual functions as "The Conjugial Angel" was. When Matty Crompton talks William into beginning to engineer his release from bondage by writing the history of the local colonies of wood ants (a person more preoccupied with slavery and colonialism would have made a quite different metaphorical structure from these natural-historical facts from the one I made), he finds a metaphor for the flight of the males which I particularly liked—and stitched together from a precise description in a modern naturalist's study:[46]

And the males, too, have become specialised, as factory-hands are specialised *hands* for the making of pin-heads or brackets. Their whole existence is directed *only* to the nuptial dance and the fertilisation of the Queens. Their eyes are huge and keen. Their sexual organs, as the fatal day approaches, occupy almost the whole of their body. They are flying amorous projectiles, truly no more than the burning arrows of the winged and blindfold god of Love. (*AI* 103)

I added both the economic allusion to Adam Smith on specialisation, an allusion to Coleridge's objections to the synechdoche of "hands" for human beings, and the mythological reference to the burning arrows of the God of Love.

One of the most peculiar aspects of analogy in the study of the Natural world is mimicry—not the mimicry of the poisonous pharmacophages by the edible, but the walking metaphor visible possibly only to humans. (Though bee orchids are metaphors or parodies visible to bees.) We see eyes in the wing-spots of butterflies, we see the deaths-head on the hawk-moth, and we recognise the mask of the bluff attitude of the Elephant hawk-moth and the Puss Moth. Very late in the writing of my story I was flicking through my insect book and saw these, and thought they were, so to speak, walking analogies, walking metaphors.

I discovered Colonel Maitland Emmet also very late in the writing of this story. When I read his accounts of the naming of *Deilephila Elpenor* and *Cerura Vinula*—both of which, by pure chance, were named by Thomas Mouffet, whom I had wanted to "fit in" and couldn't—I suddenly had the form for the story written by Matty/Matilda under the title "Things Are Not What They Seem." At the narrative level, this was a veiled warning to William not to suppose that she herself was a sexless worker, and also an even more veiled warning about the relations of his wife with her brother Edgar. But it rapidly turned out to be another metaphor about metaphor-making. It is the story of Seth (Adam's late-born son in Genesis) who is shipwrecked and trapped by a kind of monstrous Marie-Antoinette-like shepherdess called Dame Cottitoe Pan Demos who turns the crew into swine. All this mythology sprang from the discovery that Mouffet had named the snouted caterpillar of the Elephant Hawk-Moth for Odysseus' companion who was turned into a swine by Circe. Seth is rescued by an ant and let out into a walled garden, where he meets Mistress Mouffet, the Spy or Recorder and the two false dragons, the caterpillars of Deilephila Elpenor and Cerura Vinula. Mistress Mouffet helps him to escape on the back of Sphinx Atropos Acherontis, the Death's-Head Hawk Moth, and he travels to see "a more powerful Fairy" than Dame Cottitoe. She is in a veiled cavern, has a face like a fierce lion and a beautiful woman, and is spinning continuous gold thread like a cocoon. She asks him a riddle which he answers—"what is my name?" He stammers out that he does not know, but she must be kind, he thinks she is kind. It was only at this point in my narrative that I realised that I had "found" another of my own most powerful recurring figures, just as inevitable as Nous/Hyle, Spenser's Dame Nature, who "hath both kinds in one"—and whom I need as I need Sophia and Lilith as images of the female Creator.

> Then forth issewed (great goddesse) great Dame *Nature*,
> With goodly port and gracious Maiesty;
> Being far greater and more tall of stature
> Than any of the gods or Powers on hie:
> Yet certes by her face and physnomy,
> Whether she man or woman inly were,
> That could not any creature well descry:
> For, with a veile that wimpled every where,
> Her head and face was hid, that mote to none appeare.
>
> That some doe say was so by skill devized,
> To hide the terror of her uncouth hew,
> From mortall eyes that should be sore agrized:
> For that her face did like a Lion shew,
> That eye of wight could not indure to view:
> But others tell that it so beautious was,
> And round about such beames of splendor threw,
> That it the Sunne a thousand times did pass,
> Ne could be seene, but like an image in a glass.[47]

And the rather didactic, Kingsley-like fairy tale, which was a message from Matty to William, had managed to amalgamate Tennyson's statue of Truth "behind the veil, behind the veil"[48] with the personified Nature of *In Memoriam*

Are God and Nature then at strife,
  That Nature lends such evil dreams?
  So careful of the type she seems,
So careless of the single life.[49]

In the fairy tale, Kind sends Seth back with a moth (a genuine one) called Morpheus Caradris to freeze Dame Cottitoe and her retinue with dream-dust— Morpheus, the god of Dreams, is also called Phobetor, the terrifier, and shares his "morph-" root with *Aphrodite pandemos* as *Morpho* because he is a shape-changer. I realised unexpectedly that from the beginning I had set up *Morpho Eugenia*, the aphrodisiac butterfly of sexual selection, against Matty, the Sphinx, the night-flyer, who "hath both kinds in one," lion and woman, and sets and answers the riddle William must solve to be free—sending him an anagram, insect/incest, in a word-game. And I was back at the personification problem, because she is also Darwin's Nature, whom the language and the culture led him to personify when what he was telling us about the natural world required him not to, not to posit a Designer, or a Parent.

The problem for the writer, for me, is to do with Wallace Stevens's great line in "Notes towards a Supreme Fiction": "to find, / Not to impose . . . / It is possible, possible, possible. It must / Be possible."[50] Recent theories of language have presented it as a self-referring system with no necessary connection to any part of the world other than our bodies which form it. Writers like Gabriel Josipovici have analysed the Demon of Analogy—the sense that what we thought was Out There and Other is only a description of the inside of our own skulls.[51] That is why I was so suspicious of McLuhan's wish to push Hallam and Tennyson's sensuous images into *paysage intérieur*. We need to look at the *exterior*. One can use studies of ant societies to think about ants, or about ant altruism, or about human altruism. (Mæterlinck, for example, has the most gloomy and beautiful description of the inhuman functionalism of socialist communities through the analogy with termites.) I like the formal *energy* of the relations between Swedenborg's Divine Human and Hallam's insatiable love of God in "The Conjugial Angel," and the personifications in "Morpho Eugenia"— Venus, Ant Queen, Dame Kind, Matilda. I think the stories are studies of the danger of thinking with images that think with images themselves (like Derrida's *La Métaphore Blanche*), and I do think that in some curious way they find, not impose.

NOTES

1. School exams taken at age 16+.

2. Sigmund Freud, "The Question of a Weltanschauung," *New Introductory Lectures on Psychoanalysis*, Pelican Freud Library, vol. 2, trans. James Strachey (1933 [1932]; Harmondsworth: Penguin, 1973) 209–10.

3. John Cheever, "Mene, Mene, Tekel, Upharsin," *The Stories of John Cheever* (London: Jonathan Cape, 1979) 558, 560.

4. V. S. Naipaul, *The Enigma of Arrival* (Harmondsworth: Penguin, 1987) 57–58.

5. "One novel in five hundred or a thousand has the quality a novel should have to make it a novel—the quality of philosophy. I find that I read with the *same kind of curiosity* most novels, and a book of reportage. Most novels, if they are successful at all, are original in the sense that they report the existence of an area of society, a type of person, not yet admitted to the general literate consciousness." Doris Lessing, *The Golden Notebook* (London: Michael Joseph, 1963) 59. *The Golden Notebook* seems to me one of the most far-reaching examinations of the nature of fiction and writing in our time. I have written about this in my essay "People in Paper Houses" (*PM* 165–88).

6. Lessing 98–99.

7. Lessing 402–3.

8. For instance, for Jacobus's analysis of the relations between the metaphor of theatre, the theatrical nature of the events of the French Revolution, and Wordsworth's use of this metaphor.

9. Mary Jacobus, *Romanticism, Writing and Sexual Difference: Essays on The Prelude* (Oxford: Clarendon, 1989) 242.

10. Jacobus 193.

11. Jacobus 263–64.

12. William Wordsworth, *The Prelude* [1850], 3.61 and 3.63, qtd. from *The Prelude 1799, 1805, 1850*, ed. Jonathan Wordsworth, M. H. Abrams, and Stephen Gill (New York: Norton, 1979).

13. Cf. Jacobus 69–93.

14. No longer true in 2000. I have written a short story, "Jael," about an unpleasant and mendacious narrator (which prompted a scornful and hostile letter from a reader who insisted on seeing it as an autobiographical confession), and a short novel, *The Biographer's Tale*, which is about the relations of biography, autobiography, truth, and fiction and has a male first-person narrator who is a renegade deconstructionist in search of elusive "things."

15. The book in question is Michael Meredith, ed., *More than Friend: The Letters of Robert Browning to Katharine de Kay Bronson* (Waco, TX: Armstrong Browning Library of Baylor University/Wedgestone P, 1985).

16. Emily's elder son was called Arthur Hallam Jesse. Elizabeth Barrett's comments are qtd. in *The Letters of Arthur Henry Hallam*, ed. Jack Kolb (Columbus: Ohio State UP, 1981) 799.

17. Qtd. in Hallam, *Letters* 802.

18. Alex Owen, *The Darkened Room: Women, Power and Spiritualism in Late Victorian England* (London: Virago, 1989).

19. Hallam Tennyson, *Alfred Lord Tennyson: A Memoir*, vol. 1 (London, 1898) 142.

20. Alfred Tennyson, *In Memoriam A. H. H.*, 84.5–16. This and all subsequent quotations from *In Memoriam* are taken from *The Poems of Tennyson*, ed. Christopher Ricks, 2nd ed., vol. 2 (Harlow: Longman, 1987).

21. Marshall McLuhan, "Tennyson and Picturesque Poetry" [1951], *Critical Essays on the Poetry of Tennyson*, ed. John Killham (London: Routledge, 1960) 74–75.

22. McLuhan 84.

23. A. H. Hallam, "Theodicaea Novissima," *The Writings of Arthur Hallam*, ed. T. H. Vail Motter (New York: MLA/London: Oxford UP, 1943) 204–5.

24. Tennyson, *In Memoriam* 34.14–16.

25. Tennyson, "Recollections of the Arabian Nights," *Poems*, vol. 1, 228.

26. Tennyson, *In Memoriam* 88.1–8.

27. Cf. Hallam, *Letters* 423n.

28. Michael Wheeler, *Death and the Future Life in Victorian Literature and Theology* (Cambridge: Cambridge UP, 1990). See, for instance, plates 9, 10 and 11, and pp. 148–50. Professor Wheeler's book appeared while I was writing "The Conjugial Angel." I had already talked to him about Swedenborg and spiritualism and *In Memoriam*.

29. Tennyson, *In Memoriam* 82.1–4.

30. Cf. Hallam Tennyson, *Memoir*, vol. 1, 320.

31. 2 Corinthians 12.2–5.

32. Tennyson, *In Memoriam* 61.11–12.

33. "O for a Life of Sensations rather than Thoughts! It is a 'Vision in the form of Youth' a Shadow of reality to come—and this consideration has further conv[i]nced me for it has come as auxiliary to another favorite Speculation of mine, that we shall enjoy ourselves here after by having what we called happiness on Earth repeated in a finer tone and so repeated." John Keats, "To Benjamin Bailey," 22 November 1817, *Letters of John Keats*, ed. Robert Gittings (Oxford: Oxford UP, 1970) 37.

34. Hallam, *Letters* 509.

35. Tennyson, *In Memoriam* 33.3–12.

36. Emanuel Swedenborg, *Four Leading Doctrines of The New Church* (London, 1846) 46.

37. I quote the following passage from Jung, which I came across by accident while doing a "trawling" kind of reading for *Angels and Insects*, as an example of the way in which happenstance discoveries are made. I had already written most of my text and Sophy was long-since named:

These ideas are closely related to the Gnostic conception of Sophia-Achamoth in Irenaeus. He reports that

the . . . [reflection] of the Sophia who dwells above, compelled by necessity, departed with suffering from the Pleroma into the darkness and empty spaces of the void. Separated from the light of the Pleroma, she was without form or figure, like an untimely birth, because she comprehended nothing [i.e., became unconscious]. But the Christ dwelling on high, out-stretched upon the cross, took pity on her, and by his power gave her a form, but only in respect of substance, and not so as to convey intelligence [i.e., consciousness]. Having done this, he withdrew his power, and returned [to the Pleroma], leaving Achamoth to herself, in order that she, becoming sensible of the suffering caused by separation from the Pleroma, might be influenced by the desire for better things, while possessing in the meantime a kind of odour of immortality left in her by Christ and the Holy Spirit" (*Adversus haereses*, I.4).

According to these Gnostics, it was not the Primordial Man who was cast out as a bait into the darkness, but the feminine figure of Wisdom, Sophia-Achamoth. In this way the masculine element escaped the danger of being swallowed by the dark powers and remained safe in the pneumatic realm of light, while Sophia, partly by an act of reflection and partly driven by necessity, entered into relation with the outer darkness. The sufferings that befell her took the form of various emotions—sadness, fear, bewilderment, confusion, longing; now she laughed and now she wept. From these affects . . . arose the entire created world. C. G. Jung, *Alchemical Studies*, trans. R. F. C. Hull (1967; London: Routledge, 1983) 334–35.

Gnostic Aeons, according to W. R. Newbold, "The Descent of Christ in the Odes of Solomon," *Journal of Biblical Literature* 31.4 (1912): 168–209, are the hypostasised thoughts of God, and emanated in pairs, male and female, not unlike the conjugial angels.

38. Hallam, *Writings* 193.

39. Tennyson, *In Memoriam* 87.40; 14.10.

40. Maurice Mæterlinck, *The Life of the Ant*, trans. Bernard Miall (London: Allen, 1958) 48–50.

41. A. Maitland Emmet, *The Scientific Names of the British Lepidoptera: Their History and Meaning* (Colchester: Harley, 1991) 16–18.

42. Henry Walter Bates, *The Naturalist on the River Amazons*, vol. 1 (London, 1863) 103. The name Eugenia appears in the earlier edition—by the Popular edition (London, 1910) it is changed to Morpho Uraneis.

43. Asa Gray, "Darwin and His Reviewers," *Atlantic Monthly* 6 (1860): 406–25; rpt. as pt. 3 of "Natural Selection and Natural Theology," *Darwiniana: Essays and Reviews Pertaining to Darwinism*, ed. A. Hunter Dupree (Cambridge, MA: Belknap P of Harvard UP, 1963) 106–45, here 119–20.

44. Charles Darwin, *The Origin of Species* (Harmondsworth: Penguin, 1968) 218–19.

45. See Gillian Beer's discussion of Darwin's use of metaphor and personification in *Darwin's Plots* (London: Routledge, 1983). I am also deeply indebted to her discussion of the idea of sexual selection and its use in Victorian fiction, particularly in *Daniel Deronda*.

46. Derek Wragge Morley, *The Evolution of an Insect Society* (London: Allen and Unwin, 1954).

47. Edmund Spenser, *The Faerie Queene*, 7.7.5–6; here qtd. from *Spenser: Poetical Works*, ed. J. C. Smith and E. de Selincourt (Oxford: Oxford UP, 1970). Christopher Ricks refers readers to William Heckford's *Succinct Account of All the Religions* (1791) "of which a copy was at Somersby" and which describes the statue of Truth at Sais on whose temple "was the following remarkable inscription: 'I am all that hath been, is, and shall be, and my veil hath no mortal yet uncovered'" (Tennyson, *Poems*, vol. 2, 374n).

48. Tennyson, *In Memoriam* 56.28.

49. Tennyson, *In Memoriam* 55.5–8.

50. Wallace Stevens, "Notes Toward A Supreme Fiction," *Collected Poems* (London: Faber, 1984) 404.

51. I have discussed this at greater length in "People in Paper Houses" (*PM* 165–88).

Select Bibliography

Novels and Collected Short Fiction by A. S. Byatt
(First U.K. and U.S. editions only)

Shadow of a Sun
        London: Chatto, 1964.
        New York: Harcourt, 1964.
    Rpt. as *The Shadow of the Sun*
        London: Vintage, 1991.
        New York: Harcourt, 1993.

The Game
        London: Chatto, 1967.
        New York: Scribner's, 1968.

The Virgin in the Garden
        London: Chatto, 1978.
        New York: Knopf, 1979.

Still Life
        London: Chatto, 1985.
        New York: Scribner's, 1985.

Sugar and Other Stories
        London: Chatto, 1987.
        New York: Scribner's, 1987.
    Contains:
      "Racine and the Tablecloth."
      "Rose-Coloured Teacups."

"The July Ghost." First published in *Firebird I.* Ed. T. J. Binding. Harmonds-
worth: Penguin, 1982: 21–37.
"The Next Room."
"The Dried Witch."
"Loss of Face."
"On the Day E. M. Forster Died." First published in *Encounter* Dec. 1983: 3–9.
"The Changeling." First published in *Encounter* May 1985: 3–7.
"In the Air."
"Precipice-Encurled." First published in *Encounter* Apr. 1987: 21–31.
"Sugar." First published in *New Yorker* 12 Jan. 1987: 28–50.

Possession: A Romance
London: Chatto, 1990.
New York: Random, 1990.

Angels and Insects
London: Chatto, 1992.
New York: Random, 1993.
Contains:
"Morpho Eugenia."
"The Conjugial Angel."

The Matisse Stories
London: Chatto, 1993.
New York: Random, 1995.
Contains:
"Medusa's Ankles." First published in *Woman's Journal* Sept. 1990: 182+.
"Art Work." First published in *New Yorker* 20 May 1991: 36–51.
"The Chinese Lobster." First published in *New Yorker* 26 Oct. 1992: 90–
100.

The Djinn in the Nightingale's Eye: Five Fairy Stories
London: Chatto, 1994.
New York: Random, 1997.
Contains:
"The Glass Coffin." First published as part of *Possession: A Romance.*
"Gode's Story." First published as part of *Possession: A Romance.*
"The Story of the Eldest Princess." First published in *Caught in a Story:
Contemporary Fairytales and Fables.* Ed. Caroline Heaton and Chris-
tine Park. London: Vintage, 1992. 12–28.
"Dragon's Breath." First published in *Index on Censorship* Sept.–Oct. 1994:
89–95.
"The Djinn in the Nightingale's Eye." First published in *Paris Review* 133
(Winter 1994): 14–112.

Babel Tower
London: Chatto, 1996.
New York: Random, 1996.

Elementals: Stories of Fire and Ice
>London: Chatto, 1998.
>New York: Random, 1999.

Contains:
>"Crocodile Tears." First published in *Paris Review* 146 (Spring 1998): 1–41.
>"A Lamia in the Cévennes." First published in *Atlantic Monthly* July 1995: 56–59.
>"Cold."
>"Baglady." First published in *Daily Telegraph* 15 Jan. 1994: 11.
>"Jael." First published in *Guardian* 27 Dec. 1997, The Week: 1–2.
>"Christ in the House of Martha and Mary." First published in *Mail on Sunday* 31 May 1998, You Magazine: 71–74.

The Biographer's Tale
>London: Chatto, 2000.
>New York: Knopf, 2001.

Uncollected Short Fiction by A. S. Byatt
(First date and place of publication only)

"Daniel." *Encounter* Apr. 1976: 3–8.
"Repeating Patterns." *Storia* 2 (1989): 137–46.
"The Distinguished Thing in a Bottle." *Daily Telegraph* 8 Feb. 1997: A6.
"Heavenly Bodies." *Sunday Times* 20 Dec. 1998: Culture 12+.
"Brief Lives" [a work-in-progress extract from *The Biographer's Tale*]. *New Writing 8*. Ed. Tibor Fischer and Lawrence Norfolk. London: Vintage, 1999: 50–82.

Poetry by A. S. Byatt

"Metaphors: theories as nets, as nests," *Listener* 8 June 1989: 19.
"A Dog, a Horse, a Rat." *Times Literary Supplement* 24 May 1991: 22.
"Working with Clichés." *The Timeless and the Temporal: Writings in Honour of John Chalker by Friends and Colleagues*: Ed. Elizabeth Maslen. London: Dept. of English, Queen Mary & Westfield College, 1993. 1–3.
"Dead Boys." *Times Literary Supplement* 2 Dec. 1994: 27.
[Writing as Maud Michell-Bailey]. Letter. *Victorian Poetry* 33.1 (1995): 1–3.

Collected Nonfiction by A. S. Byatt
(First U.K. and U.S. editions only)

Degrees of Freedom: The Novels of Iris Murdoch
>London: Chatto, 1965.
>New York: Barnes, 1965.

Rpt. (with additional material) as *Degrees of Freedom: The Early Novels of Iris Murdoch*.
>London: Vintage, 1994.

Wordsworth and Coleridge in Their Time
    London: Nelson, 1970.
    New York: Crane, 1973.
  Rpt. as *Unruly Times: Wordsworth and Coleridge in Their Time.*
    London: Hogarth, 1989.

Iris Murdoch
    Writers and Their Work 251. Harlow: Longman, 1976.
    New York: Scribner's, 1986.

Passions of the Mind: Selected Writings
    London: Chatto, 1991.
    New York: Turtle Bay, 1992.
  Contains:
    "Still Life/Nature morte." First published in *Cross References: Modern French Theory and the Practice of Criticism.* Ed. David Kelly and Isabelle Llasera. London: Society for French Studies, 1986. 95–102.
    "Sugar/Le Sucre." First published as an introduction to A. S. Byatt. *Le Sucre.* Trans. Jean-Louis Chevalier. Paris: Éditions des Cendres, 1989. 11–19.
    "Robert Browning: Fact, Fiction, Lies, Incarnation and Art." An expanded version of the introduction to *Robert Browning: Dramatic Monologues.* London: Folio Society, 1991. vii–xxxi.
    "George Eliot: A Celebration." First published as a pamphlet for inclusion with a boxed set of George Eliot's novels (Harmondsworth: Penguin, 1980).
    "George Eliot's Essays." An edited version of the introduction to *George Eliot: Selected Essays, Poems and Other Writings.* Ed. A. S. Byatt and Nicholas Warren. Harmondsworth: Penguin, 1990. ix–xxxiv.
    "Accurate Letters: Ford Madox Ford." Based on "Impressions and Their Rendering." *Times Literary Supplement* 13 Feb. 1981: 171–72; and the preface to *The Fifth Queen,* by Ford Madox Ford. Oxford: Oxford UP, 1984. v–xiv.
    "The Omnipotence of Thought: Frazer, Freud, and Post-Modernist Fiction." First published in *Sir James Frazer and the Literary Imagination: Essays in Affinity and Influence.* Ed. Robert Fraser. London: Macmillan, 1990. 270–308.
    "People in Paper Houses: Attitudes to 'Realism' and 'Experiment' in English Post-War Fiction." First published in *The Contemporary English Novel.* Ed. Malcolm Bradbury and David Palmer. London: Arnold, 1979. 19–41.
    "William Golding: *Darkness Visible.*" Rpt. of "A. S. Byatt on *Darkness Visible.*" Rev. of *Darkness Visible,* by William Golding. *Literary Review* 5 Oct. 1979: 10.
    "The *TLS* Poetry Competition." Rpt. of "Writing and Feeling." *Times Literary Supplement* 18 Nov. 1988: 1278.
    "A Sense of Religion: Enright's God." First published in *Life by Other Means: Essays on D. J. Enright.* Ed. Jacqueline Simms. Oxford: Oxford UP, 1990. 158–74.
    "Willa Cather." Based on the afterword and introductions to *O Pioneers!*

(London: Virago, 1983); *The Professor's House* (London: Virago, 1981); and *Death Comes for the Archbishop* (London: Virago, 1981), by Willa Cather.

"Elizabeth Bowen: *The House in Paris*." Rpt. of the introduction to *The House in Paris*, by Elizabeth Bowen. Harmondsworth: Penguin, 1976. 7–16.

"Sylvia Plath: *Letters Home*." Rpt. of "Mirror, Mirror on the Wall." Rev. of *Sylvia Plath: Letters Home*, ed. Aurelia Schober Plath. *New Statesman* 23 Apr. 1976: 541–42.

"Toni Morrison: *Beloved*."

"An Honourable Escape: Georgette Heyer." Rpt. of "Georgette Heyer is a Better Writer Than You Think." *Nova* Aug. 1969: 14+.

"Barbara Pym:" Rpt. of "Marginal Lives." Rev. of *An Academic Question*, by Barbara Pym, and *Barbara Pym*, by Robert E. Long. *Times Literary Supplement* 8 Aug. 1986: 862.

"Monique Wittig: The Lesbian Body." Rpt. of "Give me the Moonlight, Give me the Girl." Rev. of *The Lesbian Body*, by Monique Wittig. *New Review* July 1974: 65–67.

"Coleridge: An Archangel a Little Damaged." Rpt. of "Coleridge: 'An Archangel a Little Damaged': An Analysis of the Power and Failure of the Poet's Mind in Solitude and in Companionship." *Times* 2 Dec. 1972: 8.

"Charles Rycroft: *The Innocence of Dreams*." Rpt. of "Downstream." Rev. of *The Innocence of Dreams*, by Charles Rycroft. *New Statesman* 4 May 1979: 646.

"Van Gogh, Death and Summer." An expanded version of "After the Myth, the Real." Rev. of *The Van Gogh File: A Journey of Discovery*, by Ken Wilkie, *Young Vincent: The Story of Van Gogh's Years in England*, by Martin Bailey, *The Love of Many Things: A Life of Vincent Van Gogh*, by David Sweetman, and *Vincent Van Gogh: Christianity Versus Nature* by Tsukasa Kodera. *Times Literary Supplement* 29 June 1990: 683–85.

(with Ignes Sôdre). *Imagining Characters: Six Conversations about Women Writers*. London: Chatto, 1995.
Published in the U.S.A. as *Imagining Characters: Conversations about Women Writers: Jane Austen, Charlotte Brontë, George Eliot, Willa Cather, Iris Murdoch, and Toni Morrison*.
New York: Knopf, 1997.

On Histories and Stories: Selected Essays
London: Chatto, 2000.
Cambridge, MA: Harvard UP, 2001.
Contains:
"Fathers."
"Forefathers."
"Ancestors."
"True Stories and the Facts in Fiction." Rpt. in this volume.
"Old Tales, New Forms."
"Ice, Snow, Glass." First published in *Mirror, Mirror on the Wall: Women*

Writers Explore their Favourite Fairy Tale. Ed. Kate Bernheimer. New York: Doubleday, 1998. 64–84.

"The Greatest Story Ever Told." Rpt. of "Narrate or Die: Why Scheherazade Keeps on Talking." *New York Times* 18 Apr. 1999, Magazine: 105–7.

Uncollected Nonfiction by A. S. Byatt
(Excludes journalism, reviews, and art criticism)

Untitled contribution. *The God I Want*. Ed. James Mitchell. London: Constable, 1967. 71–87.

"The Lyric Structure of Tennyson's *Maud*." *The Major Victorian Poets: Reconsiderations*. Ed. Isobel Armstrong. London: Routledge, 1969. 69–92.

"Wallace Stevens: Criticism, Repetition, and Creativity." *Journal of American Studies* 12 (1978): 369–75.

Introduction. *The Mill on the Floss*. By George Eliot. Harmondsworth: Penguin, 1979. 7–40.

Introduction. *Enormous Changes at the Last Minute*. By Grace Paley. London: Virago, 1979. iii–vi.

Introduction. *A Lost Lady*. By Willa Cather. London: Virago, 1980. v–xiv.

Preface. *My Ántonia*. By Willa Cather. London: Virago, 1980. N.p.

Introduction. *The Little Disturbances of Man*. By Grace Paley. London: Virago, 1980. 5–8.

Introduction. *My Mortal Enemy*. By Willa Cather. London: Virago, 1982. v–xiii.

Introduction. *The Song of the Lark*. By Willa Cather. London: Virago, 1982. xiii–xix.

Introduction. *Shadows on the Rock*. By Willa Cather. London: Virago, 1984. vii–xii.

Afterword. *Lucy Gayheart*. By Willa Cather. London: Virago, 1985. 233–40.

Introduction. *An Error of Judgement*. By Pamela Hansford Johnson. Oxford: Oxford UP, 1987. v–ix.

"Identity and the Writer." *The Real Me: Post-Modernism and the Question of Identity*. Ed. Lisa Appignanesi. ICA Documents 6. London: ICA, 1987. 23–26.

Introduction. *The Brontës Went to Woolworths*. By Rachel Ferguson. London: Virago, 1988. iii–xiii.

Introduction. *Robert Browning: Dramatic Monologues*. Selected by A. S. Byatt. London: Folio Society, 1991. vii–xxxi.

Introduction. *A Case Examined; John Brown's Body; The Gooseboy*. By A. L. Barker. London: Vintage, 1992. 2–6.

Untitled contribution. *The Pleasure of Reading*. Ed. Antonia Fraser. London: Bloomsbury, 1992. 127–32.

"George Eliot, 1819–1880 and George Henry Lewes, 1817–1878." *Founders and Followers: Literary Lectures Given on the Occasion of the 150th Anniversary of the Founding of the London Library*. Ed. Isaiah Berlin. London: Sinclair, 1992. 49–76.

"In Memoriam." *Poetry in Motion 2*. London: Channel 4 Television, 1992. 54–70.

"The Irreplaceable Importance of Reading." *Why Read?* Ed. Rachel Van Riel. Birmingham: Birmingham Library Services, 1992. 15–18.

Introduction. *Jane Austen's The History of England from the Reign of Henry the 4th to the Death of Charles the 1st.* By Jane Austen. Chapel Hill: Algonquin, 1993. v–viii. Rpt. as "Jane Austen, the 'Prejudiced Historian.'" *Folio* (Winter 1993):10–15.

"Reading, Writing, Studying: Some Questions about Changing Conditions for Writers and Readers." *Critical Quarterly* 35.4 (1993): 3–7.

"Facilitator." *A Dedicated Fan: Julian Jebb 1934–1984.* Ed. Tristram and Georgia Powell. London: Peralta, 1993. 90–91.

"Willa Cather." *Virago Birthday Keepsake.* London: Virago, 1993. 16–19.

Introduction. *Kees Fens: Finding the Place: Selected Essays on English Literature.* Ed W. Bronzwaer and H. Verdaasdonk. Amsterdam: Rodopi, 1994. vii–ix.

Introduction. *Middlemarch.* By George Eliot. New York: Modern Library, 1994. N. page.

"A New Body of Writing: Darwin and Recent British Fiction." *New Writing 4.* Ed. A. S. Byatt and Alan Hollinghurst. London: Vintage, 1995. 439–48.

"Parmenides and the Contemporary British Novel." *Literature Matters* Dec. 1996: 6–8.

Untitled contribution. *The Tiger Garden: A Book of Writers' Dreams.* Ed. Nicholas Royle. London: Serpent's Tail, 1996. 40–41.

Introduction. *The Rubáiyát of Omar Khayyam.* Trans. Edward Fitzgerald. New York: Quality Paperback Book Club, 1996. v–xii.

Introduction. *The Oxford Book of English Short Stories.* Ed. A. S. Byatt. Oxford & New York: Oxford UP, 1998. xv–xxx.

Introduction. *The Song of Solomon.* Edinburgh: Canongate, 1998. vii–xviii.

"Hauntings." *Literacy Is Not Enough: Essays on the Importance of Reading.* Ed. Brian Cox. Cambridge: Cambridge UP, 1998. 41–46.

"Memory and the Making of Fiction." *Memory.* Ed. Patricia Fara and Karalyn Patterson. Cambridge: Cambridge UP, 1998. 47–72.

Introduction. *Daniel Deronda.* By George Eliot. London: Folio Society, 1999. vii–xiv.

Introduction. *Middlemarch.* By George Eliot. Oxford: Oxford World's Classics, 1999. v–xiii.

Introduction. *The Bell.* By Iris Murdoch. London: Vintage, 1999. vii–xv. Rpt. as "*The Bell* Revisited; 41 Years After." *Kyoto English Review* 3.2 (1999): 1–12.

"Arachne." *Threepenny Review* Summer 1999: 20–23: Rpt. in *Ovid Metamorphosed.* Ed. Philip Terry. London: Chatto, 2000. 131–57.

"Half-Angel and Half-Bird." *Browning Society Notes* 26 (May 2000): 7–20.

"Nothing is too Wonderful to be True." *Times* 7 June 2000, sec. 2: 12–13. Rpt. as "Novels and Biographies." *Reader* 8 (Spring 2001): 37–40.

"Faith in Science." *Prospect* Nov. 2000: 38–41.

Introduction. *Abba Abba.* By Anthony Burgess. London: Vintage, 2000. 1–6.

Preface. *Strange and Charmed: Science and the Contemporary Visual Arts.* Ed. Siân Ede. London: Calouste Gulbenkian Foundation, 2000. 7–10. Rpt. as "Strange and Charmed," *New Statesman* 10 Apr. 2000: 44–46; and *Art Monthly Australia* 130 (June 2000): 31–33.

Introduction. *The Arabian Nights: Tales from a Thousand and One Nights.* Trans. Richard F. Burton. New York: Modern Library 2001. xiii–xx.

Introduction. *The Quest for Corvo.* By A. J. A. Symons. New York: New York Review Books, 2001. ix–xvi.

Texts edited by A. S. Byatt

(with Nicholas Warren). *Selected Essays, Poems and Other Writings.* By George Eliot.
   Harmondsworth: Penguin, 1990.
(with Alan Hollinghurst). *New Writing 4.*
   London: Vintage, 1995.
(with Peter Porter). *New Writing 6.*
   London: Vintage, 1997.
The Oxford Book of English Short Stories.
   Oxford & New York: Oxford UP, 1998.

Criticism of A. S. Byatt's Fiction

Alexander, Flora. "Versions of the Real: A. S. Byatt, *Still Life.*" *Contemporary Women Novelists.* London: Arnold, 1989. 34–41.

Alfer, Alexa. "'A second that grows first, a black unreal / In which a real lies hidden and alive': The Fiction of A. S. Byatt." *Anglistik* 10.2 (1999): 27–48.

Alsop, Derek and Chris Walsh. "Postmodern Readings: *Possession.*" *The Practice of Reading: Interpreting the Novel.* London: Macmillan, 1999. 163–83.

Ashworth, Ann. "Fairy Tales in A. S. Byatt's *Possession.*" *Journal of Evolutionary Psychology* 15.1–2 (1994): 93–94.

Bigliazzi, Silvia. "'Art Work': A. S. Byatt vs. Henry Matisse, or The Metamorphoses of Writing." *Textus* 12.1 (1999): 185–99.

Brink, André. "Possessed by Language: A. S. Byatt: *Possession.*" *The Novel: Language and Narrative from Cervantes to Calvino.* Basingstoke: Macmillan, 1998. 288–308.

Bronfen, Elisabeth. "Romancing Difference, Courting Coherence: A. S. Byatt's *Possession* as Postmodern Moral Fiction." *Why Literature Matters: Theories and Functions of Literature.* Ed. Rüdiger Ahrens and Laurenz Volkmann. Heidelberg: Winter, 1996. 117–34.

Buxton, Jackie. "'What's Love Got To Do With It?': Postmodernism and *Possession.*" *English Studies in Canada* 22.2 (1996): 199–219. Rpt. in this volume.

Campbell, Jane. "The Hunger of the Imagination in A. S. Byatt's *The Game.*" *Critique: Studies in Modern Fiction* 29 (Spring 1988): 147–62.

Campbell, Jane. "'The Somehow May Be Thishow': Fact, Fiction, and Intertextuality in Antonia Byatt's 'Precipice-Encurled.'" *Studies in Short Fiction* 28.2 (1991): 115–23.

Campbell, Jane. "Confecting Sugar: Narrative Theory and Practice in A. S. Byatt's Short Stories." *Critique: Studies in Modern Fiction* 38 (Winter 1997): 105–22.

Chevalier, Jean-Louis. "Conclusion in *Possession* by Antonia Byatt." *Fins de Romans: Aspects de la Conclusion dans la Littérature Anglaise.* Ed. Lucien LeBouille. Caen: PU de Caen, 1993. 109–31. Rpt. in this volume.

Civello, Catherine. "George Eliot: From Middlemarch to Manhattan." *George Eliot Fellowship Review* 20 (1989): 52–56.

Clutterbuck, Charlotte. "A Shared Depository of Wisdom: Connection and Redemption in *Tiger in the Tiger Pit* and *Possession.*" *Southerly: A Review of Australian Literature* 53.2 (1993): 121–29.

Cosslett, Tess. "Childbirth from the Woman's Point of View in British Women's Fiction: Enid Bagnold's *The Squire* and A. S. Byatt's *Still Life.*" *Tulsa Studies in Women's Literature* 8.2 (1989): 263–86.

Creighton, Joanne V. "Sisterly Symbiosis: Margaret Drabble's *The Waterfall* and A. S. Byatt's *The Game.*" *Mosaic* 20 (Winter 1987): 15–29.

Cuder Domínguez, Pilar. "Romance Forms in A. S. Byatt's *Possession.*" *Revista Alicantina de Estudios Ingleses* 8 (1995): 79–89.

Davey, G. "*Still Life* and the Rounding of Consciousness." *Lancet* 7 Nov. 1998: 1544–47.

Delany, Samuel R. "Antonia Byatt's *Possession: A Romance.*" *Shorter Views: Queer Thoughts and The Politics of the Paraliterary*. London: Wesleyan UP, 2000. 353–58.

Djordjevic, Ivana. "In the Footsteps of Giambattista Vico: Patterns of Signification in A. S. Byatt's *Possession.*" *Anglia* 115.1 (1997): 44–83.

Dusinberre, Juliet. "Forms of Reality in A. S. Byatt's *The Virgin in the Garden.*" *Critique: Studies in Modern Fiction* 24 (Fall 1982): 55–62.

Fletcher, Judith. "The Odyssey Rewoven: A. S. Byatt's Angels and Insects." *Classical and Modern Literature* 19.3 (Spring 1999): 217–31.

Flint, Kate. "Plotting the Victorians: Narrative, Post-modernism, and Contemporary Fiction." *Writing and Victorianism*. Ed. J. B. Bullen. Harlow: Addison, 1997. 286–305.

Fountain, J. Stephen. "Ashes to Ashes: Kristeva's *Jouissance*, Altizer's *Apocalypse*, Byatt's *Possession* and 'The Dream of the Rood.'" *Literature and Theology* 8.2 (1994): 193–208.

Franken, Christien. "The Gender of Mourning." *The Author as Character: Representing Historical Writers in Western Literature*. Ed. Paul Franssen and Ton Hoenselaars. London: Associated UP, 1999. 244–47.

Franken, Christien. "The Turtle and its Adversaries: Gender Disruption in A. S. Byatt's Critical and Academic Work." *Theme Parks, Rain Forests and Sprouting Wastelands: European Essays on Theory and Performance in Contemporary British Fiction*. Ed. Richard Todd and Luisa Flora. Amsterdam: Rodopi, 2000. 195–214.

Franken, Christien. *A. S. Byatt: Art, Authorship, Creativity*. London: Palgrave, 2001.

Giobbi, Giuliana. "Sisters Beware of Sisters: Sisterhood as a Literary Motif in Jane Austen, A. S. Byatt, and I. Bossi Fedrigotti." *Journal of European Studies* 22 (1992): 241–58.

Giobbi, Giuliana. "Know the Past, Know Thyself: Literary Pursuits and the Quest for Identity in A. S. Byatt's *Possession* and F. Duranti's *Effetti Personali.*" *Journal of European Studies* 24 (1994): 41–54.

Gitzen, Julian. "A. S. Byatt's Self-Mirroring Art." *Critique: Studies in Modern Fiction* 36 (Winter 1995): 83–95.

Hansson, Heidi. "Byatt and Fowles: Postmodern Romances with Feminism." *The Interpretation of Culture and the Culture of Interpretation*. Ed. Eva Hemmungs Wirtén and Erik Peurell. Uppsala: Section for Sociology of Literature at the Dept. of Literature, U of Uppsala, 1997. 27–43.

Heilman, R. B. "A. S. Byatt's *Possession* Observed." *Sewanee Review* 103 (Fall 1995): 605–12.

Holmes, Frederick M. "The Historical Imagination and the Victorian Past: A. S. Byatt's *Possession*." *English Studies in Canada* 20.3 (1994): 319–34.

Hope, Christopher. *Contemporary Writers: A. S. Byatt*. London: Book Trust/British Council, 1990.

Hotho-Jackson, Sabine. "Literary History in Literature: An Aspect of the Contemporary Novel." *Moderna Språk* 86.2 (1992): 113–19.

Hotho-Jackson, Sabine. "'The Rescue of Some Stranded Ghost:' The Rewriting of Literary History in Contemporary British and German Novels." *The Novel in Anglo-German Context: Cultural Cross-Currents and Affinities*. Ed. Susanne Stark. Amsterdam: Rodopi, 2000. 385–98.

Hugues, Terence and Claire Patin. "Analysis of a Short-Story: A. S. Byatt's 'Rose-Coloured Teacups.'" *L'analyse textuelle en anglais: Narrative Theory, Textual Practice*. Paris: Dunod, 1995. 189–218.

Hulbert, Ann. "The Great Ventriloquist: A. S. Byatt's *Possession: A Romance*." *New Republic* 7 Jan. 1991: 47–49. Rpt. in *Contemporary British Women Writers: Narrative Strategies*. Ed. Robert E. Hosmer. New York: St Martin's, 1993. 55–65.

Janik, Del Ivan. "No End of History: Evidence from the Contemporary English Novel." *Twentieth Century Literature* 41.2 (1995): 160–90.

Kelly, Kathleen Coyne. *A. S. Byatt*. Twayne's English Authors Series 529. New York: Twayne, 1996.

Kelso, Sylvia. "The Matter of Melusine: A Question of Possession." *LINQ: Literature in North Queensland* 19.2 (1992): 134–44.

Kenyon, Olga. "A. S. Byatt: Fusing Tradition with Twentieth-Century Experimentation." *Women Novelists Today: A Survey of English Writing in the Seventies and Eighties*. Brighton: Harvester, 1988. 51–84.

Leonard, Elisabeth Anne. "'The Burden of Intolerable Strangeness': Using C. S. Lewis to See Beyond Realism in the Fiction of A. S. Byatt." *Extrapolation* 39.3 (1998): 236–48.

Lepaludier, Laurent. "The Saving Threads of Discourse and the Necessity of the Reader in A. S. Byatt's 'Racine and the Tablecloth.'" *Journal of the Short Story in English* 22 (Summer 1994): 37–48.

Levenson, Michael. "The Religion of Fiction." *New Republic* 2 Aug. 1993: 41–44. Rpt. in A. S. Byatt. *Degrees of Freedom*. London: Vintage, 1994. 337–44.

Löschnigg, Martin. "History and the Search for Identity: Reconstructing the Past in Recent English Novels." *Literatur in Wissenschaft und Unterricht* 29.2 (1996): 103–19.

Lund, Mark F. "Lindsay Clarke and A. S. Byatt: The Novel on the Threshold of Romance." *Deus Loci: The Lawrence Durrell Journal* 2 (1993): 151–59.

Maack, Annegret. "Deconstruction and Reconstruction: Versions of English Postmodernist Fiction." *Critical Dialogues: Current Issues in English Studies in Germany and Great Britain*. Ed. Isobel Armstrong and Hans Werner Ludwig. Tübingen: Narr, 1995. 142–57.

Maisonnat, Claude. "The Ghost Written and the Ghost Writer in A. S. Byatt's Story 'The July Ghost.'" *Journal of the Short Story in English* 22 (Summer 1994): 49–62.

Marsh, Kelly A. "The Neo-Sensation Novel: A Contemporary Genre in the Victorian Tradition." *Philological Quarterly* 74.1 (1995): 99–123.

Morse Denenholz, Deborah. "Crossing the Boundaries: The Female Artist and the Sacred Word in A. S. Byatt's *Possession.*" *British Women Writing Fiction.* Ed. H. P. Werlock-Abby. Tuscaloosa AL: U of Alabama P, 2000. 148–74.

Mundler, Helen E. "'Intratextual Passages': *The Glass Coffin* in the Work of A. S. Byatt." *Études Britanniques Contemporaines* 11 (1997): 9–18.

Neumeier, Beate. "Female Visions: The Fiction of A. S. Byatt." *(Sub)Versions of Realism: Recent Women's Fiction in Britain.* Ed. Irmgard Maassen and Anna Maria Stüby. *Anglistik und Englischunterricht* 60 (1997): 11–25.

Noble, Michael J. "Earth, Water, Fire, Air, and Fiction: A. S. Byatt's *Elementals: Stories of Fire and Ice.*" *Anglistik* 10.2 (1999): 79–87.

Noble, Michael J. "Presence of Mind: A. S. Byatt, George Eliot, and the Ontology of Ideas." *CEA Critic* 62.3 (2000): 48–56.

Sabine, Maureen, "'Thou Art the Best of Mee?': A. S. Byatt's *Possession* and the Literary Possession of Donne." *John Donne Journal* 14 (1995): 127–48.

Sanchez, Victoria. "A. S. Byatt's *Possession*: A Fairytale Romance." *Southern Folklore* 52.1 (1995): 33–52.

Schmid, Susanne. "Metafictional Explorations of Realism: The Novels of A. S. Byatt." *Hard Times* [Berlin] 56 (Spring 1996): 8–11.

Schuhmann, Kuno. "The Concept of Culture in Some Recent English Novels." *Anglistentag 1981: Vorträge.* Ed. Jörg Hasler. Trierer Studien zur Literatur 7. Frankfurt: Lang, 1983. 111–27.

Shiller, Dana. "The Redemptive Past in the Neo-Victorian Novel." *Studies in the Novel* 29.4 (1997): 538–60.

Shinn, Thelma J. "'What's in a Word?': Possessing A. S. Byatt's Meronymic Novel." *Papers on Language and Literature* 31.2 (1995): 164–183.

Shinn, Thelma J. "*Possession: A Romance.*" *Masterplots II: Women's Literature 5.* Ed. Frank N. Magill. Pasadena: Salem P, 1995. 1866–70.

Shuttleworth, Sally. "Natural History: The Retro-Victorian Novel." *The Third Culture: Literature and Science.* Ed. Elinor Shaffer. Berlin: De Gruyter, 1998. 253–68.

Sturgess, Charlotte. "Life Narratives in A. S. Byatt's *Sugar and Other Stories.*" *Journal of the Short Story in English* 22 (Summer 1994): 29–35.

Thomas, Susan Stock. "Writing the Self and Other in Byatt's *Possession* and in the Browning/Barrett Correspondence." *Studies in Browning and His Circle* 20 (1993): 88–94.

Todd, Richard. "The Retrieval of Unheard Voices in British Postmodernist Fiction: A. S. Byatt and Marina Warner." *Liminal Postmodernism: The Postmodern, the (Post-) Colonial, and the (Post-) Feminist.* Ed. Theo D'haen and Hans Bertens. Amsterdam: Rodopi, 1994. 99–114.

Todd, Richard. *A. S. Byatt.* Plymouth: Northcote/British Council, 1996.

Wallhead, Celia M. "Intertextuality in A. S. Byatt's 'The Conjugial Angel.'" *Intertextuality/Intertextualidad.* Ed. Mercedes Bengoechea and Ricardo Sola. U of Alcalá de Henares P, 1997. 199–210.

Wallhead, Celia M. "The Un-Utopian Fallenness of *Langage*: A. S. Byatt's *Babel Tower.*" *Dreams and Realities: Versions of Utopia in English Fiction from*

Dickens to Byatt. Ed. Annette Gomis and Miguel Martinez. U of Almería P, 1997. 133–50.

Wallhead, Celia M. *The Old, the New and the Metaphor.* London: Minerva, 1999.

Walsh, Chris. "Postmodernist Reflection: A. S. Byatt's Possession." *Theme Parks, Rain Forests and Sprouting Wastelands: European Essays on Theory and Performance in Contemporary British Fiction.* Ed. Richard Todd and Luisa Flora. Amsterdam: Rodopi, 2000. 185–94.

Webb, Caroline. "History through Metaphor: Woolf's *Orlando* and Byatt's *Possession: A Romance.*" *Virginia Woolf: Emerging Perspectives.* Ed. Mark Hussey and Vara Neverow. New York: Pace UP, 1994: 182–88.

Westlake, Michael. "The Hard Idea of Truth." *PN Review* 15.4 (1989): 33.

Wilkinson, Helen. "Mr Cropper and Mrs Brown: Good and Bad Collectors in the Work of A. S. Byatt and other Recent Fiction." *Experiencing Material Culture in the Western World.* Ed. Susan M. Pearce. London: Leicester UP, 1997. 95–113.

Yelin, Louise. "Cultural Cartography: A. S. Byatt's *Possession* and the Politics of Victorian Studies." *Victorian Newsletter* 81 (Spring 1992): 38.

Interviews with A. S. Byatt

Aragay, Mireia. "The Long Shadow of the Nineteenth Century: An Interview with A. S. Byatt." *BELLS: Barcelona English Language and Literature Studies* 5 (1994): 151–64.

Carver, Robert. "In Pursuit of the Fugitive Good. Criticism and the Arts on the Air: A. S. Byatt in Conversation with Robert Carver." *Ariel at Bay: Reflections on Broadcasting and the Arts: A Festschrift for Philip French.* Ed. Robert Carver. Manchester: Carcanet, 1990. 45–54.

Chevalier, Jean-Louis. "Entretien avec A. S. Byatt." *Journal of the Short Story in English* 22 (Summer 1994): 12–27.

Chevalier, Jean-Louis. "Speaking of Sources." *Sources: Revue d'Études Anglophone* 7 (Autumn 1999): 6–28.

Dusinberre, Juliet. "A. S. Byatt." *Women Writers Talking.* Ed. Janet Todd. New York: Columbia UP, 1980. 181–95.

Gerard, David. "David Gerard Talks to A. S. Byatt." *Reader* 5 (Autumn–Winter 1999): 15–23.

Greenfield, George. "A. S. Byatt." *Scribblers for Bread: Aspects of the English Novel Since 1945.* London: Hodder, 1989. 42–49.

Rothstein, Mervyn. "Best Seller Breaks Rule on Crossing the Atlantic." *New York Times* 31 Jan. 1991: C17+.

Todd, Richard. "Interview with A. S. Byatt." *Netherlands Society for English Studies* 1.1 (1991): 36–44.

Tonkin, Boyd. "Antonia S. Byatt in Interview with Boyd Tonkin." *Anglistik* 10.2 (1999): 15–26.

Tredell, Nicolas. "A. S. Byatt." *Conversations with Critics.* Manchester: Carcanet, 1994. 58–74.

Wachtel, Eleanor. "A. S. Byatt." *Writers & Company.* Toronto: Knopf, 1993. 77–89.

Index

About the Contributors

Alexa Alfer is affiliated with Queen Mary and Westfield College, London, U.K. She has written on A. S. Byatt, Walter Benjamin, Jacques Derrida, Sylvia Townsend Warner, and Virginia Woolf. She recently edited "A. S. Byatt in Focus" for the German journal *Anglistik* and is the author, together with Michael D. Crane, of the first comprehensive primary and secondary bibliography of A. S. Byatt.

Jackie Buxton recently completed her doctoral dissertation on the contemporary historical novel in English at York University, Canada. She has published on various aspects of contemporary British fiction and literary theory in, among others, *English Studies in Canada* and *Contemporary Literature*.

A. S. Byatt is one of Britain's leading writers. Educated at York and Newnham College, Cambridge, she taught at the Central School of Art and Design and was a Senior Lecturer in English at University College London, U.K., before becoming a full-time writer in 1983. Her fiction includes *Possession* (winner of the Booker Prize in 1990) and the sequence *The Virgin in the Garden, Still Life*, and *Babel Tower*. Her latest novel is *The Biographer's Tale*. She has also written two novellas, published together as *Angels and Insects*, and four collections of short stories, the most recent being *The Djinn in the Nightingale's Eye* and *Elementals*. Her critical works include *Degrees of Freedom*, a study of Iris Murdoch, *Unruly Times: Wordsworth and Coleridge in their Time*, and two collections of essays: *Passions of the Mind* and *On Histories and Stories*. She was appointed CBE in 1990 and DBE in 1999.

Jane Campbell is Professor Emeritus of English at Wilfrid Laurier University, Canada. She has published extensively on A. S. Byatt, Margaret Drabble, Sarah Ferguson, and Dickens, and on the subject of women's autobiography. She is the author of a monograph on English Romantic criticism and is currently working on a book-length feminist study of Byatt's fiction.

Jean-Louis Chevalier is Professor Emeritus of Literature at the Université de Caen, France, and the French translator of A. S. Byatt's fiction. In addition to his acclaimed work as a translator, he has published several critical pieces on A. S. Byatt and is the author of many articles on nineteenth- and twentieth-century British, Irish, and American literature.

Michael Levenson is the William B. Christian Professor of English and Chair of the English Department at the University of Virginia, U.S.A. He is the author of *A Genealogy of Modernis*m (CUP, 1984) and *Modernism and the Fate of Individuality* (CUP 1991), the editor of the *Cambridge Companion to Modernism* (1999), and the co-author (with Karen Chase) of *The Spectacle of Intimacy: The Public Life of the Victorian Family* (Princeton UP, 2000).

Annegret Maack is Professor of English at Bergische Universität Wuppertal, Germany. She has published extensively on both nineteenth- and twentieth-century fiction, including several scholarly essays on A. S. Byatt. She is the author of *Charles Dickens: Epoche, Werk, Wirkung* (Beck, 1991) and co-editor (with Rüdiger Imhof) of *Radikalität und Mäßigung* (Wiss. Buchgesellschaft Darmstadt, 1993), a collection of essays on the contemporary English novel. Her most recent project focuses on utopian literature.

Michael J. Noble is a recent graduate and fellow of the University of Louisiana at Lafayette, U.S.A. His dissertation, "Belletristic Theory, Archécriture, and the Memory Theatre of A. S. Byatt: An Ichnography", further details some of the research presented in his essay for this collection. Previous publications include articles and book reviews that have appeared in *CEA Critic, Anglistik, Encyclia, Explicator,* and *Bulletin of Bibliography*. Most recently, he has been working with electronic media, designing online educational applications and development tools.

Judith Plotz is Professor of English at George Washington University, U.S.A. She specializes in Romantic literature and has recently published on Thomas DeQuincey and Hartley Coleridge. She is the author of *Romanticism and the Vocation of Childhood* (St. Martin's, 2001) and is currently working on a study of Rudyard Kipling.

Kuno Schuhmann is Professor Emeritus of English and American Literature at Technische Universität Berlin, Germany. He has published on the American short story, modern drama, and poetry in both England and America, on the contemporary English novel, and on the concept of Englishness in the context of contemporary Cultural Studies.

Sally Shuttleworth is Professor of English at Sheffield University, U.K. She specializes in nineteenth-century fiction and is the author of *Charlotte Brontë and Victorian Psychology* (CUP 1996) and co-editor (with Jenny Bourne Taylor) of *Embodied Selves: An Anthology of Psychological Texts 1830–1890* (OUP, 1998). She also edited George Eliot's *The Lifted Veil* and *Brother Jacob* for Penguin (2001) and is co-director of the electronic project "Science in the Nineteenth-Century Periodical." Her current research is on childhood in nineteenth-century literature and psychology.

Michael Worton is the Fielden Professor of French Language and Literature and Vice-Provost of University College London, U.K. He is the author of *Michel Tournier* (Longman, 1995), co-author (with Judith Still) of *Textuality and Sexuality: Reading Theories and Practice* (MUP, 1993), and co-editor of *Paragraph*, a journal of modern critical theory, as well as co-editor of the *Journal of the Institute of Romance Studies*. He is a member of the Arts and Humanities Research Board in the U.K. and general editor of the *Bloodaxe Contemporary French Poets* series. His current research focuses on reading and interdisciplinarity.